THE
CONFESSIONS
OF
Edward Dahlberg

Books by Edward Dahlberg

Bottom Dogs, *1930*
From Flushing to Calvary, *1932*
Kentucky Blue Grass Henry Smith, *1932*
Those Who Perish, *1934*
Can These Bones Live, *1940 (rev. ed. 1960)*
The Flea of Sodom, *1950*
The Sorrows of Priapus, *1957*
Truth Is More Sacred (with Herbert Read), *1961*
Because I Was Flesh, *1964*
Alms for Oblivion, *1964*
Reasons of the Heart, *1965*
Cipango's Hinder Door, *1966*
The Leafless American, *1967*
The Edward Dahlberg Reader
(ed. by Paul Carroll, *1967*)
Epitaphs of Our Times, *1967*
The Carnal Myth, *1968*

THE

CONFESSIONS

OF

Edward Dahlberg

GEORGE BRAZILLER

NEW YORK

TO

Lew D. Feldman

with affectionate gratitude

ACKNOWLEDGMENTS

I wish to thank Edwin Seaver whose pains-taking efforts on my behalf merit a "God Boke," and I pray I've not failed him. My thanks, as well, to my steadfast friend Jonathan Williams, and to Francis Brown, editor of the *New York Times Book Review*, John H. Hicks, editor of the *Massachusetts Review*, Coburn H. Britton, editor of *Prose*, and Charles Newman, editor of *Tri-Quarterly*, in whose magazines portions of this book have appeared.

E. D.

Our Muses are perished; withered are our laurels; ruined is our Parnassus: the woods are all become mute; the valleys and mountains for sorrow are grown deaf; Nymphs or Satyrs are found no more among the woods: the shepherds have lost their song.

JACOPO SANNAZZARO
Epilogue to Arcadia

I

The Prentice Years

I

---

*I owe nothing to my birth, for
I don't know who my father was;
nothing to learning, for I have
none; nothing to youth, for I was
old when I began.*

—Erasmus

At nineteen I was a stranger to myself. At forty I asked: Who am I? At fifty I concluded I would never know.

Know thyself is a wise Socratic exhortation, but how is it possible? Do I even understand a tithe of my nature? In truth, I know nothing about anybody, least of all about myself. No matter what I do it is likely to be wrong; one bungles everything, for the brain is feeble and an intuition is a saline and marshy guess. Whatever one has done he will do; that is his character, and he can neither improve nor escape it.

Who is wise, except by accident? When I am intelligent I am startled; should I be as melancholy as Avernus I am baffled. Making ready for an agreeable conversation with a friend, a seizure of unexpected spleen overtakes me. Then there are strokes of idiocy and unreasonable gales of mirth. Who can fathom his blowsy hours of vacancy, or say unto

3

himself: this moment I propose to be meditative? As to my paltry virtues, there is no looking glass in which I can observe them. Still, should a person pursue his august faults with enough resolution he is likely to become somebody in this world.

Nobody knows himself early or late, and that is his good luck and his misery. The eyes are mizzling skies, and the body a meadow one does not know how to manure. "Let the fields be free from darnel that spoils the eyes," as it is said in Ovid's *The Fasti*.

Have I not been every man's cully, especially my own? According to Apuleius, one can put off the form of an ass merely by chewing roses. I would champ hellebore could I cease to be a noddle. I never know who is my friend or foe. How often have I admonished myself: do not let your friends devour you.

Time is the draff of ennui; it is also one of the grossest superstitions of mankind. The sage still walks in the gardens of Agrippa. Yet what shall I do when my mind, usually hollow and desponding, is glutted with fright because I must annihilate a truss of apocryphal weeks? Oh, the heavy unbearable hours and troops of minutes, and all imaginary, when the heart feels barren as the region about Lake Titicaca, where there is no fuel to warm one's imbecilic existence but the dung of llamas.

When the emperor Domitian was bored he mangled flies with a bodkin. I write a book. If I do nothing I am as good as dead, for my life is my will, and then it is as if Sunday or a holiday were upon me; the shops are closed, the faces in the street are graved, and I have come to my end. A day without good or bad tidings lames my whole identity.

So I commence this memoir, which will be gorged with putid defects. "In the multitude of words there wanted not sin," said Erasmus.

4

If only I had confidence in myself and would not be a woodcock until I am skeletoned. Can skin and bones be constant? Some tremble over ordure, others fall in love with gangrened grass or feign that the Milky Way solaces their crumpled expectations.

I have always been starved. Cloistered away in emaciated pariah rooms, I have sat in armchairs stuffed with the hemlock of wretched men who once occupied them, or tossed to and fro on old dry mattresses, dying from want of wool and love. It is plain that I have no choice. Could I compromise I would be more prudent and sensible, which in Middle English means kynde wyt, what we today call common sense.

Though all has come to nothing, and I walk the orphaned leafless gutters and keep company with my own shadow, do not imagine therefore that I am without hope. I, too, have pined for Eden and for the summery flesh of women. I am glutted with the most amazing expectations. Nobody could be so nonsensical as I am without being recognized as a glorious fool who can chew merrily an aphorism, a debt, perfidy, all the gibbets men create for themselves. In this jocose vein I would advise one—I take this simple from Cato—before setting out on a journey to keep a small branch of pontic wormwood under the anus. Everything afflicts us or tickles us to death. Also do not forget the darling verdure comes up when the sun is in Aquarius, and thyme blows in our souls soon as that orbed fire in the heaven is in Taurus.

What else? I am of the mind that one ought to acquire a pensive physiognomy. It is better to sow contemplative wrinkles in the countenance than to have a *tabula rasa* baby face at fifty.

It did not take me long in this life to realize that Job's muck-heap would be my throne and his sherd my sceptre. From the beginning I had all the qualifications for the occupation of author: obscurity, penury and, I hoped, honesty, to which I could add ill hap, for he who is not enticed by the siren, misfortune, is a poltroon. I was never an opponent of the pittance one might receive from the world. What I would not do to get it was to be a sloven of Helicon. Why tell lies when one is going to die? Besides, as Euripides held, "no lie ever grows old." Would I scrabble fustian, who would heed? Echo answers, nobody, but who is he?

Some will name this the breviary of a useless man. Even now I ask: What can I do with myself? Why not go about as though I had much to do, which is the vocation of those who have nothing to do and is very esteemed nowadays? Maybe I could be an actor, that is to say one who's always acting, a caitiff profession. Or I might suggest I resembled a human being, and that also is considered an outrageous pose. This is the age of the emboweled No-Man.

I early saw that no matter how many proofs derived from seers of other centuries I might adduce, it would not help. That is the aconite one must swallow every day he wanders in the labyrinth with nothing to guide him but Ariadne's thread. Suppose I study Martial, Lucretius, Plotinus and Proclus, would I not still live and expire a stupid maggot? We must each do our own seeing and dying. Yet he who refuses to learn is in his dotage at the start. To decline to see what one must needs perceive begets perversity. I cite Ben Jonson: "*Ignorantia animae* . . . I know of no disease of the soul but ignorance. . . . It is a pernicious evil, the darkener of man's life, the disturber of his reason, and common confounder of truth."

At the age of twenty, when senile boys of letters smirk at any great mind, I opened the confessions of Leo Tolstoy and read this: "I saw clearly that art is only the ornament and charm of life."

Was this true? It is said that Ben Jonson trampled upon the proser, and John Dryden fawned upon public taste. I chose the former as my poet and teacher, but could not shut my soul to the talents of the latter. The heroic failures were my demigods. Why do I name them so? Not even the greatest Buddhas of literature and philosophy ever achieved what they aimed at, and although they may have received abundant applause for their works few or none ever took unto their hearts the ruined and blasted hopes of those men who now shed their dust, the only tears to which the deceased in their charnel houses are entitled. God help me, for seldom have I rescued my own wayward nature.

There was the dark forest of truths, and I would walk through it all my days, and never resolve the ambiguities that hardened my neck and were a mountain that crushed the shoulders of Atlas. If books were only an enchanting pastime, why should I make a gallows for myself and woo desolation simply to compose a shoal of delightful phrases and a few pelting maxims? Even if I could make a good squib or a memorabilia that was not trash, what then?

I have never scamped a sacred book, and yet what has come of it? Again I quote the master, Ben Jonson: "Grammar is the art of true and well-speaking a language; the writing is an accident." Then I could never hope to garner up much or anything from my miseries. Is this a stony negation? Ask the poor worms once called Anaxagoras, Euripides or Nietzsche, who were oracles in a poem or a tragedy but madmen in their lives. I would never be capable of sweeping the ordure of ignorance out of my Augean stables. Whatever I wrote that was good would be an accident.

Why then carry this burden of Sidon? But then, who can sit and gulp down his tedium unless he works? Since I would not be an ambulatory corpse, there was no alternative (and is there ever one?). All I could do was to wrap myself in the papyri of the sages and the folly I could not avoid. Like anybody else, I required a soft zephyr of raptures, for

7

one is indifferent until he is ecstatic. It is our habit to make an artificial division between the intellect and the body, but I assert I sometimes think because I feel.

Spite of every hazard, I vowed I would climb the alpine precipices until the Pleiades had set and snow had fallen on my top. Having no confidence in my virtues, I proposed to make every defect of mine count. By now, a good deal of my hair is famished and whited as the sepulchre, but I have never ceased to be the acolyte of the seminal Logoi.

I still remember, and after culling that scorifying sentence from Leo Tolstoy I have gone back and very often to that seer, but presently hear this: "What if I should be more famous than Gogol, Pushkin, Shakespeare, Molière, what then?"

Was it possible to achieve renown, or was I to pimp for fame? I craved an immortal epitaph even knowing that the *Iliads*, the *Odes* of Horace and *The Alchemist* might perish in a universal hurricane. Having decided to be an author to gain the affections of others, I could not foresee I must then expect to be the prey of calumniators. I sought alleviation of my hurts in *The Rig-Veda* or in a Greek thinker and laved my wounds in their counsels. Once Epictetus, asked how a person might grieve his adversary, retorted, "By doing as well as possible himself." At times, full of myself and coming to the surmise I could depend upon my wit, I believed I could oppose every slander, only to learn that I could not handle my own faults let alone those of others. I could only recall what Herodes said to Proteus: "We too have grown old, you in speaking ill of me. So be it, but why in such bad Greek?"

Would to heaven I could be reposeful. Do I not believe that nobody can really harm my soul or even touch it? No matter what occurs, there is none who can hinder you. How many will disclose to you they were ruined by women, debts,

bankruptcy, acrimony or hostile acts. Should one lose everything he has, he is still himself. Of course, one has only
guesses, though some babble about their insights or their
maturity; we are seldom grown men, and are usually peevish
and filled with puerilities. He who thinks he is continually
intelligent is a maudlin infant.

Oppressed by many vapid and contemptible encounters I
have searched for a simple to heal me. But even if I discovered a receipt for my touchy skin I rarely understood its
use. Generally I forgot what I surmised was my bold intelligence. Whatever I announce as a protection from the ser-
pents can be thrown away, but once more I take the hazard
and offer a futile admonition: take heed of your first impressions, O man who is weak of eye and judgment.

That I venerate erudition no one except a rogue will gainsay, so as I go along I shall mention the heroes of the earth
and what words they spoke, always remembering what the
haiku says, that "learning is as ordinary as eating rice at
home." Long ago I proposed to employ words that gave joy
to my ears, even if some are archaic. Never mind the jeers;
I don't care a whit about them.

Nor do I care for this century. Even as a youth I saw
that the world is a congregation of ninnies who maintain
their authority over savants by declaring they do not exist. I
claim the same right as Alexander Herzen to show my gargantuan contempt of my own day: "I feel ashamed of my
generation; we seem mere soulless orators. Our blood is cold,
only our ink is hot."

Jean Jacques Rousseau confesses that his ink was the
miserable waters of Phlegethon. Surely we live, or suppose
we do, like wailing shades. Am I endeavoring to give somebody a worm-eaten afternoon? I pray not. Everyone carries
within him countless darksome misgivings, though few recognize them. It may be cumbersome to apologize for my

negations, but were the Cosmos benevolent and could kneel to his victims, stones, flowers, herbs, animals and the inglorious defeats of all human beings, life itself would not be so unforgiving.

Little doubt that my *juvenilia* was a hemorrhage of melancholia. The young are macerated because they expect too much. Were I a Stoic I would proclaim that he is lucky who has no hopes at all. But I am filled with heady expectations that I can never control. More often than not I have been far more disappointed in myself than in the perplexities of existence. What has smitten me is that I am almost never prepared for anything.

It is not possible to relate how many times my pulses fluttered when I was making ready to see a friend or a scrub stranger. Then for nebulous reasons I fell into a passion forgetting I had sought to be congenial. Amazed at my own aberrations I tried to be the alchemist and assuring myself I should on the next adventure be delightful and waggish company I mixed the juice of the onyx with the quiddity of beryl along with granules of anise, and pounded them in a mortar with a pestle. After swallowing this hermetic medicine, I was sure no ill would befall me.

Funerary victuals. Each one pines for the musk in spite of the doleful knell that is always in his mind. It is a dull, ringing refrain: no matter what I shall do, I am doomed.

But to my tale.

2

Oh wretched clay, first formed by Prometheus. In his attempt, what little wisdom did he show. In framing bodies, he did not apply his art to form the mind, which should have been his first care.

—Propertius

Bookeless and museless, as John Milton has it, I came to Los Angeles in 1919 to drink the Pierian waters in that dump. I had become a vagabond to find those books that were as lost to me as Atlantis. As a boy of eighteen I had gone to the Kansas City library, without ever coming upon a single page I felt would be an addition to my undeciphered nature. Nor had I met one person who could aid or show me how to fumigate my galled adolescence. It seemed to me that the locality I was fastened to abhorred both my mother and me. Frequently Indians would quit one place for another, either for aliments or a more benign climate. Those who founded Darien, finding it a swamp, moved to a more salubrious site though they retained the name of the town. I had heard that California was Abraham's grove of oaks at

Mamre. Distraught, and having no inclination to leave my mother, I ran away.

For a year my belly ached for the gruel and meats my mother had provided for me. Had I been a Spaniard during the conquest of the New World, I would have eaten witch-grass, a belt or a pair of worn-out socks. My guerdon was starvation, sleet, ruptured health, and that sorriest of meals, anger. My bones were mute though they howled; I had no roof nor the sourest pallet. Dozing atop boxcars, or in rail-road yards, or under a tree, my poverty was a fiery scab. Skinny as I was, my putrid drawers hung loose about me, and I did not know where to wash or even where to defecate; the American people presumably had no inclination to furnish any sort of ramshackle privy for the poor.

Eventually I acquired a knack with hunger. What pained me more was grubby work in which I had no zealous interest. As Chaucer said:

> I wol not do no labour with my handes,
> Ne make baskettes, and lyve thereby . . .
> I will non of the apostles counterfete

With the scantiest intelligence I had already concluded that the sharper had reduced the country to a gullet and a purse. After a month as a scullion in a lunch counter on Spring Street and sleeping in alleys I had saved nearly all my wages and I quit.

With a spill of dollars in my scathed pocket I sauntered along the downtown streets of our garbaged Tophet of trade. I was jubilant, I was free; everything was dear to me that day. I walked miles, chanting: Let the Philistines tremble over lucre and make their boorish genuflections to Baal, the national idol of comfort; I shall worship a riverbank, a lorn headland and the Milky Way.

Growing weary of my spurious song of liberty I went to

a pawnbroker's shop on Main Street, where I purchased a secondhand sharkskin suit whose cloth was undernourished, a velour hat with a chink in it, a pair of exhausted suède shoes, diseased sheepskin gloves and a handkerchief for my breast pocket. Thus attired and shod I regarded myself as a fop of American letters.

Not long thereafter I stepped into the Y.M.C.A. lobby and striding toward the secretary's desk with a spruce gait demanded a room. By now I had learned that a beggar is turned away by those who profess to believe in the four Gospels, but a dandy can rest assured of hospitality.

How could I avoid wallowing in the raff of ignorance? No aged rock could have felt more senile than I who had dropped into wanton and suffering silence. Always a droll, I desired to be a thinker without having any conceptions. What was odd was that I was seeking someone who knew more than I did, which should not have given me any trouble at all. Each of us is always looking for himself in another person. Regard the remnants of Tenochtitlan or a relic of Quetzalcoatl, and a man is merely contemplating his own ruins. Human beings are more obscure to themselves than any beast on the earth. What else are the Inca temples but such an enigma? So ruminating I continued to stroll about the lobby of the Y, searching for one who might become a friend, but not bothering with any visage in which I had no confidence. New impressions are correct, and the more you know about a man the less you understand him. I was sure to make a mistake.

One afternoon I came upon a fellow member who had a beet-colored nose and a gaping mouth that showed his snoring teeth. I noticed his eyes resembled the spawn of frogs. By now I had read Oscar Wilde's *The Picture of Dorian Gray* and *De Profundis*, Nietzsche's *Thus Spake Zarathustra* and *Beyond Good and Evil*, and George Gissing's *By the*

Ionian Sea, and I supposed I had acquired enough erudition to scent an evil experience. It is a commonplace that we can learn from everybody. But who has that much time?

My sole companions for months had been Hunger, who seldom left me without returning within the hour, and Meditation, who deserted me every day because, he complained, I had nothing to say he cared to recollect. Misfortune had been biting my woebegone heels, and I was in the saturnalian throes of zero when I saw this wretch. I was of the opinion that everyone was eccentric except myself, although at rare trials of understanding I was positive I was the imperial booby.

Suddenly I suspected I saw a perfidious smile coiling about his mouth. As I involuntarily stepped toward him I took flight, but was amazed to discover I was still motionless.

Fearing I would run away he detained me by showing me his vacant purse to prove we were brothers of the saintly order of poverty. As Indigence is one of the most honest men I have ever met, I was stunned when he told me he was called Busy Perverse. However, it was clear he was no wastrel, for he began to talk earnestly at once. There is no Jacob's ladder to interesting conversation; one puts his foot on the first rung and speaks without a long ponderous prologue. Sometimes chatter eases the intestinal tract. To put both maxims together, there is as great a quantity of ass's milk in the colloquies of Erasmus as in any other memorable writer.

Avoiding any flummery proem, Perverse asked me: "Who was the first author in the world?" Without waiting for a rejoinder, he said: "Human feeling." His second inquiry was: "Who invented the novel?" and divining I was puzzled, he remarked: "Ham, who wrote the first book of fiction with his genitals instead of his head. He also started a novella which he inscribed with his hunkers."

Tireless, he continued: "Do you know who was the most stupid man on this earth?" and at once answered: "Seth, who supposed he was intelligent."

Perverse was overcome by his own eloquence. He related how Nimrod built the College of Babblers in the plain of Shinar. Mahalaleel was the chancellor and in his 895th year he gave Lamech, too blind to read, a doctor of dotage. Mahalaleel was succeeded by On-the-other-hand, who appointed four professors of rhetoric: Inasmuch-as, None-the-less, Notwithstanding, and Good Taste, who was later replaced by Doctor Addendum.

At this point I could no longer hold my tongue and I put this question to Perverse: "Did the pedant appear before or after the Great Deluge?" Paying no attention to me, he shouted: "Who built Main Street?" and replied: "Two brothers of Tubal-Cain, Sewer and Garbage." He was inclined to wander somewhat and, unmindful of historical dates, asserted that Ham bare Self-Love who begat Self-Service, who opened the first cafeteria on Sixth and Hope Streets.

Always apart from the human race, I seldom refrained from asking anybody I met to introduce me to someone I did not care to know. I implored Perverse to arrange a rendezvous for me with Self-Love, but he said he was too occupied to see anybody but himself.

"One last query," I cried out. "Who invented the bottle-head and the dupe?"

"I suppose," said Perverse, "Adam was a fool because he failed to realize he would always be a simpleton. As for the cony, he regards his trencher of gravel no supper until he has made a snare for himself.

"I ought to know something about the genesis of learning," he went on. "In the beginning truths were bound with the bark of the fir, the earliest tree in the ground. Volumes were also covered with swamp root, out of which the primitive Egyptians made bread, and so knowledge became edible. Later the rind of oaks and the grain of barley were used for the making of intoxicating papyri. When pleasure crept into men's nights, a succubus fondled sleep who discovered a wild shrub, phalaris, which resembled the prepuce, and folios were then shaped like the pudenda. Lust became so rife that men cared only to be tickled to death and nothing could satisfy the skin except pornographic dirt which was sleeved in menstrual cloth.

"Sir, what are you called?" Perverse asked suddenly, without bothering to change paragraphs. He was licking parsnips and he looked quite green; I thought I had raised his ire. Then he began munching carrots and his skin was ocherous. Proposing to reveal at least a part of my identity, though I am so impetuous as likely to disclose the whole of it, I weakly answered: "My Christian name is Anybody, but by Abraham, Jacob, and Isaac, and their seven cabalistic ballocks, my surname is Miserable Chagrin."

He considered this with more than an earnest of interest and counselled me to macerate the bark of an elm and mix it with cold spring water, then bolt this down to expel my phlegm.

Suddenly I wanted to leave. My demon tells me when to quit the presence of a person, but I have never listened to it. What should I do? Only what I have continually done. I remained.

Perverse knew precisely my inclination. He offered me a pretty conceit: "Why don't you go away? You've been leaning on me since noon, and have ruined my vegetarian diet, for now I hear gas rumbling in my stomach. Never to know when it is decorous to leave a man alone so that he can meditate is a sin against the Holy Ghost. One acquires a new ailment each time he has the ill luck to come upon a stranger. I know of no pest so harmful as another person."

Months later I would have a clever retort for this blow. According to the Quiché Mayans the black pustules of the corn smut on I Kan the Lord created anger, but I had only soft and loving emotions for my opponent although I still smarted under his quip. That I venerate a foe cannot be denied, for what a balsam is a beautiful hurt for one's uneventful days. Without adversaries I would have no memoir to compose and consequently would be a thoughtless cadaver.

As I moved with palsied legs upon the dead cement blocks I was beset with the most ridiculous vagaries I could not account for, which I regard as highly reasonable, for my digressions are the only musk of logic I know. This fume of nonsense came into my mind: The Lord God created men whose hinder parts were as seamless as Christ's coat, which made them miserable because they could not get rid of their excrements. God took pity on the human race and divided their buttocks so that they could ease themselves, which was a salacious mistake. After men had bowels each one thought the other smelled bad and this brought about hatred, war, usury, cosmetics, foppery, dandyism, malice, gossip, scandal, hypocrisy and loneliness.

Then God lamented the fact that men had hunkers; He regretted everything He had done, which made Him rather lovable. He saw, also too late, for perception is ever tardy, that soon as men knew they had hams they discovered they had four cheeks; then instead of adoring the Gnostic Ogdoad, they bowed down before the idol number 4, which is the cabalistical numeral that stands for Lucifer, and compiled a lexicon of four-letter words for lechers ordained every Ash Wednesday or Ember Week.

Though I have a scranny familiarity with the porno-

graphic dictionary I would like to list a few words I recall:
Womb, tomb, dead, Lord, JHVH, Adam, Seth, Cain, Abel,
Noah, Shem, tent, body, head, brow, hand, nail, loin, knee,
chit, tart, maid, girl, hair, dupe, fool, sink, love, hate, mind,
kind, dust, good, evil, feel, soft, heat, marl, herb, tree, lust,
just, dust, gust, holy, fond, rood, mood, lewd, nude, hide,
foul, bowl, soul, four, salt, tear, seer . . .

I could go on, for life is a four-letter word, too. God, who
is a hurricane, pretends man can be spelled with three letters although in the arcane numerology he can only be known
by the sign of four. Man is withal so obscene that his sins
were not drowned in the Flood. Since vice brings men together, which is far better and more moral than keeping
them apart, I confess we must perforce live with brimstony
four-letter words, and I admit this with a heavy heart.

3

---

*There were no dead six days and
dismal seventh in those sculptured churches; there was no
beadle to lock me out of them,
or pew-shutter to shut me in.*
                            —John Ruskin

Meanwhile I actually had gone nowhere (for meditation is
sedentary as the Buddha), and was still standing before
Busy Perverse.

My mood had altered, for I no longer cared for him as I
had fallen in love with my own excogitations far more nour-
ishing than his beets, cauliflower, turnips, carrots, grapes,
figs, walnuts and almonds. Besides, I had dropped into an
inventive vein.

I blamed God for another one of His follies. In my lenitive moods I could pardon Him for having created the world,
and in six days, as it is said, but I will never pardon Him
for making Sunday. Monday, Tuesday, Wednesday, Thursday, Friday and Saturday are well-nigh unendurable, but
who can stomach Sunday—twenty-four hours of the ague,
spleen, bile, emptiness, sleet, mildewed rest? Is God such
a dolt that He can do nothing a whole day? For me Sunday

is a rope, a halter, a gibbet, a pottle of hemlock. What can one do on Sunday except belch, sneeze, hiccough, cough, dung, feed, seed and feign to read? I abhor a book on the seventh day; it is a beadle's Sunday book.

Indeed what can one do with this burial day in the week? It is a pallbearers' festival. Have you seen these creatures in their obituary suits carrying a coffin in which God's day of rest lies? Every seventh day these mourners are attired in faces and clothes made of bitumen collected from the Dead Sea. I declare to all who will hear that Saturday, a step-dame Sunday, is more than I can bear, but Sunday is God's negative void. Why, my weeping arms and legs demanded, did God frame Sunday?

I had said nothing to Perverse, which he considered a defeat, so he leaped upon me, shrieking: "You are a master-piece of senility. I despise you because you dream, which is the grim Minos of all your secret vices."

My own victorious mood was ended. Again I slumbered, for every time we think, we are unconscious. The reflective man is a sleepwalker at noon or twilight. Endeavoring to open my contemplative eyelids I spoke without hearing myself: "Please, sir, believe me, I live alone since I do not wish to mistreat anybody so much as I have myself."

Within my closed hand was a dram of humility which stung him. He gave me a face of bile. He was bent upon flailing me, but meanwhile he said the visions of the night were a moonless bank of Styx.

How starless was my own fate, for at noon I was pur-blind. Of late my nights were pampered up with scurfy raptures, because Lilith had crept into my bed and had tightly embraced me, and when I awoke I detested that shadow of a doxy.

"Why do you grovel for a glance?" Perverse grumbled. "Woe to him who cannot endure himself. Do not suppose you can cleave to me. I have no intention of being frozen to death in the blizzard of your solitude. Why should I walk through the wintry steppes of your poverty and come down with a chilblain? Make sure of this, I don't want you. I have no difficulty in getting along with myself. Had I any desire for a foe I would long ago have acquired a friend. Besides, should I keep company with a lonely man in order to deprive him of the fruits of his character? Never do anything for anybody lest you injure him."

In a stroke of meekness I gave him my gramercy for his exhortation and promised I would live apart from the human race already burdened with one ill or another. Suddenly, without any reason whatever, and perhaps bored with my own small bout of self-abasement, I cried out: "I forbid anyone to stop me from harming myself."

When I was fifty I recalled a modicum of this colloquy as I browsed through the pages of Apuleius' *The Golden Ass*: I read that Ulysses preferred to behold the smoke rising from his native land to gaining immortality. From the start I had craved a memorable headstone. Often times I sighed for the bliss of an euthanasy, particularly during those drabbish hours when I had no belief at all in the gaudy prophetic trances that vapor off so soon.

Busy Perverse assured me I was quite tiresome and required a gamp or a lying-in hospital where I could be delivered of that besotted infant, Ennui.

Without question I detested him. But how could I satisfy my hunger for people? Paracelsus averred he knew a man who wore a clod of earth on his stomach to avoid starving. Were I to break this aguish connection with Busy Perverse would I stop searching for other trouble, another human being?

I noticed that one of my fingers was bruised, and trying to remember how that had happened I recollected I had clawed it with one of my molars. This was discouraging, but I stood straight as I could, lifting my head that had been

lobbing down my neck, and inclined my ear so as to catch
the echo of my homily: "Every hurt is a purgatory and a
revelation."

The battle was about finished, and Perverse huffing as
though I had exhausted him—I had not myself the strength
to remain there any longer—spoke with the quiet of one who
has been drained: "Are you not a different person from what
you were before you had the honor of meeting me?"

I did not dislike his condescension, much as I could have
and did the next morning when I understood it more clearly.
But for what my reply was worth, just more dross I suspected, I cast my javelin at him: "No, I am the same, but
worse than I was, for previously I had only my own faults
which are exceedingly heavy indeed, but now I have yours,
too, and since I am not Atlas my shoulders are too weak for
such a mountain of defects."

Evidently he was not delirious about my fansies. Interrupting them he insisted that I rise early in the morning to
gaze at the dawn, and also go out after twilight to enjoy a
sunset. At last I had trapped him, for I positively hate a
man who revels in sunsets, concluding, as he always does,
that such a spectacle has a potent effect upon his moral nature. I could not contain my fury: "You regard yourself as
a thinker just because you raise your eyes toward Ursa
Major."

Not liking the way I had taken command of our arguments, and considering he would overwhelm me by a surprise attack, Perverse bragged about his many interesting
friends, which I considered a personal affront. I had become
superstitious in such matters. Soon as I encounter a stranger
I hate him. Babble about a person's sensitive features and
you can be certain that the brand-new intimacy will turn
out to be a catastrophe. Then why did I keep on beating so
convulsively for friends?

There are two sorts of human beings, the hunter who seeks his prey and his victim who aches to be captured. Were I vigilant I would never show a single person an amiable face lest I be taken for a ninny. How can two be less troublesome than one?

More than a generation was to expire before a criticaster blamed me for not including a horde of fools in my milieu, adding that without them I had no environment. For this theory he received the haughtiest glance and my own terse sentiments: "I am my environment." Are not people apart even when they are together? Despite the bottleheads who are wretches unless they travel in packs, each one is separated from the other. This is God's revenge against those who are determined to speak only of man in the mass.

When Busy Perverse informed me I did not understand the world, I asked him which one, his or mine. Did I not carry the universe within myself?

Again he turned upon me with: "Why have you no dissolute connection with a trollop?"

There were instances of divine calm when I was reading *The Fasti* of Ovid and believed I could be completely satisfied with this passion. Had I not ruttish bones the pages of Plotinus would suffice. I had no confidence in the possibilities of carnal pleasure from reading.

Steeped in this speculation I considered women as nature's decoy. Adam imagined Eve was boundless joy, and once he became a libertine after he had partaken of the tree of knowledge of good and evil, he conjectured that when he entered a female he could then step beyond the bounds of his own soul. The elements that govern men have produced the flittering images, shallow pates. Who can prove that the flora, fauna and the inhabitants of the globe are not trumpery illusions?

I was wandering again, or was I? Talk is ungraspable,

yet footsteps I hear relieve me of so many vague pangs, and when someone opens my door I am ready for a visitor, and after he shuts it I am seized with a terrible flux of solitude. I wish I knew what to do with myself.

As I remained standing there I waxed colder and all the autumnal leaves were ribbed and rusty and had dropped from my branches. I noticed I was naked and did not know where to hide. Where was the raiment that covered my shame? Were it possible I might go to a yard where monuments for the deceased were cut and purchase the essence of feldspar, quartz granite and a granule of an epitaph, and swallow a teaspoonful of this remedy before retiring in order to dry up the moisture of the mushroom in me.

Perverse now complained no one should be permitted to give a man a pair of morose hours, and he offered me two crafty fingers of Judas to shake. Taken aback, I handled them. Would I ever discover how cunning is all skin? "Oh, heaven," I heard a lamentation within me, "I cry out against deception though I know I cannot understand anything about a person who has never duped me."

Soon as he had offered his two fingers Perverse quickly hid them in his pocket, the deposit box of avarice. He was flogging me and I listened to him with a fawning back: "I never shake hands. That is not hygienical. Do not come near me for you are an infectious grave."

When I proposed to depart he detained me and blamed me for being rude. I looked down at the floor, wishing I could pick up a scrap of myself. In the depths of nullity I moaned: "God created evening in order that men would be obscure to themselves and think." Somewhere I had come upon a passage that the growth of fungus on the wick of a burning lamp was a symptom of rain. What is the sign or portent of a base encounter with a shake-rag?

I dread to remain long with another. When I suppose

I am bantering, my manner is grave; or jocose, my mien is curdled and sour. After I have run out of bon mots I am blockish. To cite Milton, I would that I could always be green as the figs that grew between Bethany and Jerusalem. Was I to be whipped by a trifling failure and to reckon every hindrance a catastrophe?

Perverse was not slow to guess that I was in great trouble. He showed me a bilious beige tooth. "Why have you such ill feeling toward yourself?" he said.

I responded, a feeble smile painted upon my lips: "I once decided to buy a good disposition on credit. Could you or I trust me you would not deny that though I sow my seed diligently my crop of marvelous intentions always fails; a constant drought has eaten up every congenial thought I ever had, and the dust and wind have swept away all resolutions. One morning, full of zeal and hopes, I offered to sell my future, and at a bargain price, to a loiterer on the sidewalk who wore the most disappointed trousers and an ailing shirt for which there was no cure. Not discouraged, I tried to pawn my ethics and laid them on the counter of a pawnbroker. Blind as Tiresias he failed to find them and screamed for help, so I was forced to run out of his shop. Several blocks away I examined my wallet, and I swear it had been stuffed with all sorts of morals. When I discovered it was empty, I shrieked: "Help, police! I have been robbed."

Busy Perverse adopted a new tune: "Trust me," he said. "I now speak sincerely, which is dishonest of me. How do you live with yourself? Aren't you occupying rather wizened quarters, considering the amount of space one needs for a thousand faults?—and I speak kindly in mentioning so insignificant a number."

He had deeply bent my spinal column. I admitted I had advertised for a companion who, I hoped, would not displace my foibles. Several responded to the notice I had put in the papers, and at first they did not appear to be displeased by my exterior. But in a moment or two they spied a few devils that I had sleeved and who had hopped out, like penury, excessive tenderness, giddy enthusiasm, naïve wonder. Contrary to all my desires I have done my best to persecute or hide these demons who appear when I least expect them.

That I loved and detested Perverse is no quibble. Inflamed by his impudence which I only vaguely felt, I was prepared to chop him into small rashers. Once more I became resolute and suggested that although his company was Elysium for me, I had a rendezvous with a Venus Mandragoritis on Flower Street. This statement he did not relish, and he accused me of relinquishing his intellectual repast to browse among the violets and the lilies and to graze on a maiden's thighs. "You're full of lickerish wind no better than the slough of grasshoppers. I had hoped you were ascetic as a sea-oak or Atlantic rams or the water-ox. You're a rakish mussel."

Quite ashamed of my cormorant appetite for female flesh, I stuttered: "Should not a pebble have generative organs, or a lorn rock enjoy the rites of coition? Otherwise a boulder must be as mournful as men?"

"Fumigate your lecheries with juniper ashes," advised Perverse. "Avoid the pollen of the aspen-plum and the amorous sparrow roasted on the spit. Repent. Locusts also are an aphrodisiac. Expel from your steaming and mucksy mind words like bed, sheet, pillow, dress and the sandals of Judith. I have had enough of you. Go away, so that I can purge myself of you."

How abject and musty I was I could not tell. Almost unfamiliar with the honeyed tresses and thighs of women, although I did not care to make a full account of my dreams, I regarded myself as a debauchee who did little else but drab and drink. Nor did I show that I could handle Perverse's curt dismissal. Utterly threadbare, without a stitch of goodness to display for my bawdy twenty years, I felt as if I had crept up to him like a porker nuzzling for acorns. Whatever was my reason, I humbly requested him to prescribe a remedy for my libidinous craw. He advised me to grind sapphires, agate and amber to mitigate my venery.

Offering Perverse my copious apologies for being tiresome, I urged him to guard his health, and avoid cuckoldry. I also pleaded with him to place a sentinel over his wallet, since the best of friends steal one another's cogitations and tattered cloaks.

"I should consider it an infamy," I said, "if you were to stumble on the pavement, for you would then also accuse me of having cursed you. Would you convey my affections to your relatives and their acquaintances whom I have never met?" Then with a surge of rancor I berated him for having hoarded them up so long and hidden them from me.

When I awakened from my reveries I could see his smirking back as he went through the door. It took me at least an hour to gather up enough snow to cool my temper, but after a while I had entirely recovered, and was even felicitous, for all of a sudden I was free. Managing to dig up a consolatory adage, I subdued my boiling arteries by announcing that every act one commits, good or bad, is a portion of one's development.

Momentarily I was overwhelmed by this dismal conceit: Was I to ripen by being cast onto a dunghill every day? Still, the adventure was rhapsodic even if it was a purgatory. Once again I supposed I belonged to myself, and I went upstairs to my room and gaped at the door that was ajar—for I had failed to lock it—as though I was staring into my own abyss. I loathe any door that is open. Who has the bravery to look into his own darkling pit?

4

Whether Libra, or dread Scor-
pio, the most powerful planet
over the natal hour, controls
me, or Capricorn, the lord of the
western wave.

—Horace

Now that I had disgorged Perverse I was prepared to meet a sage. The Y coenobium was filled with orphans, cranks, quacks, pimps, panders, table-rappers and a variety of religious maniacs. Already a seasoned peripatetic I fell into a delirious friendship with a St. Louis waif who had drunken sensual lips and the plump posteriors of a Ganymede, and who played the violin. After a week's companionship he disappeared, seized not by Zeus but by an actor, an urning who fell into the arms of a lesbian every night at the Morosco Theater and who promised to secure work for him in Hollywood where he could play *Hearts and Flowers* and Stravinsky's *Firebird* while a dilapidated skeletal star was expiring of tuberculosis on a studio set.

I vowed from now on I would be vigilant all day, so that I would not be gulled, although one who has not the Lord and Christ in him has no regal destiny without the kiss of Iscariot. I remained in my room combing the pages of Flaubert's *L'Éducation Sentimentale*, Gautier's *Mademoiselle de Maupin* and Walter Pater's *Plato and Platonism*. Then I was abruptly overcome by a fit of mulligrubs. How many books would I have to read to be a cultivated bore? Suppose I ravaged thousands of learned tomes, would I ever be sensible? Vowing I would avoid Busy Perverse I weighed my desolate condition, and what a muddled mind I had as I observed: there is an enormous price to be paid for eschewing every humbug. I then recovered a saying from a Vedic hymn: "The scent of flowers does not travel against the wind, nor that of sandalwood, but the odor of good people travels against the wind." Still, I was qualmish. There was no wind that could prevail against the bad smell of Perverse.

A week later, I came upon his contemptible vertebrae, and so venomous was he that he was lacerating a casaba melon. I rushed toward him and placing one caressing arm about his plum-colored neck began to strangle him. When he raised his Delphic cane which I expected to come down upon my pericranium I was bewildered. Oblivious of all my former admonitions to myself I lent him my hand, only to have him snarl at me: "You usurer, you are looking for twenty percent interest, but I shall borrow no emotion from you."

For once I ran my swordsman's wit through his entrails: "I have no intention of becoming a free loan association for you or that abstract rabble euphemistically called mankind. Do not for an instant surmise that I shall ever greet a man unless I am guaranteed six percent interest for the effort. This is the only bargain I shall make with perfidious life."

In a more reposeful vein Perverse revealed that a squill had exquisite sensibilities and how could I mangle an unweaned calf. Was this his puce, orange or gray trance? Since his genius depended upon the daffodil or fungus or herb he had in mind or had just chewed, I wished I knew whether our colors had clashed.

Perverse rebuked me for giving my physiognomy to any passer-by I encountered. He said the face I wore now was different. He could not tolerate change, one who carried on his feeble shoulders a novel mien each time you met him. "You are as deceitful as Proteus," he declared.

Both of us were hard of hearing; we seldom listened to each other nor were our answers pertinent. Of a sudden, Perverse demanded: "Do you know whether coral and sapphire have organs, and do they use them or are they ascetic?" How was I to handle such a platter of follies? "As for me," I said, "I am a prig and dislike your goatish tinkling conversation."

He gave me the coldest look he could frame, and I complained: "What inlet is so frozen as man? Have you ever seen a crestfallen lake clothed with keening weeds?"

Perverse was mauling grapes that had never harmed him, and carnivore that I was I could not bear this gory spectacle. I gazed at him with astonishment: since we had last talked his hair had turned rotten cauliflower. But I was immune to his suffering locks, and I hurled one more declaration at him: "Hear me, surd flesh: I am the wilderness and the prophetic night, and I say unto you one of the deadly sins is to be commonplace." Not satisfied with this irrelevancy, I threw another recondite commonplace at him: "Have we broken the Pillars of Hercules and sailed over the sea of darkness to sow mediocre seeds in the New World?"

I was about to depart before Perverse could be so flagitious as to leave me first. Proudly I concealed the fingers of my right hand in the crypt of my trousers pocket, while he thrust forth his hand to clasp mine. I had ambushed him. "I despise your simpering fingers," I said.

"Go to the waters of Bethesda," he retorted, "and bathe your morphewed affection in it. I can't abide lonely clothes shambling about the world. Your jacket is a worn-out sorrow. Leave yourself before it is too late. Retire from humanity. The seamew builds its nest in rocks. The isolated plateau and the mesa expect you. Noah begat Shem, Ham and Japeth, but who bare you? Where did you get your visage? I feel so old since you arrived. Starveling that you are, you have drained me and I am so feeble I am incapable of getting up out of my chair to depart from you forever."

Perverse's fever had risen enormously; the vegetarian was anthropophagous. He who diets on nuts and raw vegetables will grow an enormous appetite for human flesh soon as some person has the ill luck to come upon him.

Overwhelmed by my insight I sped out of the lobby. As once again I walked the streets I was afflicted with the monk's disease, Acedia, boredom. I had no one else besides Busy Perverse. What should I do without him?

The palms along the way resembled shaved poodle dogs. Approaching the Pythian tripod, the secondhand bookstores, I stepped into one of them and bought Bernard Shaw's *An Unsocial Socialist*, Samuel Butler's *Erewhon* and Gautier's *The Golden Fleece*. The three volumes cost me $1.50. Having flayed that much of my scrannel wallet I would have to give up dinner. No matter; the books were a fair exchange.

After the shortest bout of euphrasia I was thrown into Tartarus. Would the crickets sing again in the balmy evenings of my loins? I had consumed a tithe of the dusk, and there were still tomorrows and other afternoons to be tediously peeled away. Perhaps there was one nostrum, and that was to kill myself. But that was a literary emotion.

I clung to life since I feared the void no less than the Lord; Pascal, according to Boileau, kept a chair on his left side in order not to fall into the void.

My chance meeting with a man named Marion was a
benison. He was in the fag-end of his forties, and his skin
was steeped in many defeats. Each of us recognized in the
other a fellow disciple of beauty. I still bend my head when
I recall that Plotinus said, "Incorporeal things are beautiful
when they make us love them." I have spent countless hours
hovering over this seraphic thought, but it only gave me
ruined wings.

Drawn to Marion since he came into the world cramped
and old, I occasionally knocked at his door. He was of the
elect; the majority of men are still babes seventy years after
they have left the womb. It was not hard for him to discern
that I was starved, and he proffered me this consolation:
"What teacher has so much understanding as hunger?" In
spite of my travail I could not suppress my brag. Sure that
the poison of genius seeped through my veins, I boasted that
the day would come when I would fill the old traditional
bottles of literature with new wine. When Marion left Los
Angeles I wept.

Friendless again, I caught sight of Reason leering at me
as was his wont. Whenever he appeared he made me nau-
seous, because he discharged his buttocks in my presence
though he had no bowels. Whatever I did to disinfect myself was of no avail; I could never get rid of the foul odor.
Under the delusion I had acquired wisdom, I never crossed
my threshold without an amulet, a sack of amber containing
the English of Gower, Wyatt and Sir Walter Raleigh.
Sometimes I sprinkled cinnamon over myself, but soon as I
stepped into the world I stank.

I could not help railing at this imperial fool and prince
of hypocrites: "You imagine you and man have something
in common. Tell me, what is it? You're as contagious as
good advice. Long ago I found out what a scoundrel you
are and how you impose on the irrational race of men. You
abhor pelagic oaks, the tunnies near Cadiz, the fat collops

of jollity. Besides, you are grum, and hurry away from a person who is arguing with somebody else because you are a turncoat. No one can win a controversy; you promise you will stand by his side when he is confused, and you never do."

Reason had a stubby infertile nose, a niggardly mouth and voracious hands. Although moldy, he wore costly jewels, yet for all his fantastic wealth was solitary as I was. Nobody wanted to have anything to do with him. This perplexed me, and I asked several thousands why this was true. Because, I was informed, soon as one was in trouble he lost his Reason. Some for this miserable condition threw themselves off precipices, others drowned, or went bankrupt. Certainly no one is so senseless as to die for the sake of Reason. A wretched Reason indeed. Besides, there are other astounding apoplexies far more toothsome, such as pleasure, ruin, litigation, blasphemy, libel, and even Sincerity, which is said to be the uterine sister of Logic, though I've never seen them together.

Suddenly I was swept off my feet by a gust of good sense, and Logic, who had never shown the least interest in my predicament, stopped and nodded. Overcome with gratulation I extended my hand, but Logic sneered at me and hurried off, moving from one hall to another. Infuriated with the boor I chased him, but I don't remember having caught one glimpse of Logic after that imaginary instant. I wept: "Why has Reason forsaken me?" Then drying my eyes I comforted myself: "Who knows when he's fortunate?"

Gossip, so dear to the nose—Erasmus goes further: "Every man thinks his own excrement smells good"—said that Reason had attended the funeral services of Feeling. The few who desired to know how Feeling had died were advised he had been trampled to death by Logic, a vicious churl who could not endure him because Feeling had no evidence, proof or statistics for his utterances.

Another day, as I was taking my customary saunter

through the lobby of the Y, more than half frozen to death by Alone who always clung to me, I noticed a lean, thewy frame slouched in a chair. His ribs stuck out of his narrow back, and I conjectured he was tall as I had already grown fond of him and was seeking a mind higher than my own. He had a masculine, theoretical nose and a thoughtful jaw that appeared to be made of vitriol, which is said to be a noble metal, and a "sauce flume face."

A gawk, I strode around his chair seven times, as the bridegroom circles the bride in Chassidic and American Indian folklore, but he merely peered at me over his glasses. Undaunted, I saluted him, praying he had a sound constitution, was not costive, and neither swallowed pellets for his rheumatism nor had loutish feet, which are a symptom of an empty clown. As he showed no surprise at my bizarre behavior I felt assured Anonymous was my kin and would deeply care for me. I detest any simpleton who loves everybody, and I could tell he did not and would select only me. That this is illogical is apparent, but everything else is and so I am not at all peevish.

As he remained silent, though every feature of his spoke, the bond between us was so close that I was quite heady. I knew beforehand that I would open my mouth, which is dangerous, but I have always taken such hazards, believing that the words falling out of one's mouth are the truth even if they are a lie. I offered him this adage: "I am the aqueous remnant of the tribe of Noah though there is no olive leaf in my destiny."

A human face is a windfall, a miracle in a faceless age, and I was reeling. On a sudden he fell upon me with this unheroic question: "Have you a moral nature?"

"No," I replied, "I'm just nervous."

He displayed his albic teeth. "Are you a thinker?"

I confessed I was obtuse all day long and it appeared to

trouble no one but myself. "I am the grub of every sapient scribe. I have no use for abstractions, what the psychologists call will, objective, subjective. I am what I am, which may be no good, but that is nature's fault. What is intellect except my anatomy? How do I know when my foot mumbles, or my legs are uttering a banality? If I have made a clever trope, how can I tell that I am not simply blowing my nose?"

By now I was so abstracted that I made this short oration: "All skin is wicked and everything we do is bad. If it turns out well, be sure that something ill will come of it. Since misfortune is a demigod, why trouble my cruddled pate about it?"

The colloquium was not going well enough for Anonymous. His steep brow was wrinkled by Minerva, who sat there as though she was an old trot. Viewing my downcast heels and the cobbled sharkskin suit I supposed was the raiment of Apollo, he was about to show compassion. Instead he pressed his pedagogic nail into me: "Would you defend a bowdlerized edition of Shakespeare?"

I had never heard of the word but I took a chance: "I am altogether against it," I said.

Anonymous baited me again: "What do you think of Aulus Gellius' *Attic Nights?*" I was fuming; had he no organs at all? As Pascal has written, men are naturally hostile toward one another. Behaving with aplomb I threw my bodkin at his groin: "I never cease thinking of it."

It took me a generation to eradicate such perjuries. One of the hardest shames for me was to confess that I was not on intimate terms with a seer or a word. My reverence for culture made a liar of me. Whenever I had a misadventure of this sort I ran at once to a used bookstore to procure the unread volume or sought my dictionary for the definition of a word.

I was the cony of my tormenting mentor, who now galled me in another manner: "Does Anatole France's *The Red Lily* arouse your testes?" The word testicles was tabu, and since I was bred a Puritan I was outraged. I accused him of being a venereal sot, and beseeched him to leave at once for the clinic. "Should I savor the discourses of Epictetus as I might taste a squab?" I cried. "Be plain: Do you expect me to lie by a volume as the Athenians did with Lais of Corinth?" Unable to repress my abhorrence of his incontinency, I added: "You will pay a heavy mulct just to be scratched."

He prodded me more: "Have you a clear mind about Bourget's *Le Disciple?*" This fiction I had proposed to get, for its author, I was told, said that if you give three books to a maiden you can seduce her. Was I such a hypocrite? Had I a damsel to ease my carnal agony I might have been more veracious and had an amiable disposition. It smote me to be guileful, but I would not be vanquished: "I accuse Bourget of robbing all men of moral conduct," I said. "He writes well, and I allow that when I submit to his periods and semicolons a soft zephyr hovers in my hair."

Tired of my deceit, he went on stalking me: "Literature void of parboiled potatoes, rice, rye bread with caraway seeds, a flitch of bacon, the cost of staples as well as the price of a plump guinea hen, is the *belles lettres* of punctuation."

I concede that an author should be an abstemious recluse who continually burns for a woman. Close to seminal insanity I never had the courage even to ask where was a bawdy house.

"Can you remember what you read?" was, I thought, his penultimate assault.

This time I was out of my shoals: "I may masticate an entire book, but what is left in my mouth when I have fin-

36

ished it is no more than a cumin seed of it. I anticipate mis-understanding Plato and Aristotle until I am sepulchred."

He tried me yet again. "What is the meaning of lemur?" This was a dishonest thrust and I gave him his guerdon for it: "I mislaid the synonym the other day, but I may find it in one of my slippers, or I might have sent it to the laundry with my pajamas."

He got up abruptly in the midst of my ranting, and to irk me or to receive a calvish reply, as he walked away he remarked: "Do you understand life?"

"How inane can you be?" I scowled. "No man may see his life and live. Were it possible for anybody to know what he was doing there would be no poetry, essays or novels." Hoping my muttering would bite his ankles, I added: "I cannot permit you to depart while my tongue is hanging out," then audaciously continued: "Who is so ignorant as a man with a splendid digestion?"

He was gone, but softly so as not to tread upon my fragile veins, perhaps realizing my lies were not bad. Like myself, he knew when a man spoke falsely he was truthful about himself.

5

I will explain things as I can; not, however, will my words be certain and immutable, like those of Pythian Apollo, but those of a weak man, probabilities following conjectures.

—Cicero

Outside on the bald pavement I was kinless once more. Yes, I had been a dissembler and had lost a friend I had never acquired. Set afire by his ribald diction I craved the tender vines of a maid. Defeat, too, was a blaze I could not quench. The same monotonous refrain beat against my temples: was it impossible to pasture upon the *Iliads* without hankering for a jill? How could I save myself? By eating the grass of Sardinia which is supposed to be the cause of the sardonic smile. My so-called cynicism was the despairing heart.

Not yet a literary upstart, with only an animal confidence in my afflatus, I vowed I would become the living waters of an American Arcady. Who will believe that an obscure and prentice waif of Mnemosyne, the mother of the nine daughters of the arts, could have such a faith? When I was lost in the Mojave Desert in my eighteenth year, and as athirst and hungry as Hagar in the wilderness, I resolved that if I could endure this I could be a soothsayer.

Without misgivings, though doubt had gnawed me every hour, I chanted: "Every genius is in the Roman catacombs of his times, but when dead is worshipped as Christ with an ass's head. This is my myth and this is my body; so be it." Still I could not placate the desponding lake and rueful hills within me. Little did I know that I had chosen bad luck as my trade. Why, then, did D. H. Lawrence, when I was twenty-eight years old and impoverished in Paris, exclaim: "Dahlberg, for God's sake try not to be so unlucky"? I made the effort, but it was an endeavor that was opposed to my being. I had to fail in order to achieve what was most necessary to my starvation. Does not Hegel tell us that "the spirit of the prophets bloweth where it listeth?"

To my amazement I descried Anonymous the following day. Without nonsense he began: "What satisfies you more, dawn-fed rosy teats or maroon nipples? Are you a connoisseur of woman's anatomy? Dare you describe yourself a La Salle, Lewis and Clark or a Cabeza de Vaca of her secret delicacies? Never become intimate with skinny haunches, for a scrag is sure to bark at you. Look at her arms before you have an intrigue with her to see whether they are malicious. A female with insipid calves will never pardon you for being unfaithful. Don't touch a wife used by a grum-jowled druggist, or lie in a dilapidated womb. It is a mistake to go to bed with one wedded to a storekeeper, for you are likely to catch feeble-mindedness."

My attention was strict, and though I never claimed to know anything about women I furtively relished his apothegms. "When I have a quotidian fever," he continued, "I want to be hampered in the spherical skirts that hide a global, dimpled rump. What can redeem a sodden, penny night except her epigrammatic teeth? She who does not appreciate wit has a vulva that never laughs."

Still the dissembler, though choleric, I offered him a mumpish sentence: "Have you nothing on your mind except your body?" Full of shame I wished I were the ancient cynic Zeno who thought one could get a maidenhead were he acquainted with certain natural laws of motion.

His pinions were strong and he paid no heed to me: "I long for every lagoon, dell and crevice of Venus." Then changing the subject brusquely, he examined me with a plethora of pity: "You're unemployed. What would you like to do?"

"I would like to be intelligent," I said.

He showed his mordacious teeth and kind lips. Then he removed his glasses and I stared with astonishment at his eyes. I had the most crumpled feelings as I stood there brooding on his deeply set oracular orbs. Had I such profound, burning sockets, I thought, I could be a writer. Never was I to see such adustive brown eyes again until I met Sherwood Anderson.

After we parted I went upstairs to my room, and hopelessly looked in the mirror at my nose, brow, cheeks, hands. Were my eyes shoaly, life was finished. Doing my best to regain my arrogance, I pondered: could one make his own face while he moldered? Had not nature been a skinflint with me: boredom, helplessness, no prospects of any sort, completely useless—such was my lot. What else could I be but an author? I stood erect and took the oath of poverty in order to be honest. But that was a redundant pledge.

I considered all that Anonymous had said and borrowed whatever from him my body could accept. Those who fear influence lack the intelligence to realize that one takes from a book or a friend only what is essential to his flesh, and automatically rejects what he does not need for his life. I vowed to keep his name close to me as I could, for he was an autocrat of the intellect.

After he left me I felt lost and I feared I would never find myself. I had another sorrow: a vacant mind. A writer is broken to pieces when he has no thoughts. I had all the grief of a thoughtless man who imagines he has an imperial destiny. I suppose I am just as stupid now, but is it not faith in destiny that redeems all erring skin?

At the start of my apprenticeship I disdained our indigenous children of the arts, although I knew paragraphs of Ralph Waldo Emerson by rote and was to give my genuflections to Thoreau's *Week on the Concord and the Merrimack Rivers.* I remarked to myself that the U.S.A. scribbler was still asleep in the matrix, and making a tremendous effort to encourage the weakling in me I roared: "I am different, for I have come into the world like the four elements: emotion, strife, remorse and chagrin."

Now without Perverse and Anonymous, I walked the streets and pulled my nether lip which is the more cogitative of the two. With no one at my side but Alone, I asked: "Why is man just as solitary with his friends as he will be in his shroud?" Had not Flaubert in the nineteenth century complained: "What grieves me most is the appalling solitude in which I live. I have no one to talk to any more, absolutely no one. Who is there left that cares for eloquence and style?"

Days passed, and weeks, and months when I could not even find a gentle smile on a human face. I was treeless as the bleak *puna.* What is the physic for those humdrum negative days that cover us with scoriae? So far I had found nothing but to be a drudge in the kitchen of a lunch counter. Not wishing to be otiose I loathed work I could not enjoy doing. Apart from such reflections I knew I had to exhume myself each day or be a senseless grub.

Was I putrefying in my humors? Perhaps. "When philos-

41

ophy had sung this stave," said Boethius, "she began to make a discourse." I had fallen apart and nothing was of any importance. I wondered how Diogenes had dunged. Natural appetite was regarded unlawful by the political spado. Penniless I could not purchase a sop of pleasure.

The American amazon with the pitiless paps, as Caligula described Roman Livia, was a Ulysses dressed in woman's clothing. A desperate and famished urchin, I was prepared to diet on curried paps. Brillat-Savarin has written that medlars and woodcocks should not be tasted until they are somewhat decomposed. A splendid observation, but where was I to take hold of antiquated nipples? Giordano Bruno had said that nature itself is profligate, and Queen Elizabeth the First was no less wanton, for she beheaded her paramours whom she could not enjoy because a membrane covered her secret part.

Wherefore all this maundering? Those who think it puerile are boys who never committed a prodigious folly, nor have they known real want. What teacher has so much understanding as hunger? Despised by the human race, I offered this pronunciamento to my raving skin: "Cato fell on his sword, others drop into the vulva, and all are doomed."

How enchanting it was to hear that certain beasts couple thirty days before the rise of the Dolphin, but what good was that to me? I could seek companions at the Y but such company is solitude unless there is a woman in it. Spite of all my seminal fantasies I was a prude. I also had a horrid fear of venereal disease. Had I not been warned at the orphanage that one could grasp such an infection by sitting on a public close-stool, or by handling a towel used by many, or even by breathing the air issuing from a house of ill fame? Should I be so unlucky as to come upon a wench whom I could lie by, I would be amerced for a number of ticklish seconds with a large dose of gonorrhea or syphilis.

Inconstant every hour, I said good-bye to all lecherous desires, and shortly after this valediction found myself in front of King Solomon's temple of fornication. I had never had one voluptuous meal and I felt the urge to yield to incontinent idiocy. Yet what could I derive from one of these rancid dowds? One acquired a dance partner for a penny, but all I could manage was a gawky fox trot, and even if I spent a dollar leaning against her I would still be an unsatisfied lunatic. I tried to overcome my unbearable passions by reciting the "Over-Soul" of Emerson. Whenever I encountered a person capable of making a paradox I became his vassal. I was now the slave of Oscar Wilde and the wit of Anonymous, and emulating the latter I muttered: "It is easier to discover the Mississippi, Kansas, or the seven cities of Cibola than to locate a pair of sapid hams."

Full of spermal auguries I was rapt like one of the Old Testament prophets about to be translated from earth to Ursa Major. I would be content with a cut-rate Ashtoreth as any palmer is with the sacral joint of St. James. Simultaneously I detested my ardor.

I could not quell my drasty goat-toothed madness. Why should I not gather into my arms the loins and belly of a maid? Standing there on the curbstone I blamed every writer I had read for having forsaken me. Was there not a tinsel recipe or even Homer's Nepenthes that might assuage my sensual sorrow? I recollected a Christian Scientist who had forbidden me to be a flesh-mongerer, though I had not revealed to him I had any fever at all. He said he knew how youths were troubled by seminal demons, and mentioned an antique author, Dioscorides, who related that when one was overheated he could pluck white asphodels during the vernal equinox. After swallowing these flowers one would be cured of any barbarous emotions. He believed in the laying on of hands and so did I, but after all his boring elocution

43

I hated every philister who had passed statutes forbidding underground sensations. I gave the lot of them this brimstony epitaph: Here lies Father Phallus who gave up the Holy Ghost before his puberty.

It was useless. Like everybody else I sought those verminous delights one gets from that scabby goddess Psora. Would I ever enjoy the wide-hulled hips of any trull?

But could I afford to marry some woman solely to be quiet enough to read books, would I not be tied to my worst enemy? There was another American riddle: Why did people marry in order to sleep in separate beds, when they could be just as apart from each other by remaining single? Was not American literature so antiseptic because of twin beds? There was no solution; life was an enchiridion of errors, and all legends the result of human foolishness. Who can forget the one about Ocnus, who never ceased weaving a rope and could not see the ass, who was himself, just as busy unraveling it.

To be laconic, and I am as garrulous as Democritus of Abdera, I went inside the Hadean tickler.

composure, or that a north wind of health might brace my higher faculties.

I was in the midst of a charnel house of morbid gaiety, and though I wept for Phyrne's thighs I declared to myself that all men are disorderly beasts. I stared at the lewd skirts and factory suits rushing about the floor in a dry copulative dervish, and threw this at the giggish swarm: Call no man happy until his prepuce is dead.

A puny six feet tall, I weighed a hundred and eighteen pounds, and felt as decayed as one of Columbus' carracks that had been eaten into by worms. Just then a damaged jay passed me and gave me a spiteful face, and I was slain. The most ordinary insult or slight is unendurable; on occasions I have vomited after a pedestrian has jostled me without turning to apologize. What could I do in this counterfeit whorehouse? I shut my eyes to see. Could a farthing of darkness furnish the light for which I sighed in vain?

Now a dancer with two hundred pounds of lubberly self-assurance tiptoed by with a malkin. What a rotter he was! Would that I could support that much weight. Was not Mark Antony coarse and pursy, and he had Cleopatra?

How grubby it was. I seldom got what sharpened my appetite. If I craved a buxom lass I received a skeleton. When I coveted silken threads of hair I fell in love with a woman who was balding. Gasping for small feet I noticed too late that I had gotten involved with one who had loutish ankles and skulled toes. I detest a woman with a wide slattern mouth. As Chaucer affirms in *The Wyf of Bath*, "a likerous mouth moste han a likerous tayl." Imagining I had acquired a plump fundament, what was my amazement when I saw she had flat buttocks. Or realized I had not measured her nose. A small nose is best for erotical bouts, while a woman with long agaric nostrils is argumentative, and a crucifix in the boudoir. Thick arms are gorged with spleen, and a widow

46

EDWARD DAHLBERG

will never be content until she buries her new husband since
people want to do what they have done. It is a gargantuan
risk to marry one who has divorced three husbands; no matter what her most recent mate does for her, she prefers the
dead bridegroom who did nothing. A woman dislikes any
sort of change, and if she is accustomed to a scoundrel she
cannot abide a man who has principles.

It eventually became clear to me that no matter what I
did it would be a mistake. Soon as I met a female who
kindled my whole body, after we had decided to live together I regretted it. Should I broach a maidenhead I was
deluded; when my mind was clear I knew I had acquired a
dry and passionless concubine. Defeated each time, I wondered how I could eschew disaster. I was prepared to carry
about with me scales so that I could know beforehand how
many pounds I could expect. Were I sufficiently common I
could also inspect her. I panted for well-fed calves and a
pair of roseate, orotund teats. Such a woman is a philosopher
of amours.

Now a stale doxy whirled by showing a snippet of her
puce shift. She scalded me by pretending I was not there.

I am inflamed by colors and forget to see what is inside
the seductive material. The Roman matron adored orchida-
ceous hues, though the mud-purple feeds on slime. I swoon
over a vermilion chemise though it covers a carrion Aphrodite. A green hem is the verdure of the libertine.

Ovid reminds us what women used to arouse the booby
and the rake-hell; Poppea, the sexual swill of Nero, employed as her cosmetic that part of the sheep that sweated
most. She and others darkened their eyelashes with charcoal. Brantôme was certain that "by dress we are enchanted;
by gems and gold all things are concealed; the fair one herself is but a very trifling part of herself."

The human race is mad, and he who questions this belongs in Bedlam. Thinkers especially are lunatic, or drop into seminal rages. According to Rabelais friars have long and large genitories. Ignorant as I am of the other sex, I admit I shall never understand the female of the species. Can it be that she must remain forever a riddle to me because she has a matrix instead of a pudendum?

My reverie was interrupted by a sloven who stared with disdain at my clothes. Since I rarely got out of my suit we had become very close to one another, and I was not as defeated by her contempt as she had anticipated. Was it not Rousseau who said that a crone with six teeth in her chaps still imagines she is an appetizer for a Don Juan?

A drab stepped on my toe. At once I begged her pardon and she paused to ask what a relic like myself hoped to gain by flirting with her. This remark ruffled me. I had on several occasions been rebuffed by crumpled jades to whom I had made no advances. Examining myself narrowly I concluded my blood had spoken. Even when a male is apathetic he is lickerish.

Tired of these rammish skirts and senile trousers I was determined to leave, but remained to howl: "Oh, maggoty, dollar wombs, may you be bald in Gaza, have vinous piles in Ashkelon, and be ulcerated as Francis the First." Overcome by my reflections I loudly announced that she who has pinched lips is a snudge. Avoid a slut with unforgiving shoulders; a hard, savage neck is made for a halter rather than embraces. Do not cohabit in a room with an open window; you may get a draft on the small of your back and be flaccid. Don't mingle with one in a basement, for man is melancholy enough. Should a woman tell you she is truthful, shun her, for pleasure is dishonest.

After mumping these maxims I felt the manager touch my cringing sleeve; material is exceedingly sensitive. He said that if I continued to conduct myself without regard for the virtues demanded of every clean and righteous dancer, I would have to leave.

I crept toward a seat, seized by a quartan fever of Humility. I did not care for Humility from whom I had been hopelessly estranged. The word originally meant creeping on the ground. Indecisive, I wanted to be sensible and go back to my Y.M.C.A. hole where I could be the proud disciple of Nietzsche's *Beyond Good and Evil*, or his *Birth of Tragedy*. Who could mangle me as long as I had as my protector Friedrich Nietzsche? Why, then, did I not leave at once this grievous hysteria of dust?

In a fret I happened to turn and saw a maid about twenty years old. Modestly I looked at her; now I was beset by Compassion, who hardly ever visits anybody. She, too, was a gull of nature and I guessed that no one looked after her but Alone. I thought I saw a wizened smile creep around the corners of her mouth.

Instead of rejoicing I grew plaintive. Was this scrag the prize I was to get for all my struggles? Straightway she made it plain she trusted me, and I thought that another flaw in her for I had not the same feeling about myself as she had. At least I could trifle out my night with her, though my fingers were already smitten with sorrow since they acknowledged that after they had caressed her they would be widowers. Still, Alone and Want dearly loved both of us.

7

*Let her head be from Prague,
paps out of Austria, belly from
France, back from Brabant,
hands out of England, feet from
Rhine, buttocks from Switzer-
land, let her have the Spanish
gait, the Venetian tire, Italian
compliments and endowments.*
—Robert Burton

Outside with this timorous sparrow I stopped my ears with
my fingers to escape the hoarse, coughing sounds of Avalon.
We sauntered toward Echo Park, a nocturnal garden of lust
for those who could not afford a cheap whorish room. I
strolled along at her side, wondering how her famished arms
and skinny dress could nourish my tumult. Her face had
not been hardened by the usurious demands of a lewd drummer although her lips were a spinster's lamentation.

A rake adores a stale chemise, others faint with joy at
the sight of a sharp elbow. A slovenly mouth arouses some
amative gourmets; pimps dote on any scrap of a frump in a
trencher. But what was I to do with this puny?

This was a bad moment in my life. I felt I was betraying

her, and I wanted to be kindled by her in order that she might not believe she was forsaken! In sore need of counsel, and utterly lost myself, I saw a dry figure grinning at me. It was Reason who forced me to confess that after such a snack I would be as starved as I was.

We sat on the grass, a midnight sky covering us. I placed my benumbed hand on her breast but could not find it. Despondent I touched her knee and there was no musk in it. I was swindled! Then Pity, who seldom visits men, came to me, and I looked at her and saw that Alone was with her. We were both decoys of nature, and had been cheated by the elements and the four corners of the earth. I could hear her small-born wings fluttering and her flimsy petticoat bleating. In a rage I kicked Reason hard as I could for he had deprived me of compassion.

I have heard that the worms sing like the viol, and that it is a libidinous song. She was listening to my blood speaking though I believed it was mute. Her fright troubled me, and I blamed myself since all skin is lascivious; my feelings are sly I am always guilty. Baffled, as I did not know how to reassure her, I looked for Intelligence, who was seldom around when I needed him although he doesn't require a calling card to visit me.

Meantime, I thought I had gotten rid of Reason; why should he pester me now when he commonly considered me a nuisance. Besides, I detested him. He stood there, brushing his bowler hat, polishing his cane and snickering. Born to be gently stroked I cannot suffer my rational faculties that have not a farthing of affection for anybody. I laughed, and her fear rose. I wanted to flee; sensual I also have an ascetic strain, and hold in real account the *Resolves* of Felltham: "I would not care for too much indulgiating of the *flesh*, which I must one day yeeld to the *wormes*."

Would that I could watch myself more narrowly; sometimes I shake hands with a woman so fervently she supposes I am making advances to her, and although I am not, am I? What a festering dilemma. Or if a female offers me a gloved hand I resent it, and she assumes I desire her when I didn't, but did I? Of course, I've consulted Reason about this countless times, but what did he ever do for me? Nothing, that's why I'm always guilty.

Meantime, I had forgotten her although she was on my mind. She sat there hurt by my silence which can be extremely uncomfortable.

Trying to console her I lipped her skirt she had bound tightly around her whimpering legs. With no intention of possessing her I could not retreat. For no reason at all Reason stood beside me. When I'm irascible he's never there to advise me to be rational; should I be in the Dionysiac throes of an argument I lose because he is absent.

There were two waifs I could not handle, the one on the grass and me.

Did I hear her getting up? I stared at her defeated skirt. Suddenly she covered herself with her arms. She believed she was naked. Desolation is always nude.

Had I removed my clothes, for I was ridiculous and an eccentric man is bare as his skin? I began to recite a love song to her:

"I prize your celestial documents, your hips and potable nipples. Without lawless passions I swear by the discretion of your feet and your continent legs I adore you. Guileful as I am I shall never forget the forgiveness in your loins. I admit I become excited when I consider the rakish flea that perches inside your blouse."

That made her scratch herself, and I regarded it as a hopeful sign, since Scratch sired Eros.

As nothing happened I continued: "I could lie by you roasted, baked or sodden, as the olden poets speak. Hear me. Merlin was ever prepared to waylay a maid, and I too crave your smiling navel. Quiet the wanton in me, otherwise I am beyond all help for the world eats the inner life. A ragged pilgrim I beg you to offer your toes which are the Canticles of Solomon. A religious, I will turn the leaf of your petticoat just as I might a page of Genesis. Or by your leave, I'll be the mariner who tacks about your anatomy and finally anchors in that cove where one can doze and wonder until he is oblivious of the Many, the foe of the One. Let us gabble about maidenheads, the phallic turnip and the Pythagorean vetch. Have all faith in my swoon, for your matrix is as sacred as the Book of Psalms."

Slowly she walked away, which made me morose. What cruelty there was in that. I never wanted her, yet she had plainly rejected me. Women spy on emotions men don't even notice. A female knows a man has hidden a crafty feeling in his slipper or in one of his socks, but he has one triumph, his sole secret from her—what's in his brain when he imagines he has a marvelous thought!

Breaking out in wrath I told her she was the plagiary of all the exhausted virtues of society. She was placid and quietly took my arm as we left Echo Park. Nearly conquered by this soft gesture, I reflected: It's a ruse.

On the porch we sat on the steps. I looked at her room through a window empty of expectations; it faced flowerless Figueroa Street. She was in my lap, and without concern she raised her slip to fasten her wrinkled stocking with a safety pin. I was undone; where were the wimple, the tire, the lining inside the silk garment Plautus said drove Romans into a frenzy.

I arose and kissed her insipid wrist and pleaded I had to go back to my books that grew very lonely without me. After she timidly closed the door to her room I knew I had abandoned her. Crestfallen I trussed up myself best I could by the observation of Baudelaire: "To fornicate is to aspire to enter into another; the artist never emerges from himself."

A vagrant was standing on the curbstone, and I dropped a tear because he was with Nobody. When I joined him he looked at me warily; to allay his suspicions I offered him an acre or two of my most arable friendship. Certain I was about to rob him, he fled.

I limped along, seeking to fathom the cause of his flight. True, there was a mortal disease called good advice which was rapidly spreading everywhere. Some referred to it as the Los Angeles plague of 1920.

Deeply puzzled I wondered how I could prescribe for people who were so suspicious. I suspected everybody also, for though I am different from others I have the same sickness. Considering that a pretty fair insight, I swallowed it and for a while was cured, but I believed I ought to go to a herbalist to remedy my sagging devotion to others. However, I was not without medicine; had I not gained two new experiences although they were similar to old ones? I insisted they were novel; otherwise, what had I to look forward to except a monotonous life?

Presently I descried a pariah doing nothing with his time but losing it. This made me somewhat acrimonious, and I was determined I would do nothing for him. I went off, cursing him, and was surprised that I was standing alongside him. His jacket had no confidence in anybody, and it cost me no meditation to assess his condition. Since man is gregarious even though he is forsaken, it was obvious that he was being cared for by Poverty. He spat in the gutter, which so repelled me that I assailed him because I no longer had any compassion for him. At the same time I railed on Good Manners, an amiable but shallow fellow who has no Pity.

Soon as I came to this unsocial judgment Reason capered

toward me and warmed his hands in my cold pockets. He found nothing in them but misery, which made him quite jubilant. I misliked his familiarity and shoved him away.

Then I listened to Abel crying up out of the ground. I had met this unusual creature when I was born, and his presence brought about a change of mind and I said to the vagabond that though we were strangers to one another he could feel free to help himself to my prospects. Expecting gratitude and a tittle of affection for my generosity, I was hewn to pieces when he showed such a fear of me that he hurried down an alley. I threw my rancor at him but missed. My leaven of pessimism was rising and discontent was hanging at my sleeve and nagging a button on it.

8

*Will you be an ass, despite your
Aristotle?*

—Webster

I returned to my room, expecting to be the reposeful calybite,
but I had another stout foe, Belly, who was grumbling at
me. I tried to quiet him by chewing one of my sacred books,
but he did not stop growling and finally he began to howl.
"Be quiet," I commanded him. "Lao-tzu is present. How
can he teach me ethics when you are screaming?"

There was an impostume on my neck, and viewing it in
the mirror I saw that after months of starvation it had begun
to suppurate. Meantime, I studied my situation. Where could
I get purgative work? To be a grub in an office was repulsive to me. Nor could I be a busy idler in a plant, producing
baubles and pillaging my life to increase the cupidity of the
fat Jeshurum of commerce. What was I able to do with
the wisdom of Ecclesiasticus: "The chief thing for life is
water, and bread, and a house to cover one's shame."

I paced the room. Everything was finished but at the
same time maybe there would be a windfall. My blood was
virtiginous as my mother's, who never let a day go by without looking for that stranger, Good Luck, but he was too

occupied with other persons to bother about us. Yet to be idle was a yoke, and just as bad as this I still could hear Paunch tumbling about, rumbling and raving. I sank as I muttered: fortunate is he who has no hopes at all. But this was a tiresome quibble that I rebuffed.

The next day I encountered Anonymous in the lobby of the Y. He appeared to be expecting me, though I had been sure he wanted nothing of me. At once he imparted to me that an Edenic part-time job was available which would only require three hours of my sun. He showed me the advertisement in the help wanted column of the Los Angeles *Times:* "Must be young, congenial, educated, suspicious and experienced in handling cash. $60 a month and climate."

What qualifications had I for this position? Always old and of a decrepit humor, only on rare occasions did I not quarrel with myself. As for education, I had misread forty to fifty books whose authors had made me absolutely useless. Small wonder Cash was disappointed in me. I had the wrong foibles for this world.

As for the other asset I needed for the position, who can gainsay I have not suspected myself and everybody else?

Without waiting to discuss my qualifications Anonymous left me, and I was so perplexed I went downstairs to the gymnasium to weigh my irascibility. I jumped off the spring balance; it was so patently dishonest. How could my faults weigh so much? After counting them I had not an ounce of virtue. As I carried no more than one hundred and eighteen pounds, how was it that my spleen weighed ninety pounds, my mistakes two hundred, my character nothing at all? Still, I considered I might make a clever appearance, and I departed from the gymnasium walking upright, resolved to be what I was not.

I was doomed. It was clear that Money could never afford to keep me. I did not see the employer who had apparently expected me; I stared at his illiterate teeth and slobbery shoulders and felt he abhorred me, so I hated him right away. But before I could begin my diatribe he said I could start the next day.

I was to serve as a clerk in a public venereal clinic. Most of the patients were Mexicans; those who had gonorrhea paid twenty-five cents for treatment—a dose of Argyrol— and syphilitics half a dollar. I had never anticipated I would secure such a jovial position.

The first day I was there a Harvard man with a Ph.D. arrived for treatment. I had not thought that a Doctor of Philosophy could have the pox. I was very impressed by this unusual man and spoke to him with the awe of those who cannot mention education without crossing themselves or kissing the toe of Ignatius Loyola. I also prattled with the unfortunate Mexicans who forgot, whenever they could, to give me the quarter or fifty cents. An enthusiast, I never had the incivility to ask for the money. However, the physician proved to be quite churlish and after counting the silver pieces in the drawer he accused me of stealing. Always resolute about doing anything that was to my disadvantage, I called him a liar and was straightway discharged.

Where should I turn? Anonymous had forsaken me, and Marion had left. I still envisage his flat, hopeless face, and his nose that was not prehensile enough for this world. There was David Josephus, who had a mulberry-colored mouth and who had introduced me to Walter Pater's *Marius the Epicurean*, William James's *Varieties of Religious Experience*, and Josiah Royce, but he had gone to Monterey to be a waiter at a hotel facing the water, where he received fabulous tips. He would not relinquish his job until he had earned enough to come back and read for several months. I realized I was too clumsy to carry dishes.

By chance I ran into Anonymous again. His body seemed

more of a rib than before and I gazed at him with all the pity I had for my own peaked condition. He asked me to join him in a chat and soon as we sat down he demanded to know if I had heard of Leo Tolstoy. I retorted that I had. With contumely he told me he had no intention of discussing my hearing. Examining his ocherous pimples, I nearly bowed down to him. A congenial despot, he was ready to help any man who acknowledged him as the autocratic mind. I was gloomily pothering over my future and as I continued to poach into the wet mire of my desolation he suggested without wasting words that I go to college.

How could I do that? My mother was a hard-working lady barber in Kansas City, who scraped chins for ten cents and cut hair for fifteen pennies. Of late, I had now and then asked her to mail money to me, assuring her that I would be a genius very shortly. Two people had faith in me: my poor, torn mother and myself.

I was such a bizarre noddy that Anonymous saw I was not mediocre and might become a rare failure were I able to pocket up all the disadvantages I needed. He was sure that I could gain the obstacles essential to me.

"Speak plainly and without any pettifogging," he exhorted me. "Have you read Tolstoy's *What Is Art?* Is literature honey in your mind?"

"No matter how many books I put my nose into," I mewed, "why is it that I can never profit by them?" And meandering I went on: "To misunderstand a book comes from a spinal defect. One seldom has the strength of the poet to disinter his own tombs in order to feel his verses."

"You fret me to the guts," Anonymous whispered, although I thought he had shouted. Tired of wasting his oracles on me, before he departed he announced: "Hegel reveals that goodness and beauty are similar. Good-bye. Go to the University."

9

I aged as I read Tolstoy. Art, according to him, was only
a decadent pastime. Why should I then write? I have
never been able to answer this question. Before I was familiar with Tolstoy I dropped into the fatuous conceit that
a book of mine might have a beneficial effect upon some
torn and outcast reader. I might gain petty triumphs, or
make a squib, but how useful would that be? The Spaniards
who came to the New World caulked their boats with moss,
bark and very tough grass; every pore of my anatomy was
filled with satiety and the muggish plants of death. Craving
a simple existence I was in more respects than I knew froward. I tried not to say what I did not believe or know, but
I said it.

I fell into Styx as I studied *What Is Art?* and *My Confession*. I recited sundry lines from these two volumes by
the master of Christian nihilism that larded my woe. At this

point I parted from Emerson. The "Over-Soul" could not truss up my grief, and I detested "Self-Reliance." I cared as little about the universe as it did for me. Utterly tired of the cosmos, nature, the firmament and such flummery words, I had only one ambition and that was to flee from the most tedious person I knew, myself. He was just as much of a bore as Alone.

Days followed one after another when I could not force out the futile words. My mouth was tombed. There was a god of old time who had no mouth. Everyone has heard that people who are reticent are wise, without considering that if they do not speak it may be they have nothing to say.

I thought I could be amiable and tranquil were I stupid and seeing that I was stupid I took up simplicity, but people I met by chance thought me affected. Though a curmudgeon was the one thus to describe this pose I was no less stung than had Lao-tzu corrected me. I had wallowed in the paradoxes of Oscar Wilde, and could not tolerate anyone who did not accept my dogma that there was no literature superior to *The Picture of Dorian Gray* and *De Profundis*. In the suds I set myself up as the intuitive artist. Preoccupied with atheism, spiritualism, Christian Science, I happened to catch sight of one of Spinoza's observations, that remorse is a cardinal sin. Oh, go grind your lenses, Master Spinoza; what else is there?

Put off by this wayward remark of an unusual thinker, I again sought my redemption in Tolstoy's works. I had the audacity to disagree with some of his dogmas, but never with him. A real book flames within me like Ilium. In essential matters he was right. Maybe I was never to be simple, but I realized that plain ignorance is as hard to come by as wisdom.

The wormwood in *What Is Art?* was better than the anile sports of the middle class. Never was I to renounce *My Con-*

fession, a scaffold that Tolstoy had created for me. Pensive worm that I was, I would walk to it until the end. From the Russians I had gotten the knack of accepting pessimism without flinching. I would also treasure *Thus Spake Zarathustra*, that desolate, bacchic laughter. That I shall never know the truth is obvious, but he who ceases to strive for it is as good as dead; his oracles have dried up in him.

Unable to commit Shakespeare and Beethoven to Bedlam as Tolstoy did I could not then foresee that painting would be the belly of Moloch, and that the artist would be selling waste and foolery while doggerel would be praised and George Herbert become as vacant to readers as a cenotaph.

Always I returned to the great Russian who had banished Sophocles, Euripides, Aeschylus and Aristophanes whose works I had read in the Bohn Library edition. What fever drove this Slavic soothsayer to such madness? I declined to wage war with Homer or Aeschylus, but allowed the poesy to pass through me and what was not essential for my singular necessities I would automatically reject. This kind of cerebral passivity was best understood by Ignatius Loyola, who said "a pupil should be a corpse in the hands of a teacher."

In a muddle, I was likewise startled by Gautier, one of my demigods, who stated that Baudelaire had attempted to excise eloquence, passion and truth from *Les Fleurs du Mal*. Could Baudelaire, one of the most naked sufferers in our Arcadia of poetry, be so artificial?

As an antidote I became an acolyte of Pater's *Marius the Epicurean*. But Pater could not take care of my desperation. It was my resolve to abide by principles, but when I had the vapors I forgot all about the *Analects* of Buddha; what I promised myself I would do of a morning I violated by evening. Should I assert, this day I shall be kind, I was waspish; or witty, a dunce.

EDWARD DAHLBERG

Tolstoy wrote: "I fell ill . . . gave up everything and started for the steppes, to breathe fresher air, to drink mare's milk, and live a mere animal life." By now I was as good as a relic, a part of my head in one sacral vault and half a foot in another crypt. I could not put myself together. I mourned over the disappearance of Busy Perverse, Marion, and Anonymous. I blamed them for having neglected me, and I said: "A friend creepeth into your soul and there excretes all his foxes, and then everyone who approaches asks: 'Why does he stink?'"

I pined for the genius of touch, though I vaguely suspected I would relinquish everyone who called himself friend. After that, where would I go? Never to the rout. Rather the stone than the bread of opinion.

Then I ran out of doors, for no logical purpose except that one is always doing the same thing and the snare prepared for him by the furies is that he is forever having brand-new experiences that are only the lees of the old ones. After walking the streets I returned to the lobby and stood alongside myself.

Whatever illusion of space exists between my young manhood and the present, I would never go back to such a miserable night of puberty. I was ashamed of my childhood; smothered with humiliation, my youth was a glut of unwanted degradations. Although I venerated my mother I sank when I thought of her barbershop, that dungeon of morose vulgarity. As her hair thinned I was mortified; when her melancholy deepened I was sure her nose, shaped as the tent of Kedar, had grown longer. I fell into despair because she could not govern its length. Then there is no more Stygian trance than youth. He who would go through it again is asking for two scaffolds, his past and his present.

I continually strolled, spoke to myself, sat, studied; all this was the mull and herbs of doubts essential to me. In the streets I mistook a strange face for a familiar one, and approaching him and holding out my hand I saw I had come upon human rubble. He who has seen a mountain that appears like the visage of the Creator will have the same disillusion soon as he has come right up to it and sees that it is a pile of dead sullen dirt. I venerate all distances, for they are the only images I have ever had of infinity.

My appetite declined, and though I did not know it my sharkskin suit looked as starved as I was. By now I had the notion I was meek and ascetic, but I continued to have those visions of beasts who had the leering eyes of the succubae. One would arrive and another depart, and each one opened her white alb and showed her breasts, wild wanton apples.

I thought words might be as healing as the garment of St. Martin. Sir John Mandeville's "lust is a kindly sin" comforted me. Then there was Ignatius Loyola, who dreamed he saw the Virgin Mary and after that considered the honeyed pleasure of mingling legs together as unaffecting as a woman at her loom, or a tailor threading a needle. Yet I could not dissipate those nocturnal brutes; I was still libidinous as Ignatius himself, who had his broken leg reset by a surgeon so that his stockings and boots would fit better and give him a pair of handsome calves.

Could it be that everything I did was solely to vanquish my venereal conceptions? Does man go to and from Capernaum, Bethany and Tarsus to govern his phallus? Each morning I stood in the corner of my room so that I could not be observed by the walls, or my chair, formerly straight and austere, that had since been transformed into a hilarious gargoyle, or the carpet I had so often trod upon and that now coiled about my bellied large toe. Mindful of these devils I cried out to the four elements: "Let me not be gross, and prevent me, I beseech you, from having any commerce with Touch, for as soon as I finger anything the most infernal and involuntary vices crowd in upon me."

Constantly vigilant of my deeds, I was low when I expected lofty emotions, and complicated when I had every belief I should be simple. Enraged, I took up affectations, wit, then naïveté, indifference. When I showed pity for others I blessed myself, and if put out I was argumentative, unpleasant and finally a horror to my own nature. He who imagines he is better than this is worse. Obviously, my harvest was stubble. Renouncing good and evil principles alike I pursued beauty and was depraved for searching it. Every enthusiast is a droll who is under the smart of a jibe.

Talking to myself as usual, while rambling on Hope Street I contemplated a pair of old, forsaken shoes lying in the gutter, waiting for any two feet to come along. Gaping at them with compassion I noticed the broken despondent latchets. I stood the shoes upright and exhorted them: "Though I pity your predicament I demand that your strings cease sniveling. Are you so beaten and fateless as to asylum any poltfoot?"

Gingerly tiptoeing away from the vagabond shoes I looked back at them and each showed me a mocking tongue. I constrained my spleen for I knew that though they were together each was alone. Then they brayed at me until I was the laughingstock of the street. A horde had heard me; some howled, some threw sticks, and numerous chuffs kicked me. Each blow stung and blistered me until I bled with joy.

Ravished by melancholia, I uttered these words of Tolstoy: "I hid away a cord to avoid being tempted to hang myself by it to one of the pegs." There is no reason to deny that I had killed myself several times. That I could not go on in such a desolate vein obviously is untrue had I not proved that this is what happened.

Youths are filled with unlimited expectations and skulled

laughter. Woe sooner or later is the father of pleasant tidings, but as the cosmos is envious of a mortal's good fortune
I was on guard against the universe all day long lest I be
smitten. What I fear most is unexpected calamity.

Suddenly I dreaded that my mother would die, and when
I got out of bed in the morning I took hold of her dear face
and gathered each feature in my hand. When I saw the
whole of her perishable being I knew then I was ready for
the sudden attack which brings the pile of griefs.

I became the adamant enemy of the cosmos and grieved
for its victims. Had I not seen a pond with thick guts of
ice covering it on wintry days fail in health in March and
dwindle and perish from the raging blasts of Sirius? A stout
warrior rock that has defied rain and winds becomes a crum-
bling dotard? Since man himself is the most superstitious
brute in any meridian, I imagined that the only way to guard
my mother from an unpredictable assault was to think of
her all day long. Could I sustain an unsleeping vigil she
would live.

What, I mused, is the difference between the phantasms
we observe and those that tenant cemeteries? After a parent
has moldered for a decade the memory becomes so dim it is
nearly impossible to piece together the entire visage. No
matter how great is the emotional struggle the image is
painted in the mind for the shortest winter.

Then I forgot to remember my mother, which was a stroke
of blasphemy, and caught sight of a worn-out periodical
slumbering in a cane chair next to me. Glancing at the title
of the magazine, *Bedlam*, I picked it up and held it close to
me. Among the advertisements I noted:

"Two million Americans die of loneliness each year. Free
consultation . . . Subscription to *Bedlam* $100 . . . Learn
to be satisfied with yourself; only your friends can kill you
. . . Be courteous to the pickpocket: he is only trying to

warm your empty wallet . . . Do not be afraid of the germ, love. Man himself is ten thousand diseases . . . Be old-fashioned. Those who exchange buttons for zippers are likely to geld themselves . . . Health cafeterias for desponding pre-puces . . . Meet your right mate. Most people live out their lives with the wrong bodies. Liaisons arranged, fee $200 . . . Optimism lectures . . . Herbs for those who have an excessive abundance of pity for others . . ."

I continued to scamp the advertisements: "If you have a splendid digestion you will care for nobody. Be sick once in a while so you can be human . . . Learn how to make a plain remark in six weeks . . . Ill-humor atelier: specialists who cobble up a bad disposition . . . Study ceramics and you will be gregarious . . . Learn to shake hands and make a fortune doing it . . . Self-knowledge reading room . . . Sanitary bibs for professors who soil themselves . . . Upper and lower colonic irrigations for mildewed maidenheads or retired wombs . . . Visit the hypocrite shop where one can wash his hands of the Truth in Pilate's basin . . . Laugh emporium. Nominal fee for grins . . . Higher thought jour-nal. Subscription $5.00 . . . Logic dry goods store . . . How to maintain a business face during office hours. Ten beau-ticians will arrange your features for you . . . How to win friends without acquiring enemies . . . Chiropodist pares calluses on doctorate theses . . . Perversity study group . . . How to be wise without alienating 200,000 U.S.A. citizens . . . Cockloft for rejected human emotions . . . Don't sit at home and maul your feelings. We have ten adjustment rooms. No couches. You will stand on your own feet instead of others' . . . Nursing home for millionaires. Purses and large bank accounts fumigated every week . . ."

When I grew tired of fondling my follies I read what I had written recently in my notebook. From Samuel Butler's *The Way of All Flesh* I had acquired the habit of carrying

10

---

*They may, for want of better
company,
Or that they think the better,
spend an hour,
Two, three, or four, discoursing
with their shadow.*
—Ben Jonson

Los Angeles (I read) is a crazy, quacksalving town. There
are shoals of widows immured in seedy rooming houses,
who have nowhere to go but say they pay visits or expect
guests and have a few teabags on the shelves of shallow
clothes closets, which they generally serve themselves.
Should they have inherited a tiny patrimony, they buy themselves a suitcase which they keep in their sitting rooms to
prove they are about to travel to a foreign country. About
half or more of the town is full of kennels for widows, spinsters, divorcees and bachelors. They are the forlorn ghosts
of the left-handed part of Los Angeles. The others are
sharpers, quacks, spiritualists, brokers, doctors who use their
surgical instruments to probe consumptive wallets, legal
liars called lawyers, and bankers, euphemism for usurers.

There are also a million cats and dogs that comfort the

peeled spinster, the cautelous widow and the bachelor. These people venerate their pets no less than the Egyptians who wept for the crocodile or the ibis, and built a feline sphinx. They dine with and sleep with them and cocker them as if they were infants.

There is nothing that so awakens the negative spirit as watching a spinster who has been mewed up until late afternoon allowing her terrier to dung on the pavement while the finical gentleman warily goes around these foul droppings. Grass widows and divorced males stop in the middle of the street to permit a cocker spaniel to acquaint herself with a pedigreed sheep dog as they snuff one another's scent. Once this habit between the two curs has started it is more or less a certainty that it will be continued. Nobody knows the time as well as such a pair.

The animal lovers sneak out of their thin lodgings to stroll with a Maltese or a terrier who bites the heels of passers-by, thus giving the hag or toothless jade jubilation. The curses of the man or woman are about as good as the smiles they never observe. Should a man stoop to stroke the back of a cat, and get for his solicitude a scratch long as the life line on his palm, the animal's owner will show her gums; the more rebukes she gets the more hysteria her old, greased dress displays. Oftentimes the encounter is a glory and the victim goes to her lodging, while the cat hisses and claws him. Since men in America are born to be mortified, such an encounter may be the origin of a beautiful friendship.

The next day she is expecting him. She pounces her wrinkles, rouges her flagging and shrunken lips; when he arrives he can smell her even before she opens the door. There is nothing so offensive to a male as a crone who sprays him as though she were a syringe of every perfume in the garden of Eden.

The talk, no less queasy, is about her four-legged Lucifer. His mind strays while he covers his nose with his hand lest he be overcome by the odor of cat's urine, worse than the stench of Acheron. She chatters: "What shall I do about Dolly? She is afflicted with arthritis, the rheum, has chills at bedtime and shakes at the edge of my bed; if I try to take her close to my young, swelling teats she leaps out of my arms and goes—pardon my language—to her bowel box. Then she chases a moth or a fly for a pair of hours, and I have to turn on the lights to see whether my love is ailing of Parkinson's disease. You know, I took her to the optician to get a prescription for glasses for her as she is extremely near-sighted, and when he refused to give her an examination I went to a chiropractor to straighten out her spine. He said it was affecting her brain, and would you believe it, she thinks more quickly than she ever did.

"Cats are really philosophers," she goes on. "I have heard the ancient Chinese told time by looking into their eyes. One veterinary, of more repute than my spiritualist or Plato, told me she had a venereal disease. I assured him she had been altered, but he said a cat can get the pox from—I beg to apologize for my English—snuffing up the anus of a stray who has no shelter but an alley, or from eating garbage in our hygienic gutters, and even—O Lord, heal my mouth—syphilis if I take her out for the air. Dolly does pass water often, and I suspect she has heart trouble, or is suffering from the stone."

When this crumpled udder takes Dolly for a walk she prays she'll meet a man who does his own cooking and darns his socks and who'll stop to caress her companion. Should nothing come of this, wearing the same deceased dress and withered felt hat she visits her faith healer. To take up as much time as possible she catalogues her complaints—insomnia, trench mouth, ungovernable saliva, oversweating, palsy and premature baldness—and beseeches him to cure her. Perhaps she needs more iron in her blood. Could he not prescribe for the apoplexies of old age which come upon her when she is disappointed or receives a letter fringed with funereal black?

Of an afternoon she goes to a meeting for civic improvements, or sits with a group of gammers one of whom has lost her geranium pups, or attends a gathering of a reincarnation society she has joined. She subscribes to the *Christian Science Monitor*, the reading of which affords her much solace, and when boredom hangs heavy on her back she visits the graveyard.

Although she has no kin beneath the ground she studies the epitaphs and turns her back on one headstone that imparts this information: "Mamie Dullife—Born 1898, Died 1919." Her own crabbed bones have lasted seventy years, but she dreads she might suffer from that cruel affliction of mankind, a short life. Standing before another burial plot she reads with jubilation: "Eve Nonesuch—Born 1826, beloved daughter of Mathilda Nonesuch, left her venerable aunt in 1910." Praise be to Eve Nonesuch for having had the intelligence to stay alive for that length of time! Our lady paces about seeking another sacred site where she hopes she may find an interred one who was even more sensible.

As one who has lived apart from men she reproaches every one of them for having abandoned her. Who can console the matrix? O God, must I speak aloud to Thee who knoweth one organ from another? She sings a hymn to atone for this obscene idea that came into her head without her knowing it. A devil must be slinking inside her musty skirt. Does he not linger about jakes?

Church is not so much a relief or pastime as a cemetery. She sits alone on the bench and not even pious Martha, too busy lifting up her craw to heaven, speaks to her. Again she thinks of all the sins that attack her; even her dug whimpers for a hand. She goes out and prays to Him who hears nothing and embraces herself.

Was God a tailor? Her throat is so seamed and miserably stitched together. What a malicious mirror she has, and why is she so ignorant as to look at herself in it? How a looking glass ages the beholder.

One afternoon, while Dolly was sprinkling the street, she forgot her own name. Paralyzed, she begged Dolly to stay close to her. Then she went through the alphabet to discover her Christian cognomen and dropped into a liturgy of anguish:

"Anne, Bertha, Clara, no. . . . What comes after C? Or G, girl, once she was a maiden. . . . H, Hanna. Let me see . . . M, Maude. P, urinate. God help me, what dirt there is in language. Q . . . that won't do. P . . . Oh, I am back to that profane letter. Don't, O Lord, let me pronounce it; my bones are not a morsel for a cur. Q . . . Didn't I say that before? G . . . G . . . What unshriven ghost is G. Ah, grave, granite. My mind is blind. Where are my glasses? My nose mizzles. I am December's sapless buttocks. What ragpicker would buy my killed chaps, my slain hair, my sunken mouth, my unbudding loins, my unused maidenhead. Old age is Golgotha, the skull of the body . . . S . . . No, R. Ah! R, Roberta Olive, that's it. The Mount of Olives. I drop no blood nor sweat upon thee, only my loose scriptural saliva."

At dusk she repairs to her bare impotent room, her dry vacant womb, and falls into her own arms.

Roberta Olive goes abroad with Dolly every day, and when an Angora accompanied by a celibate pauses to sniff Dolly, the lady and the gentleman chat. He walks with her to her room, and they drink tea, and when one of the cats wets the carpet each imagines the other smells.

I I

*I joye in grief, and doo detest
all joyes.*

—Sir Philip Sidney

I had disclosed to my hard-working mother that I hoped shortly to be a famous man of letters, and with charred distrust asked her if she could send me fifteen dollars a week. When word came there was a money order for me at Western Union at first I tarried. Should I refuse to accept it, for was I not filching her poor savings? Such was my plight: I had to gull my mother so that I would not be a gross person. I have always burned in the furnace of shame when I recall how I diminished her addle purse.

At last I bent my way toward the telegraph office, asking my mother to forgive her son. I wore my guilt on my face and on my back.

A young woman behind the counter asked me to identify myself. Absorbed in her toothsome, plump hands and the cleft in her dainty chin, I began to gently boil and my head turned to other impressions. As I gazed at her chin, and the glen in it, I was sure this was proof of a blessed cranny. Yet esteeming her chastity I misliked my riggish heat.

Awakened from this sleepy vagary I heard her say: "What

is your name, please? Sir, will you kindly show me your driver's license? Doubtless you are a propertied man."

"Lovely Madonna," I said, "I am Anybody's Miserable Chagrin."

"How much life insurance do you carry? Perhaps the company will guarantee that you are Anybody's Miserable Chagrin."

My tone altered. "Lady, I belong to the wormwood fraternity of penniless authors, a parasite according to our shop-keeping nation." Then with more bile I said: "Do you expect me to own a twenty-story building in order to collect fifteen dollars? How can I prove that I am I? So many parts of me are dissimilar I believe they must belong to someone else. I beg you on bended knees, don't ask me who I am; I really don't know. Let my countenance deliver the angelic or brutish message."

I handed her a card on which a printer had engraved:

ANYBODY'S MISERABLE CHAGRIN
Castaway Author of America

What delicate pips she had, a pair of roses or two bunches of violets, I guessed. And the little nose of a Sabine virgin. Already I chanted Chaucer's "For pitie renneth sone in gentil hearte."

She turned from the counter to go to her desk, and I devoured her milked calves and was set afire by the rump Venus had given her to placate the hungry tribe of males. Filled with her untasted myrrh I yearned to gather her mouth unto me.

Giddily I told her my imperial companions George Gissing, Flaubert, Gautier, Andreyev, Gogol and Baudelaire would not be reluctant to be a surety of my character.

The manager, who had a bean-shaped nose and vulpine mouth, picked up the phone and asked for the number of the charity hospital for the insane, but she stopped him from proceeding further. After she had given me the fifteen dollars I called out to him: "Do you know *The Death of Ivan Ilyitch* by Count Leo Tolstoy?" Bewildered, he gave me several low bows, declaring he had not realized I was on intimate terms with the nobility.

As I stood by the counter, for I was loath to leave, I considered the difference between her seraphic hinder parts and the pin-buttocks of Aeschylus and Euripides, which a poet must have to compose *Prometheus* and *The Bacchae*. Immune to a female with stingy flat posteriors, I was now full of my knowledge of women, the cause of so many scabbed follies. My easily stung flesh was my sole hovel which was never sufficient to cover my feelings. Still what a delightful udder she was.

My hesitation to ask her name was so thinly wrapped up that she herself told me she was Mary C——, and that I might call on her at her home the following evening. When she opened her lips I inspected her teeth as edible as the inner white skin of an apple, and noticed with a quantum of despair that one of them was fungused. Then to reappraise her and sustain my amorous desires I observed her wrist, for women who are hairy are as unpleasant to kiss as Methuselah in his nine-hundredth year. My heart was mirthful; her skin had no bristles and she did not secretly shave herself.

I walked away in my sodden shoes with a spruce gait. What a windfall the hour had been. A superstitious animal, I was minded to believe that good luck is gregarious as evil occurrences. Why does one receive five letters from different people on a single day, and then none for a fortnight? Should one receive a civil salutation from a bare acquaintance that also was a good sign and likely to be followed by another agreeable incident. Then if a passer-by steps on your foot, and you apologize to him, and he scowls at you, be sure the entire day is a fit of gloom. Doubtless nature is as unreasonable as man. I had won this virgin, and so pampered up was I by my triumph I now felt I was to acquire some credit in this world.

The night I was to visit Mary I polished my secondhand shoes so that they would not appear to be a pair of misfortunes. Then I spat on my sleeves and endeavored to sharpen the crease in my trousers, for I did not want my pants and jacket to show their murrain traits at once. Yet my clothes did not despise me, for my crumpled sharkskin suit and I had grown so close to one another we could be said to be blood relations. My cravat gave me a musty look, but I let that pass. I hid the ragged end and was ready to be the fop and beau.

Deeply smitten, though somewhat unnerved by the memory of that fungused tooth, I had the most pious faith in my lady's body. As I gazed out the window of the streetcar I hoped she was an orphan. A family was sure to be a galloping consumption to a mendicant suitor. At last the tram was near the city's limits; I got off and strolled, having an unusual fondness for the trees because they were neighbors of humble cottages. No avarice could dwell here, and the air was not pestered with the rotten fever of wealth.

At the door I was introduced to a slight stump of a father who straightway took a rare interest in my suit. Neither he nor my suit seemed to be getting along together. Fingering my coat he asked: "Where did you get this drowned animal?" With a vein of hauteur I quoted a sixteenth-century author: "The richest garments are subject to time's moth-frets."

My cravat also was scornful of him; it was still damp with my saliva. "Has your necktie a bad cold or bronchitis?" he asked, and without warning he put his nose against my sleeve. Dolefully he shook his head. "Never have I seen a coat so filled with sorrow. Was it beaten up lately?" Then with some display of propriety he touched the spectral seams of my trousers.

Without further preamble he stated that he was a tailor and demanded that I be plain with him since I showed myself all too clearly.

"Sir," I replied, "I did not come here to deceive you. My sharkskin suit is just as sincere and outspoken as I am."

The tailor was himself a piece of tallow wrinkled dotage, with a hump on his back and a head scrawled with a few miserable hairs. But Mary was standing close to me and I was so delirious I begged the universe for help, little knowing that he who looks for alms is certain to receive carrion woes. I was resolved to marry her, though my purse suffered from catarrh. I felt sure we could maintain ourselves with the fifteen dollars I would receive each week from my mother added to Mary's wages.

Shortly I heard her father saying: "I didn't catch your name." Misliking this fetid obstacle to my ecstasy, I gave him his deserts: "I don't lend my name at once. Wait until I am assured we can rely upon one another." Then in another mood I answered him: "Suppose you borrow my name, and then discover you are holding Mr. Hypocrisy, or Mr. Deceit, or Sir Knavishness, what sort of a match would I be for your daughter?

"We've had a bad start," I began again. "Now let me be frank with you. My prospects are more than you could discover at first blush. I have a score of glorious disappointments. Don't be put off; you can't imagine what good can come of bad luck."

In return for my efforts to please him the tailor gave me a smile that had long since died. Then he proffered me a mawky grimace, but I was in a high gale of self-confidence.

"To repeat," I said, "I'm not promiscuous, and just don't allow the first person I meet to handle my name. Such a name is a whore, a summer resort companion, a pimp. Look, I am ready to esteem you. After all, now that I think on it, you are Honorable Father-in-Law. Please bear in mind I offer your precious flower all that I possess, good clean poverty, a carcass of my simplicity and my clove-scented anticipations. Don't frown on such Arcadian gifts. Now that we know each other better, you may use my Christian name, *Anybody's*, and when the occasion is ripe you may disclose to a few intimate friends my surname, *Miserable Chagrin*."

The fuddled tailor stared wildly at me, and then in a vein nearly humble, beseeched me: "Have you a family?"

"No, sir," I replied, "I live with me."

He nodded. "That must age a man. Your face seems to gray your hair."

Musing, I said: "Well, so much has happened to me though there are no events in my life. I'm not a mediocre tradesman. I account bakers, dairymen, cobblers, robbers, and though they grow fortunes Venus shall hate them and the caterpillars devour their houses, wives and mistresses. As for my own vocation, when the spell is on me I go out into the streets bawling: 'A harp for sorrow, a sackbutt to soothe those diseased with melancholia, and true fresh garden maidenheads for the impoverished.' "

"You call that work. A man must sweat for a living."

"Sir, I perspire for your daughter."

"Look to your manners, lunatic. This is not a sporting house. Simple-minded as you must be, you know where the door is."

Mary stepped between us, and the tailor lowered his tone: "Let us pass that over. But tell me, who takes care of you?"

Somewhat battered, I asserted: "On Sundays, when I have totally forsaken myself, I write a letter to my mother. I have learned it is human nature to abandon others. A few months ago, realizing this, I got a divorce from society."

"How is your health?"

"I'm in poor shape, but I despise a man who has a sound constitution; he is sure to take advantage of it and have a short life. Besides, he is so concerned with his diet, digestion and how many bowel movements he should have a week that he has no time for others."

At this point the benumbed tailor pinched himself. "What have you done with your youth," he moaned. "You look a good sixty to seventy to me."

"Tell me, what has my youth done for me? You're seasoned enough yourself to understand how experience ages a man."

"Yes, but who gave you the right to be that experienced? If I may say so in a word or two, you've been hard on life. I can't help pity you. Your sharkskin suit looks homeless, pain has peeled most of your socks, your shirt is a waif and should be sent to an orphanage. But don't come to any fond conclusions. Be truthful and soft-spoken: how long have you worn your clothes? They are ailing if not dying. When did your shoes have their last meal? Never has a customer handed me such a pair of pants. Does your jacket give up bile before breakfast? Could you see the back of yourself you would carry your suit to a charity ward. Why are you so unkind to your collar that it hangs so hopeless about your neck?"

Mary had disappeared, and I felt as though I had gone back to my own cell supperless. Had she that feminine comprehension of a long rapturous quarrel which cannot be interrupted without causing more quarrels? Whatever was occurring within her swollen breast I feared the planet, Cancer, had affected me and would presently eat up even foul denials. Oh, the influences of storms, winds and constellations opposed to my manly purposes. Then I caught sight of her primping in the bedroom, and I was stirred up as I saw her put on a violet-granite blouse.

Meanwhile our argument had so heated the tailor he had removed his shirt, and when Mary came out she scolded him. "Father," she cried, wringing her tender palatable hands, "are you out of your head? It is not eleven o'clock and you act as if you were in Mother's bedchamber. You show not a whit of respect for her household, and she cleaned and scoured the walls and floors all morning. Good heavens, you're as naked as Adam and in your wife's own home."

By now this unboweled cottage had chastised me. Certain venomous spirits haunted the furniture and the mourning December drapes, as the tailor continued his monotonous catechism: "Why is the seat of your pants so tired? You do nothing, and yet your suit is all in. Wake up, mister. I can hear the threads snore, and wheeze in vain for a needle. Everything you're wearing looks dead. God forbid, I should have a corpse in my house. You keep on rattling about books that probably died centuries ago. Are they buried or lepers, for I never met a single person who touched one. Does reading make a skeleton of a man?"

"What can I do?" I muttered. "I'm thin as dust. Like the Essenes I eat so little I have evacuations only once a week."

This seemed to infuriate him. "Idler! Don't tell me your bowels are too lazy to move."

Mary was once more in her boudoir powdering her face and completing her mouth. Slyly I peered at her, while I watched an apocryphal mouse playing in the muggy, sour channels of her father's right chap. I was stricken by the shameful works of my blood. No wonder it is fabled that Venus has her abode beneath the celestial roof of Scorpion, who stings men until they are covered with love scabs which they scrape with Job's potsherd only to burn the more. Give me danewort, I silently begged, or a purgation, or let me vomit forth all my salt deprivations. Where is there the physic for my corrupt sighs? What ravenous beasts are within proud upright citizens who go abroad like counterfeit principles?

The tailor had not lost sight of my furtive gaze and was determined to protect his fledgling, but I not noticing him tottered about in an amorous swoon—yea I was love drunk and there was no help for it. "Are you a street animal," he exploded, "that you dare enter my front room to suck up the breath of my daughter's skirts?"

"Forgive me," I begged, "but I could be the lamb of God did she not move about so much. It's the motion that makes me lewd. She takes one tiny step and I'm ignited. Oh, Father Tailor, give me leave to touch her finger, but that will fury me the more. Who can deliver me from this venereal affliction?"

"Mary, open the windows, I'm suffocating," he cried, and turned to me and demanded that I go outside and throw my mean and sotted desires into the street. Then abruptly he altered his tone. "Perhaps you're unemployed because you've just got out of college."

"Sir, I do not propose to be textual and have a student address me as Professor Footnote. All is over if you expect me to be a university buffoon with pocky wits."

"How did you get an educated language? Simply listening to you has made a lunatic of me. I'm so dizzy I forget what we were talking about. What did you tell me your occupation is?"

"I think."

"Is that work? Explain, what do you think about? And don't load me with any more of your piggish feelings."

"I think about thought. Believe me, there's no more cruel

labor than that, for no matter how hard you think, you're likely to be thoughtless. Suppose one has an idea in January, by February it has chilblains, bunions or is gouty. Although I am by nature and creed pensive, what is the result? Nothing, which is as good as thinking about something. With all veneration for you, what do you do that's better? You toil to make a suit to order for a glutton, a miser, a usurious banker, a shark in a life insurance company. It's your turn, Reverend Tailor. Is it right that you should labor to cover the seven cardinal sins?"

He was pacing the floor to tether his irritation. Now he paused abruptly to turn to me. "Loafer," he screamed, "don't let me lose control of myself. I'm gentle, tender—ask any customer how soft and amiable I am—but am I to stand here while you expectorate on my sacred trade? Right from the start, I believed you were so bad you couldn't be worse, but who doesn't make mistakes? Come to the point. Don't you even like money? Be careful, you've already gone the limit."

"The real question is," I protested, "does money care for me? Besides, the sight of it makes me squeamish; everybody handles it. Wouldn't you admit it's like a secondhand womb? Would you marry one? Could you fall in love with what's false and sneaky? Look at it this way; whenever I happen to clap my eyes on money it slinks into somebody else's pocket. Without any cant I am able to admit I never wronged lucre. Answer me, why does that creeping mole despise me? I have more charity than you'll ever know, yet though I pity everything on this earth I abhor money. Anyway, since I'm more out of this world than in it, I decided to be a foundling singer of the purgatory of poverty."

Seeing no way out of this enigma, the tailor waxed insolent. "Do you know what you look like?" he said, to which I weakly replied: "Who is brave enough to see himself?

Not even Helen of Troy had a mirror. Could a man know his own face it might ruin his whole life. Regardless of your uncivil manner, I am a religious of fanatical fancies that don't thrive in a merchant's lukewarm land. We're a carcass of a nation, a decayed lion where businessmen, electricians, plumbers and landlords get their money; American morals are Cash on the Spot, respectability. Whatever you call me, don't say I'm Mr. Shrewd Mammon."

"Never mind Grace, Sarah or Helen and their looking glass. Just reply in three words: you're self-employed."

"Who else would hire me? Despite all my crushing doubts, I trust myself more than society does, and so I work for me. You ask why? Once I took my head, by no means brand-new, to a junk dealer who obviously was on the lookout for exhausted goods of any sort. When I offered to sell him my head at a bargain price he called a policeman, and not finding one, bellowed: 'Madman, criminal, murderer, thief, spoiler of our country's virgins.'"

Panting, I continued: "Why should a peddler of junk, who buys up scrap iron and lead pipes, refuse to give a penny for a brain? Why, I could sell unkindness, knavery, dissembling, savagery and every quibble could they be marketed as wares. At times I have the most woeful shrieking dreams that gush up out of my sleep, and when I attempt to slubber over the miserable remnants of such a dark watery agony that has been pictured upon my closed eyelids I am certain this is the paint of death. The whole dismal globe is in a suffering and slumbering grave daubed in divers colors just to befool maundering dunces who have not even the skill to perceive that the sun merely rouges the sky, and that the morning's crimson-robed light and the white evening stars are funeral torches. We are and we are not, and this is the disease that killeth up resolution.

84

"What pains I have are in all greedy, shaking limbs. Remember, this is a tale of worshipful books and a maiden chaste as a ring dove. The game is at an end; shrive my authors and me, for Nature is our enemy. Not all is my fault; your bed and hinges have eclipsed my sober hours. Already past my prime, I bring you the ashes of my youth in an urn. Still, one writer, Porphyry of sacred memory, has said that a crab is lured out of a chink by sounds produced from reeds. Since I am your obedient servant, why can't I enter one?"

The tailor was in the throes of melancholia, and he muttered, with some hardship: "Do you live for flesh and bed, mister?"

"No, I die for it."

"Ancient boy, I doubt you know the time."

"A time-server either wants to get rid of you or himself. It's his manner of hurrying into a winding sheet. Besides, clocks are likely to render a man impotent."

He gasped at this. "In truth, you're God's riddle, you come out of nothing. Have you any character references?"

"Just write to Hunger, Desolation and Rueful Expectations, three doughty and steadfast citizens of our republic, and you'll see I'm no ordinary gutter bird. You should bless me, for as one poet of olden times says, 'Poverty is hateful good.'

"Nor am I so indigent as you deem me," I went on. "I have bountiful compassion. How I pity a weeping, vacant purse I see lying in the gutter. In a way, I could be the compendium of perfection did I not want to void my seed in one glorious vessel. Tell me, why did you beget her? Oh, proud cloth-mender, you've been lofty with me, but I could not even patronize a slug. I know I'm a bladder of arrogance. I only cleave to my raffish foibles because they are so devoted to me. But I apologize, and pledge that solely because you produced such a tasty morsel of a minion, I'll compose a dudgeon epitaph for you. I admit I am of contrary moods. Would that I were a jot whimsical, and gentle and lamed in the middle." And I recited this:

"Christ was a mayde, and shapen as a man."

Again I shouted forth: "Take a caveat from your son-in-law: avoid your closest friends, Greed and Optimism. Never set foot in a bank. As you can see, I have a pocket full of precepts, and you consider me a pauper."

The fuddled tailor was running around the room; my words were driving him senseless. But then it is said that commoners cannot understand Angels who only talk Latin.

"Daughter," he howled, "not even I can stitch this fool together. What man in my trade ever had material like this to mend?"

Mary hastened to us, and overwhelmed by the sight of a snippet of her russet petticoat, I vowed I would walk barefoot to the sepulchre of Christ and lay a gillyflower there as a jot of penance for my unruly corporal desires.

The tailor reeled. "Daughter, his eyes are sewers gluttonously lapping you up. Is it too much to expect that he show some skill in hiding his disrespect?"

"Gentle sir, pardon me," I begged. "I cannot stop up my pores. A blind man taps the pavement and knows where he is going, but to see hurts me. What can I do? My shoulders, my neck, my feet have ferret sight. Soon as one announces his morals his vices appear, and from nowhere. I would be virtuous did it not become a vicious habit. All precepts I have studied have racked my sore pulses. What lilied lepers of human goodness range the town. Oh, God shame good conduct, lest bare grinning principles show themselves."

The tailor's spleen rose and fell like the Ephesian sod.

"What do you expect of a reverend father? Everyone wants my daughter's precious vessel. Either I guard her virginity or let her be a streetwalker."

"A pair of whoremasters, I swear," whimpered Mary. "If I repeated such unclean toilet language to Mother her blushing ears would flee."

12

*What eyleth yow to grucche
thus and grone?
Is it for ye wolde have my
queynte allone?*

—Chaucer

The tailor was listening to himself, a custom that dulls and depraves the spirit. He looked around to see if Mary had left the room, then moping he commenced a coltish oration:

"For forty years I've kept the old baggage. Her hair is so thin on top you'd take her for a skirt-chasing fur operator, or a member of the Garment Workers Union. Her unhandled breasts failed five years ago come next February. She's pure, too; if I try to tell her of my troubles at the shop she complains I am bent on forcing her. The hag's out of season. Why should a man wish to commit a nuisance with her? But by my ancestor's foreskin I confess I crave her sour nipple. To have worked my fingers to the bone for a pair of revengeful, hanging dugs, how's that? Such is a laboring man's lot. Sometimes I listen to her snore, or if I'm lucky, belch, but simply for the sport of it. Ah, the bedroom, what a sweetmeat it might be did she not save up her unkind, villainous body.

"My brain is loaded with the chicken feathers in our un-

88

fed marriage pillows," he went on. "The blankets are rotting rinds. When she accuses me of wanting to use her I'm dirt and shame, and can't get a mum out of my cheeks. Every night the she-miser is on one side of the bed while she keeps me to the other. If I pretend to be asleep, and reach for her, she's already standing on her feet and snorting: 'Get the air, take a walk. My private room is entitled to a bit of rest.' Either she's got hot flashes or heart palpitations. A good sixty-three, maybe seventy, she snivels at having a change of life. She lies and lies, but never underneath me. Can't you take a lesson from my mistakes?"

"Yes," I said, "if there were a soft mild clime where all our errors are white as lilies. You speak, sir, of poetical conceits that graze our veins like zephyrs from Eden. But is not all advice a bastard issue of our own unclaimed infirmities? Each man has title and deed to his woes, and neither the sheriff nor the tax collector, not even the Lord God himself can deprive him of them. I would heed you and be a paradigm of modesty were it not that my unforgivable past has stirred up so many unwanted pains. Oh, I have prayed for quiet, since the least noise overwhelms me and raises up a ghost of lechery. All blood is debauched and constantly haunted by nocturnal specters that slay the will. Long ago I sought to be a thinker so that I would give no thought to copulation. Doomed, how often I have railed on the maker of the universe and implored: 'Tell me, by the bolts from other planets that strike us, is everything we do a sin?' The unlucky truth is that any unsought issue, and is not each one a grimacing devil, harasses me. Yet nothing is of great moment to my deceased being. Would that I never knew a dram of emotion, or as Sir Philip Sidney puts it so bravely: 'Happie, happie be they which be not: and the blessedness onely is this respect thou maist feele, that thou hast no feeling.'"

Emboldened by my own avowals I concluded: "Would

you suggest I chew a few mucky crones so that your darling may be continent? Give me gutwort for my spermal aches. Why am I denied what any sow or broodmare can have without lucre or license?"

The tailor's ire could not be contained. "Take your garbaged desires out of my home," he cried. "Go, O louse, to a lechery house."

Ready to chime the funeral of our relations, I rang out: "Must we rest in this mock canting society? Don't be so cringing. You can afford to acquire other melting arms, two new, swelling calves and a voluptuous belly that could purge Jehovah of his massy seed. Do you not merit even a syllable of a caress? Dear Father Tailor, we are closer than you know. I esteem you, so do not disdain me because I reel over the smallest finger of your nymph. Although my head is ghostly, I rage and roar like a robber in my own thickets and hedges for your Mary. Pardon me, sir. I kneel before each scrawled hair on your head and bow down before your holy age."

The tailor's tone was murky: "You'd be a pack of sorrows to me. If you remind me of my years again I'll show you out. I wish you were one of my deceased relations. In one month I buried an uncle and two insolvent cousins. What a relief; you can't anticipate good news always. To come to the point, how can an educated man like you be homeless? Be truthful; should I permit my only daughter to marry a twenty-year-old man without a past, present or future? Ha, ha, with several thousands of you around a watchmaker would have to close his shop."

Now I was distant from him and could only sigh: "I'm the last supper of the worms. You cannot imagine how many poets have sung for a headstone. By your leave, may I deliver well-nigh two lines from the Middle English bard of blessed poverty: 'In a somer seson when soft was the sonne, I shope me in shroudes.' "

He shook his skimpy hairs. "Since I met you I'm all mixed up. Are you trying to persuade me that to be poor is God's gift? Intelligent as you are, why are you stupid? Can't you do anything at all with yourself?"

"Really I can't," I confessed, "for myself won't allow it. It's too severe for the intestines to be reasonable more than five minutes a day. Isn't Vesuvius itself a miraculous failure, for after it destroyed olden Herculaneum what did it acquire for its amazing performance but a heap of ruins? You've worked all your life and have nothing to show for it save dim sight, and doubtless hemorrhoids. You're no more prosperous than I am. So what's your brag? The owl requires no thread or thimble; he does nothing for a living but hoot. I'm utopian and would camp out with the bramble-frog had I the knack for doing it.

"Often I drudge a whole week for a trope," I continued. "So nothing comes of it, what then? Besides I sit, stand, lean, crouch, and walk seven to eight miles to the outskirts of Los Angeles, and were it not for witless money I could piss just as freely as you. Aye, it's a frosty and putrid world when a man has to hold his tongue in court and his urine on the pavement."

The color came back to the tailor's shrunken dun cheeks. "I'm strong for labor," he said, "but I believe in courtesy." Then without warning he reverted to his dismal stave of married life. "Besides, she hasn't a scrap of memory. One day she misplaces her spectacles, the next her keys or pocketbook, and if I'm around she cries out I've stepped on her nerves. Who could believe me? Once I caught her crawling on her knees, and when I asked her what she was looking for she bawled and said she couldn't find her body. Admittedly, low feelings are illegal; sometimes I could put a rope around my underhanded appetite and hang it. I have a few animal fancies. When I can't get rid of them I take a short sniff of her dime powderpuff. Some mornings when I'm out of my head I tiptoe around the bed to catch a simple husband's glance at the skinny remnants in her night shift. How is it she's always awake and prepared to trap me? What a herring mouth she has and how she uses it: 'So,' she says, 'at your time of life you won't let me or the sun that's dozing on the screen have a little peace.' After I've relieved myself she rushes to throw open the window, puts the rugs on the clothesline and beats them to death, fumigates every corner. It hurts a man to think he smells so bad. Only last Thursday she noticed a tiny crack in the ceiling and accused me of having a filthy mind. It's hopeless. On Sundays I drive out to the mountains to observe a cave, and mourn because it's vacant. For a holiday I attempt to cool myself by going to a lake or pond. A month or so ago a man informed me the world is round. No wonder I'm so restless.

"When I was courting her I could not get over her smooth, fat neck. Now, though she wails and screeches, I cannot help grieving for the seams in her throat which I would patch together and run through the sewing machine could I do it. It's a sorrow to look at the shriveled mouth of a woman, or her sagging, crumpled body once so well knit together. Skin and cloth alike become threadbare and are scraped away long before they are middle-aged. I can't tell you when I had the whole bill of fare with my wife. What's so special about a uterus that a husband can't occupy it? Don't I pay the mortgage and meet the bills for it? It may be blasphemous, but does God understand Himself any better than men?

"That's not all. The crow calls me old. What a heavy

word is old. When I heard her say it, I was green moldy bread for a week after that. I see myself when I shave, and wish it were somebody else that was looking. My back is cranky as a creaking arthritic hill. What's become of the rich flow of blood in my lips? My joints are brittle autumn leaves ready to break into many pieces.

"Don't repeat all this to a soul. Remember, I never said it. But where is my July and August bloom? Tailors are a hot groaning lot. They sit all day long and get vile visions. What a pile of grief it is to shake for a pin cushion, a hair comb, a yard of ribbon, a sample of silk. Believe me, it inflames a man to be seated for twelve hours in a shop. Makes me think of a joke: life is pointless though a needle is not. Pretty good, eh? Never mind, I do all I can to forget the sly winter missus. Does that keep me from brooding on her corset cover or her chemise? Listen to this: the nag once raved: 'Wake up, shrimp, and never forget; my parts are my secret and not yours.'

"Were I not a coward I should have packed my valise and moved into a hotel room. I couldn't face it. What a stroke of life's spite it is to lie in a single, unseasoned cot with no mate to comfort the stiff, blue bones. Don't misunderstand me; I've a pinch of pleasure, too. There's more to my working hours than you might suspect. What a dizzy flutter I have when a widow enters the shop and she leans close to me to ask: 'Do you press and repair ladies' underwear?' I'm in heat if I am running the steam iron over a skirt, and I spin when I have to darn the plackets of a dress because I know the lumpy-hipped matron who's been in it. Once I held the odor of a virgin blouse in my hand until the store closed. On dull afternoons I stand by the hour smelling the racks of women's dresses and skirts. I'm most excitable during a long downpour. If a rough snow is beating against the windowpanes I broil, and when business is slow I have the most impolite feelings. This is what comes of spools of cotton, a thread and a needle."

The tailor could scarce govern his moan. "Had not my wife lost her merciful figure I could endure several more tough, bitter years of slime in front of the steps. I don't understand people of too strict principles. Why can a kettle of water boil over without being accused of irreligious fever? The kitchen pot may burn until it's black and who says it's disreputable and dirty? What's left? Steep, uncharitable wrinkles and a few ragged teeth that were never properly nourished. Heaven provide me with a whole cloth of quiet that I may soon retire and look out the window and watch without shameful pestering stings garments and stockings walking by."

Sorrowing, I thought of that poet, still so ill-known, who held that "Eche kynd of lyff hath with him his disease." I was overthrown by the tailor's amorous woe, the stint of joy that had been his, and was near to sobbing as I mumbled: "How impure are the pure. Could hyssop cleanse the plain bread of flesh?" Inept, I proffered him this: "Sir, there's an occupation no less lecherous than a tailor's. You allege you simmer as you sit. Shakespeare wore out his hunkers to compose the sonnets. Beaumont and Fletcher were word-tailors, sewing lines together and dyeing and pressing a secondhand Horace or Marlowe. By dusk, having finished their repair work, they went to a hedge-tavern for a bragget and chat, and afterward to knock up the room of a doxy in whom they could sink their debts and stricken moods. It's either the vagina or a lifelong grave."

The tailor's humpback was swelling. "Please have a little respect for this home even though you are only half a guest. Do I have to repeat the door is waiting for you?"

Reduced to a whinling I said: "Nobody expects me. I'll

go soon. But where? I thought a sinewy friendship had sprung up between us. I wager you don't even remember my name. Since venerable words are for hearses and the grave, here's my epitaph: 'Don't pass by Anybody's Miserable Chagrin, eternally Sir Dust but once purulent lust.' "

"See here, penniless fellow," the tailor shouted, "I'm married and have a real name to protect. Don't get glowing notions and think you're about to eat up my daughter without lawful wages. In my wife's holy home you dare mention womb to me. That's no common public matter." He was perspiring with wrath and suddenly removed his shoes.

Just then Mary came into the room again. "Father," she exclaimed, "in your indecent socks in Mother's house!"

The tailor was convulsed. "What is a husband's reward for removing his clothes in this unmarried home! It's always Mother and never Wife. In our prime we sweated without being smothered with shame, and without having a scold for a daughter."

"Don't blame this young wondrous tidbit of innocence," I broke in. "It's a Mother land, Elohim and the Matrix reign, for Abraham, Isaac and Jacob have vanished. We've said good-bye to the Father. The Bitch ruleth the cottage, the savings account and the purgatorial boudoir."

"Where did you find this urchin?" the tailor demanded of his daughter. "Are you a ragpicker? He says he lives by himself. What frightful company he keeps. I'm not a pitiless man, but how much sympathy can one have without dying of it?"

"Sir," I protested, "I'm in the lost and found department, since no one has ever claimed me. Hear me, I belong to the prophetic host of outcast Ishmaels."

Abstracted, the tailor was wiping his torso with a tape measure, and Mary, endeavoring to placate him, seated herself on his grumpy, puling lap. Somewhat assuaged, he addressed me anew. "Be straight with me; don't be bashful. Maybe you're ashamed of your job. Are you a night watchman, a shipping clerk, a handyman, a porter? Do you sell mops, brooms, buckets from door to door on a commission basis?"

"No, sir, I read."

"Could anything stop you from reading?"

"Well, yes. What you call work."

"What have you to offer my Mary?"

"Nothing, sir."

"Is that a bargain or an inheritance? Are you laughing at me? Who can afford to possess Nothing?"

"The Truth," I replied.

"The Truth," mused the tailor. "I once met an old tramp by the same name. I was quite young and green, and I strolled with him a couple of times until I learned I was being friendly with the worst circumstances imaginable. How was I to know I was going about with a vagabond who had no rubbers, umbrella or winter topcoat? He even slept in the same suit he walked in—sound economy, no doubt, if it hadn't stunk. Aside from that I noticed that well-to-do or commercial persons whom I introduced him to either turned their backs on him or rushed off. Naturally, I was worried and began to wonder if he had an incurable disease.

"At first he seemed amiable enough. Until we went to the grocer who forgot to give him the proper change. Then he began to rage about injustice, and I questioned him timidly who was this Mr. Injustice. You can't make the acquaintance of every stranger and keep physically fit.

"Soon I found out he had a bad disposition. If I was in the street and my mind was elsewhere—you know what a traveler the mind is—and I didn't happen to see him, he lectured me by the hour about being polite, gentle, and shaking hands. He was in a fury and told me that the next time I

went by him and didn't take off my hat he would have
nothing more to do with me. That was the limit. So I was
expected to remove my hat and bow to a street urchin like
Mr. Truth. What really put me out was that he was always
talking about dying. I couldn't help saying to myself: 'He
looks as though he's been dead for thousands of years and
is still wandering about hoping to find a funeral parlor free
of charge.' Once in a great while I wonder what's happened
to that fellow, Truth. Perhaps a tornado or a strong wind
has carried him out of this world."

"I can't laurel you for dropping Mr. Truth," I said. "As
for Nothing, it is so plain, honest and clear that you can see
right through it. Whereas Something is a thief, a liar, and
exceeding covetous. Once one has Something he isn't satisfied until he has something else, your mortgage, your spouse
and your property. There's something about Something that
he will deprive you of Nothing if he can do it."

"Stop confusing me with your philosophical somethings
and nothings," the tailor bawled. "Speak out: can a nothing
like you be a faithful husband?"

"Dear sir," I sighed, "how can you speak of faithful when
you know how changeable women are. Of the two sexes,
they are the more discontented."

The tailor's chaps glowed. "As patient as I am, I am compelled to repeat: What are your prospects?"

"My present condition may be better than my future
which might be worse. Even a pessimistic outlook decays."

The tailor groaned. "I need a headache powder," he
pleaded. "Mary, an aspirin."

"I am almost speechless," I said. "It appears I have no
rights at all. The wind sports with Mary's underclothes, and
the sun teases her jocose knees, while I am forced to stand
aside and grieve for her very breath. Consider what pleasure
men get from a trifling scratch. A louse bites you and when

you take off the scab the skin is delighted. Rather disgusting when you think about it. A bedbug is the botch of Egypt but people crave it and bungle everything for such infamous happiness.

"Give me license, O Father," I cried in the heat of my passion. "Let her breasts flower and prosper in my hands. You want me to be locked up in an office until five or six o'clock and come to Mary and simply sit and eat my own plate of boredom. Then we'll go to bed with our backs to one another; even bears face each other when they are ready for their naughty game. Like Giordano Bruno I am guided by the constellations, Ursa, Gemini, Perseus and Hercules, for though I am repulsed by what I need I always shall follow in the libidinous footprints of Eros."

Delirious by now, I could not contain myself. "As for the books I haven't written, do you realize that no weasel, spider or gnat toils so much as I do for my ghosts. Although I contradict myself I beg you to let me labor in the sweatshop of Venus. I'm not as imprudent as your suspicions indicate. Your eyes are perfect testimonials of my flea'd caution. I wear nothing that's brand-new, and decline to grasp a hand that's not been used by others. Moreover, at this instant, anyway, I do not care for the unthrift virgin. I'm quite willing to squander all myself upon your daughter."

The tailor guffawed. "What have you to spend except your misery?" He took the aspirin tablets Mary had brought him and swallowed them fast, for he seemed anxious to gather her into his raw lickerish arms. As she seated herself in his puny lap I goaded him: "Would you grave your daughter's maidenhead beneath a grum stone? Thou piece of savage dotage and incest, I'm the one to be consoled, lest I perish of insufficiency."

"Have you no morality at all?" he demanded.

"All I possess are my habits, and I don't trust them or they me."

"You're an atheist," he shouted. "A free thinker."

"Forgive me, sir. I erred in speaking so to you. I have the most religious emotions for Mary. I cast myself at her delicious feet just as the prophet Daniel prostrated himself when he espied the Angel in the river Tigris. Know how I mourn for hills torn away from their mountain. Can you understand what a devout tumult there is in me when I observe a lorn shingle deserted by the sea?"

The tailor was obviously prepared to put an end to this folly, but he had still another query. "Have you ever had a hundred dollar bill?"

"Although I am a quack metaphysician of love," I demurred, "don't mention first causes to me. Suppose I invented an imperishable thought. Could I exchange it for a bowl of porridge or one artichoke?"

He shook his head hopelessly. "Don't you regret your life?" he said.

"Who doesn't? I think such emotions belong to the deceased. The sole remorse the dead have is that they ever lived."

The tailor's nose was pressed against his daughter's blouse as though he were sniffing all the delicacies in her secret archives. Blasted by what I saw I felt I was being cuckolded. Without receiving any warning I heard one of my graves divulge: "Only among the Judases will you find your life." Mary had abandoned me. But then it is fabled that maids have slow phlegmatic bodies.

"Tailor," I cried, "you've won your small triumph, but there are no victories. My desolation is potable as muscadine."

How moldy I was. Was I in the house? Feelings are very

99

sly. I was startled that the tailor had not perceived me. Who has sufficient energy to see one human being? A stranger, was I already too close to him? It has been said that sapphire may cure the infirmities of the eyes. Why is it that men worship the remains of flagitious Emperor Commodus just as deeply as they canonize St. Augustine?

Weary of these vagaries, I looked about me; the room was empty. Had it ever been filled? O rivers, estuaries, and banks of fogs, people are confused because they think. I softly left the cottage so that I would not hear my lacerated footsteps.

Stoical for four to five days, I then commenced to haunt the office of Western Union. She had left. I waited for hours outside that merciless slab, the door to the cottage. She never appeared.

A dry-goods storekeeper pitying my plight said her parents had sent her to one of the canyons.

In the evening I sat on the curbstone, my cankerwormed head in my arms. The Mojave Desert always would be within me. Clad in dust I chanted: "And as a bitore bombleth in the myre."

13

Our sins forbid Jove to lay aside his thunderbolts.

—Horace

I was torn as that martyr, a part of whose skull and all of whose face except the lower jaw lie in Amiens, and the rest elsewhere. But who is what he is at any instant? Most of our faults lie buried since there is often no occasion for them to appear. Some ripen their defects, others suffer them, but none cast them away.

Shambling along I considered what a stupid suitor I had been. Could I have been adroit with the tailor? I never could handle people. The others invariably won in the penny gamble. Encountering a stranger I fell upon his neck; were he startled I felt base; when he fled I was defeated. I craved affection and yet was wretched and dirty when I sought it. I was always humiliated, for I depended upon those who needed me. I could not pardon life because I was the beggar.

I wished that I had never met Mary and her father; I grieved because I had ever met anybody.

Living in the town of quack angels, an older man at the Y told me he desired to start a universal religion, and hired me as his secretary at eighty dollars a month. A religious vegetarian, he was parsimonious and never paid me a penny. After listening to his endless and tiresome discourses for a week I quit; out of pocket I had besides lost six gallipots of meditation. As Le Sage held, I was again the bookkeeper of the other world.

Shortly after this I attended a séance by a woman who promised a small audience of crumpled men and women smelling of the dregs of coughs and moldy rooms that they could converse with the dead. Soon as she said this I dreaded my mother had died; from the time I was seven years old I feared she would leave me. This fear is perhaps the purest sensation I've ever had, the impressions of a child before he is soiled by sneers and sophisms.

The medium, a plump leaven of fanaticism, asked each one to scribble on a piece of paper the dead person with whom he desired to speak. All people are superstitious, and philosophers and poets are, in part, credulous.

I said I wished to hear the voice of Anatole France. He was still living, but I always thought great men were among the deceased. The medium assured me I could listen to Edward Dahlberg, and I told her I didn't care to hear from him.

Meantime, I had boiling seething dreams, involuntary sins, which shook my faith in sexual morality. I drank barley water, went to a barbershop for a tonsure so that I could feel ascetic, and took the Pacific Electric train to Redondo Beach to hear the howling costive tides excrete millions of yards of surging ocean. I imagined sea salt, essential to the metaphysical mind, would fumigate my blood. Ocean is the first cause of philosophy. For hours I sat on the sands watching the fluxional pelagic robe of God, and supposed I was calm. A week later I went back to listen to the thundering sea-foot of Jehovah. Some while my mind was concerned with water, and I thought: brooks remedy little pestering griefs; channels relieve jadish days, swift streams encourage the sullen legs.

Did I receive alms of quiet? Presently I thought of rocks that groan, and ravines that are hoarse. Dust growls and excitable worms tickle the skeleton. Lust is the Father, the Son, and the Holy Ghost, and the Universe is a mad, seminal creature.

I studied the *Gita*, but was an ant of concupiscence. I seemed to be getting on and off streetcars, falling into the arms of strangers in the Y lobby; the hours hacked me to pieces, and I found myself chasing away Loneliness, who ran off, hid in a hallway, and then rejoined me. How galling it was to be beside myself.

Helplessly I lingered over the memory of Mary's carmine petticoat. Men wax delerious over beads, gauds, a wimple, or crisping-pins. Venereal fools wonder why they had not purchased taffeta, satin, silk, linen, cotton instead of a trollop. The same libertines would yawn over Helen of Troy in grogram.

Once more I saw Mary's fungused tooth which ruined my desires though I ached for her small nose. Oblivious of my resolution I fell into the most sorrowful error, and considered how marvelous was a downpour or a fog for coition, and what a soft fallow twilight can do for the passions. There was libidinous excitement in a cough, and sneezing was extremely agreeable. Remembering another one of Mary's petticoats, black with a ruffled hem, I recalled that in old literature Pluto's horse is black, the color of death, but a very licentious hue.

Pigments plague the philosopher no less than a bumpkin. Different shades of feeling come from diverse colors that adorn the female. It is hard to be immune to the luscious rump of a trull covered with a red kirtle. The skin is grum and papaverous until it is awakened by a painted garment. According to antique poets there are many names for red, a few of which are rutilus, rubidus, luteus; flavus signifies red and green.

Marvelous writers select words with the appetite they savor the various parts of Aphrodite. Virgil speaks of a green horse, perhaps a synonym for glaucous; he used *flava* to denote blond hair which inflamed the Romans. The poet of the *Georgics* wrote: "Sandyx itself shall clothe the feeding lambs." Sandyx means yellow, and now red. The fleece of sheep at dusk is yellow and red. Heliogabalus, a scholiast on profligate sensations, wore saffron slippers. Purpure, or murex, the Tyrian purple, concealed lubricious Messalina; Merlin in *Morte d'Arthur* is garbed in an almond cloak as he waits beneath a tree to ambush a maidenhead. An olive blouse increases pleasure; all colors, including white or alb, are songs of desire.

I did my utmost to banish from my eyes and ears the round, flowing sound of Mary's skirt. Not only did I give over mutton, liver, beef stews, filet of sole with tartar sauce, but I vowed to abstain from amorous fruits, and shunned the Pythagorean bean which when eaten expels wind often mistaken for a sovereign conception. Nor would I have any part of a fig, the shape of the holy womb, and declined to pick up a comb, which has to do with the ancient ritual of the muliebrity, meaning womanhood. I remained in my room three days without food, studying Epictetus. Moreover, I refused to use words that might provide me with a ferine sting: bread, fed, wed, bed.

Call this a spurious calendar of ten thousand tombs; no matter. I sank into a murmur: "O earth, rivers of this unfortunate globe, I sorrow for you, but you are older and more sage. Confide in me; tell me what I may do so that I won't be torn to shreds."

How unbearable it was to think she would cease to flail my senses. That was contrary to the oath I had taken; and what else could I do except bawl out: "Nature, what reason have you to beat my back and belly and chest?" Saints mentioned their seasons of dryness; how sacred dearth could be. Origen claimed he was haunted by a succubus who crept into his bed every night, and though he flogged her he discovered his own body was full of welts.

Finally, I learned who was troubling me—the low god, Scratch, and his uterine brother, Touch, for whatever one handles is certain to wreck his nervous system.

But I was not yet undone; I could become a celebrated author. All I had to do was ravish a few more books. An infelicitous verb, and I regretted it. Villiers contended no poem should extend beyond a single line; with luck I might invent five. There was no doubt I longed to be different from others; I already was and that was my stumbling block.

Meanwhile, my face was peaked, and my nose waxed longer, and I was only able to afford Y cafeteria fish, Plautus' "cattle of Neptune" once a week. How could I squander money on food when I required books?

Natural for me to make mistakes, I joined a correspondence school for scenario writers. Perusing sundry booklets I learned there were only thirty-six different situations in human existence, and I had believed there was only one, failure. Still I was confident. After all, I had studied Thomas Hardy's *Far from the Madding Crowd*, knew by rote hundreds of lines of Emerson, venerated the *Gita*. What then would be hard about scribbling a story for Mary Pickford or Douglas Fairbanks? My manuscripts were instantly rejected.

Unable to get into a studio, I went to a Hollywood casting office, and got a part as an extra in *Beverly of Graustark*, starring Wallace Reid. Once I had seen him in a fashionable automobile and gaped at his Grecian nose. At another time I had seen Fatty Arbuckle sitting in a Rolls Royce; the number of his license plate was 606. It did not occur to me then that the number was a comic allusion to syphilis.

Informed I could earn $7.50 a day in the cavalry, and $5.00 as a foot soldier, I became a rider although I had never mounted a horse. Before dawn hundreds of extras were taken to the desert where scenes were to be taken. Though the sun had not yet come up the mesa was broiling, and I melted in my vagabond clothes. Nobody was doing anything except waiting for food and water. Now it was two o'clock in the afternoon and still neither was available. My mouth was parched and my stomach rumbling. I sat down on the dashboard of an automobile, and opposite me, also seated, was the very popular character actor, Theodore Roberts. He, too, was the proprietor of a Rolls Royce. He had snowy hair, a terra-cotta complexion, and a usurious mouth. In a little while he took a pearl-handled knife out of his pocket and, placing a watermelon on his obese lap, cut dainty rectangles from it. Not once did he glance at me. Each swallow he took was a stone thrown at me. His gluttony infuriated me. Now, as he rots somewhere in the ground, with an expensive sculptured saint guarding his vault, I cannot dispel my hatred of him. Actors have no conscience because they are always acting, are continually somebody else.

Later that afternoon I took my station with the others. I looked quite nervously at my mare, but she did not notice me, and I did not care at all for her indifference. An easy mark for anyone, I had uneasy feelings about her; she was the shrewdest beast I had ever encountered. When the horn blew I mounted her, and she galloped off with such fierce and mirthful speed that in five seconds I lay bleeding on the ground. Managing to get up I hobbled toward the infantry.

An Indian prince was staying at the Y. He was hirsute as Esau, and I fancied he was impressed with my bookish conversation. I told him I was writing scenarios. Oddly enough he never referred to Far Eastern scriptures nor did he give off the sleepy fumes of incense. I liked him since he was gifted enough to believe I was a superior person.

Once he asked me for the key to my room to borrow a book. I loathe lending books, for one will return a watch, money, or a loan, but never a volume. The Hindu prince craved to prove he had a head. Previously he had disclosed he was on intimate terms with motion picture directors and had been in the bed of the star, Olive Thomas. His hair was coming out because of his lecherous nights and mine because I had none. I did not care to hear of his boudoir happiness, and I recited words that I hoped would banish lust and be a theriac: briar, thistle, nettle, sherd.

For a month I did not see the prince and I concluded he was bald and ashamed to present himself. Of course, I missed him, and conjectured he was avoiding me. Why in the first place had he attached himself to me? Finally, when he turned up, I commenced to count the hairs on his head; the more his hair receded the fonder I became of him. Suddenly I grasped his thick maroon hand with tender firmness and was about to embrace him when he repelled me. At once I reprimanded him: "There are so many stillborn un-people in the world. Have you also the insolence to disavow true warmth? I challenge you to a book." (This came out inadvertently.)

Not at all abashed by his vicious deportment he called me a rogue, serpent, moneylender, and impostor. From the beginning he had known I was a fraud, for he had the most subtle emotions about charlatans. Liars were a choice delicacy, and that is why he had not abandoned me. He alleged

I had no talent, an intolerable accusation. He had brought a scenario to the director of the Thomas Ince studios and had been reviled by him as a vendor of unspeakable trash.

I pleaded with him to explain the cause of his spleen. He railed on me; it was my scenario he had stolen when he feigned he wanted to borrow a book of mine. But it was I who was guilty; why had I written such rubbish? His rage increased. Did I not roam the lobby duping guileless Y members? Had I not told him I was a writer; was that scrupulous?

One must admit the prince had the nicest ethics, and to show him the respect I had for his moral denunciations I gave him a low bow and apologized to him repeatedly, but he spat on my shirt which had just come back from the Chinese laundry. After this episode I felt I should renounce the thirty-six classic situations.

14

Always have a good opinion of yourself. Nothing more improves the appearance.

—Erasmus

What should I do? Savage work was hebenon for me. Moreover, I was not only in need of food, but was hungry for headlands, coves, the sight of a sea hare, the lantern fish, plateaus. I had never seen a widgeon, tern or a booby, but the names helped to fill my empty spirit and belly. People can be content with little; the islanders whom Columbus found at the Antilles were satisfied with a calabash of water and brown earth crumbled into small pieces kneaded with leaves.

Western man wants everything that is useless. Why not, I speculated, go from door to door selling hiccoughs, yawns, belches, dysentery, colic, impostumes, virility, infidelity, and granulated eyelids? I considered other wares that could be sold: a cask of Reason seasoned with muscadine, hundreds of sour syllogisms, a pleurisy of unkindness, rashers of apathy, a barrel of pitilessness, or a trencher of mediocrity dressed with oil and watercress. Maybe I might open up a

Logic Shop, since so many were convinced they were rational, particularly those afflicted with intellectual cramps, or were suddenly seized with information-colic, or who take to bed ailing of statistics. One could go into business as a professor of humility or a dean of sycophancy. I myself could use a ninety-nine-year lease on amiability; what about starting a bile emporium? There are always customers for ferocity, hatred, quarrels, libel suits, slander. Or I could be a drummer for goods like bad health, chills, insomnia, hysteria, since people with a sound constitution are just as discontented as sickly persons.

Maybe I had found the sort of work that would not harm me. Could I not stand on street corners and hand out kindness, spices of wit, honesty, truth and understanding? To earn a living I could sell impenitence, inflammation of perversity, apopleptic nonsense, strong oaken inhospitable doors with hinges wrought of the jaws of Cerberus. There were other necessities people might accept, free of charge: affection, love, embraces, soft sighs, warm salutations, and friendship.

Had I found my vocation? I prowled the streets putting into the hands of passers-by my wares of genius. Rushing from one block to the other, and in and out of shops, I was shoved, kicked, beaten, and thrown into the gutter. My courage lagged.

Then I had another resolution. Furtively I packed my suitcase, laying inside it my beloved volumes. I am a secretive person; if I ever acquired a wife I would never show her to anybody, fearing that such a public display was merely a wanton advertisement of private fornication. What I did was my own clandestine affair.

I had put into my suitcase Nietzsche's *Beyond Good and Evil, Genealogy of Morals, The Birth of Tragedy;* Anatole France's *Thaïs, The Red Lily;* Oscar Wilde's *Dorian Gray;*

Bourget's *Le Disciple;* Andreyev's *The Seven Who Were Hanged;* Maupassant's *La Maison Tellier;* Amiel's *Journal;* Jakob Burckhardt's *The Renaissance;* Chekhov's *Short Stories;* Dostoevsky's *Poor Folk;* Lombroso's *The Insanity of Genius.* Looking about surreptitiously I peered into every cranny of the lobby, thus attracting the attention of the majestical clerk at the desk. He demanded my weekly rent, but I did not owe the Y anything.

My integrity pained him, and he reprimanded me: "Why must you be so sly about your honesty? We're burying one of our members Sunday; you're cordially invited to attend the funeral service. After the hymns there's to be crullers and one cup of coffee for each mourner."

Unexpectedly I ran into Anonymous. I told him I had studied the books he had suggested, and intimated I had in my possession some other titles he did not know. He accepted my braggadocio, for I was no soft-going man. Had I not learned that the word humility came from *humus,* to creep?

I was not slow to tell Anonymous that I had gotten the most acute disadvantages from reading. He showed me quite plainly his thin, perspicacious nose, and informed me once more that I should go to the university for an education. But I emphatically asserted I did not want to spend four years in order to be more useless than I was. Nor had I any intention of becoming a doctor of mishaps.

Anonymous then asked me whether I had any recreations. I was very embarrassed; yea, I had ruffled Mary's skirts, fondled her stockinged knees, but was otherwise abstemious. Never failing to be senseless I at the same time quoted George Moore: "The bold and fearless gaze of Venus is lovelier than the lowered glance of the Virgin, and the blood that flowed upon Mount Calvary." He let that pass.

A scholar of female flesh, Anonymous said I was a true mystic. He congratulated me for being obtuse, and added that only when a man is stupid with a woman is he really virtuous.

Taken aback by this Don Juan's paradox, I had not time to reply before he picked up my suitcase and dropped it on my foot. I howled, and he wanted to know what I was hiding.

"My books," I exclaimed.

"Is a book a mistress?" he demanded.

"Yes. I lie with a book, and rummage its pages as one would ravel the undergarments of a paramour. I lift each paragraph as amorously as one would elevate a delicious shift. Love is lifting, uplifting, elevating, construing and misconstruing. I am an incontinent adorer of any volume I consume; soon as I have finished my intercourse with one book I instantly forget about it and hurry to another despite the fact that I cannot remember what I have read." With shame I avowed I was a whoremaster with books, and I was such a fop I could not be faithful very long to any literary masterpiece.

Anonymous relished my conversation, but not well enough to hear more. All of a sudden he walked away, and I was dismayed. Then he returned, which was the first occasion he had ever repeated himself.

Anonymous was a Mason, and quite confidentially disclosed that each member was entitled to his winding sheet. Aside from this questionable Masonic benefit one could get credit, let his rent go for six months and hear of recondite business opportunities. Whenever the clerk had the brutal effrontery to request a small down payment for what Anonymous owed for his room at the Y, he showed him his Masonic card whereupon he was immediately shriven, and the clerk fled to a chair far to the rear of the counter.

I vowed I possessed the true principles essential for a Mason. Anonymous was skeptical, and he made it clear I

EDWARD DAHLBERG

could not niggle with him. My motives were immaculate,
I assured him, but he shook his augurial nose; he declined
to sponsor me. Before he quit my dust I hurled a diatribe at
him: "I'm past my twentieth year, and I own everyone's
indigence. Look at my poor, groveling eyes and arms; observe the wit of my white teeth. What learning do you demand in order that I can be a dishwasher and pick up the
filth in the plates a noisome dowager has left?"

Then I grieved: All of us are saprophagus grubs; only a
trifling oddity in a man makes him Ben Jonson or Paracelsus. Some fail because one finger should have been longer,
or lack the extra toe of Alexander's horse, Bucephalus. Defeat, O wretched worm, is thy sole insight; God save those
who cannot help themselves. You say you do not look for
wormwood, but he who feeds upon it is the hot Vesuvius.

It was the same question: What could I do? I had not
the knack to be a shipping clerk. A needle-throated lady advertised for a listener, but she did not want me. Whatever
I applied for I was refused although I mentioned my valu-
able stocks and bonds, my books, and added I came of the
royal lineage of Cain and Abel.

Was there nothing left except to cocker my foibles?
Could a ragged soul, a shoeless spirit have any profit in this
world? I carried the suitcase filled with venerable works to
the Los Angeles *Times* and asked for the book editor. She
had a fat face and several chins, but two chins are kinder
than one. Very giddy, I opened the suitcase and showed her
my precious stones, the sapphire, the onyx, the chalcedony,
Pater's *Plato and Platonism*, Gautier's *The Golden Fleece*,
Abbé Prévost's *Manon Lescaut*. Of a sudden I recited various
bizarre words: gabber, gammer, hugger-mugger, sib. She
gently stopped me and asked what she could do for me.

"Madam, just about anything; though worthless I'm an
absurd enthusiast. Once Gautier was asked whether he loved

113

dictionaries, and he passionately answered, 'Yes'; Rabelais said to offer words is love. I have more feeling than a knot of ninnies in Hollywood, yet I can't get past the gate. I can't do the usual brutal work. Jesus made plows, Joseph was a carpenter, and Pantagruel acknowledges that Lancelot of the Lake was a flayer of dead horses. I think I could be a writer would God give me the chance."

She wiped her damaged violet eyes, and I was ashamed of my parched socks. She was about to say she had never come across anybody like me, but I guessed her thought, and said, "Nor have I; I've tried to handle my nature, but it won't let me do it."

She gave me a letter of introduction to the head of the scenario department of the Fox film studio. Most people cannot abide a benefactor, but I have always been very lenient with anybody who rescued me. Taking steps backward, I said: "All my fingers will never be able to discharge their debt to you. Pardon me for squandering your time, but did I not do so I would be rude. My gospel of love is to spend other people's hours, for I can do it better than they can."

The epistle was sufficient and I was hired at once and given a desk and a chair. Instead of scribbling stories, I was asked to pore over Wild West magazines and search for a narrative for Tom Mix's horse. I was in a scribbling infirmary and mauled for eight hours a day looking for a story for a film cowboy's beast. Soon I had sinus trouble and a stale migraine. Boils grew on my arms, my hair receded more, and my nose got in the way of my face. I could find nothing for Tom Mix's brute.

This was my second episode with a horse, and I was miserable. The Eohippus chewed plants; the horse of the tertiary period, no larger than a fox terrier, was satisfied with sand and grasslands; the extinct Mesohippus of South

Dakota adapted themselves to hackberries. Had I four legs instead of two might I be content?

I received forty dollars a week, a fortune. Suddenly I had an original idea. I rose and walked straight toward the head of the scenario department and demanded fifty dollars a week. Thus I provided a solution to his own conundrum. He discharged me and I embraced him and called him a human being.

Had I been a disciple of Samuel Butler's *The Way of All Flesh*, Thomas Hardy's *Jude the Obscure*, Emerson's "The Over-Soul," Oscar Wilde's *De Profundis* to be a scribbling yahoo? Or had I avoided being corrupt simply because I was bored? I was not virtuous; I simply had bad nerves. What particularly troubled me was that I could never stop worrying. Even in pursuit of the profound life I would be taken for a sham. One interested in learning is sure to be considered a poseur. I was doomed to walk upon my hurts and cherish them.

A suicidal feeling came over me as regularly as the four seasons. I do not remember how many times I have killed myself. Anyway, I said farewell to Eohippus and to Tom Mix's horse; both are buried and the world ought to be the better for it.

Out of work I could continue to scrape the sores of impecuniosity with Job's sherd. Still, I did not snivel; had I become a hack I would have spoiled the land savagely as Hannibal devastated Cannae. Momentarily I had a seizure of humility certain to be followed by wily, bombastic emotions. I was the dupe of my own rodomontade, as Le Sage remarked. Humble or arrogant, a palmer of thought travels to Gethsemane every hour.

Born to be a regal simpleton I thought I could be wise although I cannot define wisdom. What is it? Ariadne saunters upon the shingle to feed the swallows; that is poesy, and is as far as I can go. My ribs howled, and I was nowhere, which is Capernaum, a New Testament trance. So far my worn-out youth was a breviary of books and stupidity. It is said Zoroaster laughed when he was born. Is that a laughing matter?

Something else bothered me: Was I an imperial bore? I fear to close a conversation lest I seem rude; nor do I know when to say good-bye. What a tedious ceremonial I make of it; first I rise from a chair, which I may have desired to do earlier; then I look for my coat though I know where it is. I embrace my host, and gabble a while longer to reassure him though he has the utmost confidence in himself. Finally, I reach the door, much to his relief and I slowly examine his countenance. Should I see trouble there I question him narrowly; has he enough money for supper or has he been jilted? By now he is somber and I am awkward, and both of us wish we had never met. I bow, telling him not to be uncertain about his natural charm and intellect, and I grasp his hand in both of mine and beseech him to forgive any inconvenience I have caused him. By the time I have gone down the steps and am outdoors my chagrin is intolerable. Had I stayed too long? Hereafter I shall absent myself altogether.

All I had for my existence were disconnected reflections and chaotic incidents. There is no cause and effect; only character binds life together. Whatever I do, good or ill, it is I. There are no accidents either; we attract events and color them. Let it be; Sirius dries up the moist man; there is no tomorrow since one is always in the present. It didn't help to admit I was unsure of everything.

What was I about to do? Venture upon the pikes of American education.

15

> He abandoned all honorable
> studies and exercises, and ban-
> ished from his court, as insidious
> persons, all that had the least
> measure of honesty and learn-
> ing. But buffoons and debauched
> miscreants were (as his chief
> minions) most powerful with
> him.
>
> —Herodian

Graveled by many nebulous purposes I traveled north. Already I moaned for the sun and the caitiff two years in that
ramshackle garden of Sodom, Los Angeles. There is a Spanish proverb that a man always returns to his slop. Never
wise, at best I was an astral clod. Never knowing whither
to go, elsewhere was my Elysium. I was always to be nature's
cully.

Now Rabble University loomed before me. And as I stood
at Wether Gate viewing the disorderly horde of students
anathema was on my lips. "What is the easiest digestion and
excretion?" I asked, and replied, "The crowd." Then I recalled Le Sage's description of Academe: "A common sewer
of erudition."

I heard the saints in my suitcase grieving, and I opened it and stroked their woes. There was Theophrastus, who at one hundred and seven years, and dying, revealed to his friend that could he live longer he would be sagacious. Regardless of my veneration for this shade I was forced to chide him: "O glorious Theophrastus, thou wert the third head of the academy in the outskirts of Athens, yet with all thy knowledge thou, too, art a ninny."

What wormwood courses would I take? I had not forgotten that Plato asserts once men received their education from Apollo and the Muses.

Approaching a student, I inquired of him where I could find Diogenes or Buddha, and added: "I am looking for Thucydides to teach me how to become one of the logographoi." He was an old child with the white hair of the emperor Claudius, and he stated dolefully he had aged in the department of psychology.

I wandered past a pylon to the rear of which was the marmoreal Hall of Pedagogy. One academic sepulchre after another rose within me as I walked in my sleep. (Dreams tire the blood; what a rotting, tottering river is sleep.) Now Lucian appeared, and his specter spoke: "Teaching is a sold virtue, and schools are shops and shambles."

I asked the ghosts within my suitcase, "What is knowledge?" and Sir John Mandeville answered: "And a myle from Ebron is the Cave of Lothe."

Once more I had to console another of the manes, Gustave Flaubert, who formerly had been a solitary and now wept because he could not join the human race. Gently I reproached him, reminding him of his letters. Plotinus was shivering in the Antarctic Regions of Indifference, and he begged me for several clouts to clothe himself. I pondered: How naked is he who thinks and feels, and enjoined him to apparel himself in his Absolutes. Then I smelt the gaunt cinders of Giordano Bruno. I was almost prepared to revivify them but did not lest a knot of pedants reward them with the sorriest footnotes. This came to my mind from Erasmus: "They have their syllogisms, their majors and minors, inferences, corollaries . . . and they interpret it allegorically, tropologically, analogically. . . ."

Other sacred remains trembled. Propertius stirred, Theocritus got up and sat down, declaring that was just as good as making verses. Ovid still lamented at uncouth Getae, and Plautus was minded to compose another comedy for nobody.

Now I came upon the president emeritus who was addressing an ailing citrus tree with senile branches. At his feet were skulls resembling withered gourds—the worn-out craniums of students.

Then I espied a band of youths flogging a professor. When I endeavored to stop them, one brawler scowled, declaring: "This noddle greets us each morning with, 'Sophocles wrote 127 tragedies, 7 remaining, and Cassandra was ravished by Ajax Oileus. I pray all of you've been continent.' "

"Don't forget," I admonished him, "literature was once referred to as polite letters."

He was fuming. "Good manners are effeminate. Besides, he's a dotard, in his thirty-third year, quite useless to our age of the New."

"In a trice we shall all be gray-headed thistles," I said. "Euripides tells 'how morose is old age to men, and sullen to the eye.' "

A decrepit doctor hobbled by, bent over to sow Dragon's teeth and two thousand textbooks were born.

Meantime the youths continued to beat their professor until he pleaded, "Sirs, please leave off," but exhorting him never to be gentlemanly with them again, they kicked him.

I objected. "You'll kill him," I said.

The wide-shouldered student retorted: "We murder him once a week, but he insists he's alive. That's a pedant for you. He says it's his point of view against ours. We're destitute. Who'll listen to us?"

Before I could answer the students abruptly left to take care of a shoal of diviners they called economic weather forecasters. They were especially incensed with a sharp-pated statistician who had stated the week before that unemployment had risen 1.0073 owing to the summer doldrums. Furthermore, the rise in the cost of living, although higher, was less, and consequently people could look forward to some degree of relief when the Pleiades set.

Little doubt I was asleep. My breath was brackish as the sea, and I could not caulk the seams of my aqueous body. What was I doing in this sweatshop of degrees? Still, I hoped a pupil would approach and cry out: "I thirst for the living waters of your miraculous errors."

None did, and I considered how each one is Procrustes who wishes to cut off the feet of another so all may lie down in one common bed of Opinion. Yet I hoped I might renew my virgin senses each hour.

Suddenly Nietzsche called to me: "Everyone being allowed to learn to read ruineth in the long run not only writing but also thinking." My sleeves were swollen with loneliness. I had no receipt for my desolation but a pelting maxim: "Woe unto him who craves to be liked by everybody."

I saw another throng of pupils issuing from the Composition Surgery, but they spoke an inexplicable jargon I could not understand. Passing the Infirmary of Liberal Arts I was stopped by a young man who said: "Why don't you register for Professor Smallhead's course in the humanities? It only lasts a short college week. Monday will be devoted to the Old Testament and the four Gospels. Tuesday there's to be a forty-five-minute television program on Leonardo da Vinci,

Michelangelo and Dante. On Wednesday he'll cover the medieval ballads, Langland and Chaucer. Thursday there'll be a class discussion of Shelley, Keats, Byron and Coleridge, and he'll finish up Friday with Pound, Eliot, Stevens, Cummings, and existentialism. Meet me at seven o'clock at the Pelops Ambulatory; Jack Dempsey is receiving a Doctor of Letters."

Going by Pornographers Hall, I regarded the stone figure of Billingsgate. Hard by was the Doggerel Dormitory. There was a gracious abstract sculpture marking the site which bore the cryptic title, LSD, and standing before this deity with heads bowed was a horde.

Two furlongs removed was a statue of Hecuba blowing her nose, and over against this image was a lavatory bowl called Hecate. Amazed at the abundance of art on the campus I next regarded the statue of Insolence in the form of a lead pipe. There was also a figure of Slovenly Dress, made out of ill-smelling laundry wrapped around a broomstick.

A league from this I discovered a colossus of Zeus Saliva which stood before the Caligula Forum, the school for stage players, acrobats, jugglers, circus riders, mimes, and bowling alley athletes.

Forlorn, I tarried near the Human Nature obelisk that I might overhear Pedagogue George Fundament discourse on the two hundred and forty-eight meanings of nature. He extracted a porringer of blood for every hour he was heard.

A student drew apart from the group of listeners, reeling with nausea, and I begged him to retire to his room and repose there. He jumped up and down on my feet, and walked away erect. I confess I learned much from this experience and readily advised myself: "Do not meddle with another's life. Remember he, not you, must live it." Soon as I met somebody else I forgot this unusual precept and forthwith began to counsel him.

For a few minutes I was an auditor in the class of Doctor Burden Greybones who was thoroughly bottomed in the *materia medica* of syntax and who had recently been given the Sophoclean Honorary Degree in Diction. After that, I stood in awe before a tiny pebble on which was inscribed: "Malcolm Kine McStupid, poet laureate for one day and honored for his immortal quip: 'When I think about thought I know I never thought of thinking.'" Dropping my hot rheum I paid him my funerary homage, mournfully referring to the Dhammapada: "Men who have not observed the proper discipline perish like herons in a lake without fish." Nor could I repress the conceit that a fool is the hardest to discover.

As I passed by the Castor and Pollux urinal I lowered my head. My whole existence was Sunday, my brain feeble as the cony, and no bread or marrow in my legs. I saw a parcel of naiads with uncovered, wrinkled breasts soured by a seminar in social studies. They were carrying textbooks bound with the skins of gnats, spiders and ants.

Oppressed by these unkind volumes I beseeched the shades of literature to give me a book clothed in a hair shirt whose pages were wild honey and locusts. Thomas Wyatt succored me with his own dolor:

> *And yet my mowthe ys dome and dry;*
> *What menys thys?*

A doctor of Dotage was staring at me, but I averted my eyes. When he evaporated I was gazing at the figure of a great mime of the films, Douglas B. Mindless. He had contributed his papyri, and all his correspondence from flatterers, forgers, widows, barbers, and dancers, and his papers were stored in the Archives of Immortal Men. In his own *Confessions of a Famous Mummer* he admitted he had been

christened when he was seventy-six years old, for he was
still an infant.

Over a baroque portal there was a notice: Entrance Ex-
aminations. I entered softly, took a seat, and tried to answer
the following questions:

Was Cyclops a hairdresser? Why was he more content to
eat human flesh after his diet of stags and lions?

Did Nestor die of a hernia after lifting a Minoan jar?

Did Peter Tubal-Cain, the building contractor, take
bribes from the bricklayers' union?

Name your favorite teacher and his chief feature. As an
example, Dr. Orpheus Bitterneck was a zealous mentor who
demanded that students bolt down a Restoration play a day.

Would you say that Associate Professor Marcus Unmen-
tionable had constuprated Ben Jonson's *The Alchemist?*

Why is it said that August Harmless spayed diction for
half a century in the Roman Hall of Articula?

Why was Professor Warmtouch dismissed?

Are the members of the faculty of the department of
English Bibliophagi?

Did Lot drink Pramnian or Thasian wine when he lay
with his two daughters?

Name the four best scenes in *Murder in a Purple Gown*,
played by Marvel Rotgut who won a triumph in the quin-
quennial games, and received the Benny Trifle honorary
degree.

Are you registered in the political science dung shop? If
yes, explain why?

Was nylon invented before or after Arachne discovered
linen cloth?

Are vowels the uterine letters of English? Do you consider consonants gravel in the craw?

Do you believe the four-letter word scribbler can father
a spermal sentence?

There were many more such profound questions, but I was in the suds and I left the room, wondering where I might find the remains of erudition, the small toe of Porphyry, the sacred anklebone of Plotinus, a chine of Webster, a joint of Dekker's *Plague Pamphlets*.

By chance I wandered into Rabble Cemetery, and there I found the headstone of Tale Unborn, the most eminent short-story writer in America. A few aisles down in this charnel was a boulder, and I read the epitaph: "Martin Morethan Mouldy. His untimely death was caused by extroversion complicated by behaviorism." Piously I fingered these words for student Philip de Chinless, deceased in 1922 before he could complete his dissertation on public relations. A stone of good worship was devoted to Professor James Muddle, who had been found dead in one of the drawers of Economics. After that I came upon the massive tomb of Henry Poultfoot, deified by his countrymen. A glorious football stood above the marble over his benevolent remains, and somberly I read: "Henry Poultfoot, Ph.D. in Soccer, Swimming, Basketball, and Pleasant Social Feelings for his Classmates."

Unable to observe all the solemn burial sites, I took a brief glance at a stele over the grave of Dean Percival Unconscious. On my way out I nearly missed the ossuary of Merton Welldeparted, the distinguished collector of gramophone records and the earliest sewing machines; he had been a Doctor of National Usefulness.

Walking more slowly I managed to catch a glimpse of the Herbert Fun Pythian Coliseum, and the hundred-story high fratry commemorating the lifeguard, Junius Moribund.

By chance I encountered a very old lady. She had evening sight, and though extremely deaf heard what was essential to her spirit. She informed me that she was the librarian, and graciously asked me to accompany her to the Funeral Parlor of Books. Following her with tender tread, for I feared to bruise her intelligence, I observed a crowd of students, who were taking their Master of Arts in Remedial Reading.

Soon we arrived at a small hovel built of rough-hewn fir, said to be the earliest tree on earth. Before stepping across a wooden bridge that almost hid the emaciated pond of Helicon, I discovered the statue of Jonathan Swift whose words I immediately stored in my breast: "I believe it is with libraries as with other cemeteries; where some philosophers affirm that a certain spirit, which they call *brutum hominis*, hovers over the monument, till the body is corrupted and turns to dust or to worms, but then vanishes and dissolves; so we may say, a restless spirit haunts every book, till dust or worms have seized upon it; which to some may happen in a few days, and others later."

The cottage was no larger than a shed. This then was the Necropolis of books that Callimachus at Alexandria alluded to as "the healing place of the Soul." I entered, dipped my fingers in a basin of sacred water, genuflected, and was conducted down a wizened corridor where the shelves were loaded with burial urns.

Here was the prime nobility of the human race. I asked my guide why the abode of literature was so tiny, and she answered that most of the sages had died from moths, rust and caterpillars.

The ashes of Sir Thomas Wyatt, Surrey and Raleigh lay in jars as close to one another as were the remains of Achilles and Patroclus. Those of Gavin Douglas lay on the floor, and the librarian came with a besom of gold and gingerly swept them together, after which she deposited them in an alabaster vase.

"Down this cobwebbed lane," she whispered, "you'll find George Chapman. The vellum binding has perished and the flyleaf was torn out by a student named Bibliophobe."

A few paces from there I came upon the vault of Philomen Holland, who had Englished Suetonius' *Lives of the Caesars* and was recently assailed by Carl Vacuum, curator of the Hemingway collection.

By the time I had browsed and knelt at the graves of Ovid, Philostratus, Herodian, Porphyry, Eunapius, Diodorus, Strabo, Thucydides, Alexander von Humboldt, Buffon, I had the ulcerated camel knees of St. Jerome. Several times I was bold enough to open a page here and there. They were empty and I uneasily asked the librarian how could a sage be vacant. She replied: "When books of old time are not loved and read they are hollow as the Ephesian Sod."

Sorrowfully I departed. I had forgotten to ask her what had become of Livy, and realized he had been forsaken since Caligula had said Homer couldn't write.

16

Man is the head of a woman,
and without his management it
seldom happens that any under-
taking of ours succeeds well.
                              —Boccaccio

As was my wont, the day I registered at the university I regretted what I had done. I had left behind me my studious waifs at the Y, the sole human terrain I ever was to have. Always homeless, I could not cease seeking friends who would sow snares for me. Was there another kind of arable soil? Was my exhortation also futile: Why had we clapped up the Mesopotamian valley in a plastic bag to be placeless in the New World?

Looking for room and board, I espied a ramshackle three-story house, and nailed to one side of it a sign: Russian Students Club. I went indoors and found a burly Slavic dowd in the kitchen. Slops were piled up everywhere and I was about to flee when she stopped me. As I lacked the courage to leave I said I wanted a room. She showed me a cot, one glum broken chair and a morose table in the attic, then scowled as I seemed disappointed.

"The White Russian Club is on the opposite side of the

campus," she said. "Don't worry, we have very wealthy Bolsheviks living here, not White Russian taxicab drivers."

"Madam," I replied, "I'm poor as St. Francis and have only a tiny crust of money, two shirts, an extra pair of socks, and the books I keep in my two old peeled suitcases." Then assuring her I was acquainted with Karl Liebknecht's *Militarism* and Rosa Luxemburg's *Letters*, also a few other lawless tracts, I gave her seven gangrened dollar bills. She still suspected me, for I had, as usual, a guilty face. But I told her how I had gone from one wooden hovel to another until my feet groaned, and that as Hippocrates advised, the only medicine for woebegone feet is rest.

She let me have the room and I unpacked my books and sat down and read. When Plato grew weary of me, I went downstairs to the first floor, where I found a chair in a corner and listened to a squab Russian from Tomsk, Siberia, playing Tchaikovsky. Nearby other Russians from Vladivostok or Harbin, China, were engaged in a marvelous literary game. One questioned the other: "Why did Rozanov say he had become a revolutionary?" And the other answered: "I became a Decembrist because she had such wonderful shoulders." Again, "Who wrote the following, a disgusting decadent of the upper classes or a friend of the Russian working classes: 'Every day he forces himself to vomit for the sake of his health, on the advice of his friend'?" "How about this line, did one of the scum-proletarian scribblers pen this: 'The parlor maid Nadya fell in love with an exterminator of bugs and beetles'?"

What a revelation it was, and to boot I was astounded because those involved in this pastime were not seers; actually they were quite commonplace. Having a fixed conception of the lofty, the noble and the sagacious countenance, I asked myself: Is it possible for hackneyed blood to be passionate?

Oblivious of my misdoubts, I fell under the spell of these Russians who considered all Americans lackeys dozing over their ulcerated middle-class newspapers, having nothing in their minds but the treacle and rot of motion pictures. After several weeks one who had been to a czarist military academy before the revolution lashed me with this observation: "Capitalism wears a man out before his twenty-fifth year. You're as unhealthy-looking as a toad."

His remark enfeebled me and I told him I had long ago dried up, and my legs were weak, but I was only an unmonied street Arab in the American society. "You can find me in any sough, alley, spittle, or just dig me out of a cemetery. A muckhill orphan, I read, and swallow oil of niter or a dram of hellebore to purge a halfpenny of the petit-bourgeois in me. Sometimes I drink barley water to clear my kidneys so that I can think. Now and then I catch a capitalistic cold, but after I have come to my working-class senses I cough up the phlegm of any social ambitions I have. Believe me, I own nothing, am nothing and will never be anything but a miserable glut of nothing."

I esteemed each boarder at the Russian Students Club as a Pushkin or a Gogol. Though I longed to disclose what a tumult Dostoevsky was for me, and that I had written a novel using *Poor Folk* as my paradigm, I had not the boldness to reveal myself.

After occupying my worn-out attic for a number of weeks I discovered there was another tenant in the room. I had been so busy with my reading I had failed to notice a mouse that frolicked from one corner of the room to the other, or just stood on his hind legs and pulled a thread from the dead carpet. Ever since childhood a rodent had been a misery to my imagination. How often I had implored my faculties to rid me of this cringing fear and illness. If I happened to see one of these brutes garbed in detestable gray skin I could not touch food, or lift a spoonful of soup to my mouth. Even when I walk the streets now I dread seeing one of them, knowing that for weeks I shall have a thin sickly appetite. On occasion I can still hear these animals gibbering in the morbid room behind my mother's lady's barbershop. To this day I loathe any hue resembling dust. Had I never seen a rat I might believe in God.

Each afternoon I observed the harmless mouse sporting with the carpet string. My stomach wailed and my intestines groaned, but I could not hurt it. When one day the creature vanished I only hoped it had not been destroyed.

In the mean space something quite droll was happening at our Russian barracks only three or four blocks from the campus. Some of the Bolsheviks were the sons of extremely wealthy Siberian merchants, while others received a puny stipend from their families. One of the former, the son of a timber merchant reputed to be worth twenty-five million rubles, had a sister anxious to marry, and he was exasperated because he could not find a man who desired her.

This daughter of a multimillionaire had a polite, well-fed leg. Her hips were wide and rolled slightly as she sauntered, a sign of a most agreeable bed meal. Indeed, it could be said that from her waist down she had not been flouted by nature. Nor did she perspire copiously. The sea sweats, and man is drawn to its saline odor; some lechers are carried away to Paradise by the rammish armpits of a woman. But she had not this corporal advantage or bane. She was short, which gratifies many a long man, and swart, especially during the dog days, but for an adventurous galliard this was not a defect. Her hair, rough as bitumen, was no joy to hungry masculine fingers; still, a man could accustom himself to that. The lady's real trouble was that she was a female Esau. She had a mustache on her upper lip. There are no explanations for human desires. Why hair in the wrong place diminishes venery is a subtle riddle.

The brother had spoken to almost every student in the club, but no one was willing to be his sister's legal bedfellow. He brooded over her misluck and asked himself endlessly: "She has a fortune, is a vestal. What's wrong?" Alas, what is wrong may be right, or the other way around.

Now among the Russians in the club was a wrestler. He had mahogany-colored hair, a nose of some feeling, and a vigorous mouth. Many, if not all, viewed him as a buckram Ajax. But how could the brother ask a wrestler if he wished to wed his sister?

One rainy day, as he sat by the piano, Chopin's *Études* before him, he was startled to descry the fellow listening to him, but the likelihood of this stupid colossus being moved by the music of Chopin was no more to be entertained than his possibility as a bridegroom, and the brother dismissed him from his melancholy thoughts.

Such a damp fell upon him that he began to eschew everybody at the club, although he was often seen of an evening in a tuxedo, rushing off to one stylish party or another in San Francisco. By day, as he roamed the streets hard by the college, he wondered if his sister was to be a spinster with the mustachio of a braggart sergeant. She had already stepped into her twenty-seventh year and soon who would care to finger her wintry flesh? Even now when she was seated one leg was so faithful to the other that not even the most libidinous suitor could part them. Yet has not the porcupine quills, and the boar bristles, and they do not sorrow for a mate? He pondered human physiology. Why should massive hair on the head and murky eyelashes excite men, while what was only nature's brushwork on a feminine upper lip repel them?

Passing a boardinghouse he imagined he saw a sign supported by a wooden stake, with the following notice printed on it: "*Wombs Available.*" As he was a puritanic Communist this becrazed vision disgusted him. Returning to the club he almost shouted: "What about that sloven giant? Sure, he was a moujik, but were not such the elite of the revolution?" Yet as he clattered up the wooden stairs his courage flagged. How could he approach this dolt? The brother was not bookish, but at least he revered Pushkin, Gogol, Goncharov, Andreyev and Gorki, whom he doubtless never had read.

For ten days nobody knew the whereabouts of the wrestler. Then it was learned that he had won a match with a Pole. "Very fine," thought the brother dismally, "but can he put down my sister?" When he encountered the victor on his return to the club that vascular Cyclops had a hiccough.

The brother was done for. "I esteem the proletariat," he thought, "but if this lubber can do nothing in the bedchamber except belch or clear his throat then my sister will expire on her nuptial night." His mind was positively wayward. He considered the wrestler's past life: No doubt this bulk of a fool had a master for whom he scoured pots and cleaned the privies. One could tell that he slept in the soup vat atop the kitchen stove. Probably he drove the hearse for a Siberian landowner. The sister would faint soon as the clod approached her.

Then another whim came to him: a powerful fellow like the wrestler, who probably never even caught a cold, was sure to die young suddenly. The sister would be a bride and widow almost simultaneously.

Nevertheless, the brother asked the mountain of sinews to come for a glass of tea or vodka on Thursday. The wrestler accepted the invitation, but said he never touched alcohol, at the same time adding such petit-bourgeois words as justice, kindness, idealism and, worst of all, virtue. The brother could scarce govern his ill temper. "Who can trust a man who pretends he hasn't vices?" he muttered. "One way or another, he's a rogue."

He realized he had made a boorish blunder, and was stupid, which is all the learning there is; he knew he was utterly despised by the university morosoph. Few are benumbed by their imbecility; the brother at least was startled. He felt he had duped his sister.

The visit was a dunghill failure and he tried to forget the debacle. Perhaps it was not altogether the wrestler's fault. One conceit after another raked the brother's entrails. Had not his sister been a maid overlong? Now only a bed-mariner, descrying a frozen narrow fret, would be able to tack about until he managed to pass through it.

Meanwhile, gossip that has a wrangling and malicious tongue had found his ears: his sister had discovered a Casanova who took her to the theater and concerts every week. Thank Marx, Lenin and Trotsky, was his first thought, the wrestler has been eliminated. What if the fellow could lift iron weights and run several miles each dawn? What need has a man of the gymnasium for the marital couch?

Still, the brother feared the rake was a fortune hunter who might not have marriage in mind, and this made him sorry he had been unjust to the wrestler. Presumably the peasant had a sound head and did not care where a woman had hair so long as she was not without it.

One dark afternoon when the brother was at the piano playing Tchaikovsky's *Barcarole*, who should be seen standing beside him but the wrestler, with tears flooding his tawny cheeks? Some people don't like any sort of noise, even the melodies that come from Apollo's reedy lute. The brother apologized to the athlete for trampling upon his sensibilities; he was well aware that the wrestler was no effeminate, or likely to be seen carrying a violin case.

Imagine his astonishment when the wrestler roared, and said he would be willing to have the short life of Achilles, to become a concert pianist. Dumbfounded, the brother gaped at him. Was this a capitalist's joke? Then involuntarily he embraced the wrestler and both wept.

Now he was in a new muddle. How could he get rid of that mountebank cavalier who had been his sister's consort for above three months? Sheepishly he confessed his error and admitted that first he would have to persuade his sister to renounce her false romance with the humbug Romeo he had not even seen.

The wrestler was positively giddy. Humbled by the thought of the brother's immense inheritance, "Sir," he said, "I'm no Don Juan. I adore your sister. I beg your forgiveness for my boldness, but I'll be overjoyed to wed her if you'll purchase a grand piano for me. I promise I'll practice all day long until I can play Chopin. Believe me, I'm not an upper-class parasite. A man with my strength doesn't require much sleep. Only wastrels slumber most of their lives, doing nothing but imitating the dead."

The wrestler was embarrassed by his own eloquence, and his muscular chaps were flushed with a deep blush. He had so much respect for the brother, how could he reassure him he was not an ignoramus? For his part, the brother felt he was seeing the wrestler for the first time, and now as he scrutinized his physiognomy he wondered how any person on earth could understand the human visage. How he had misjudged the fellow. Actually the wrestler had a kind forgiving mind; he was no sycophant.

The wrestler, still misunderstanding the brother, assured him he could support his sister; he was not looking for a scum-proletarian's dole. He had read a book on natural history and knew that a harp fish lives on seaweed. As for himself, he preferred to subsist on a leek, a head of lettuce and a plate of soup a day.

The brother, seeing how much in earnest the wrestler

was, felt it was time to temper the seriousness of the occasion with a little humor. "A husband," he said, "is an absolute ninny, otherwise would he ever have gotten married?" The giant, not too uncouth to appreciate the joke, prodded him so affectionately he nearly lost his balance.

And so the Russian wrestler married the heiress, and they occupied a plebeian, wooden cottage which contained a large Steinway. He practiced fourteen hours a day, and in the meantime maintained his wife by wrestling. He had become the champion of Oakland.

Not only was he a tender lover. He grew positively fond of his wife's mustache, which he considered an aphrodisiac. Every time he kissed her the hair tickled him so much that he took her to bed, and she was ecstatic. She had never supposed that a man who had so much force in the gymnasium would have any left for connubial delights. Though ugly women can seldom endure their own defects in a man, and are the most difficult to woo and win, she thought him clever. No matter what he said she described it as an epigram. He could, she felt, be a Chekhov if he cared to, and would one day be a rival of Paderewski. She was beside herself all day long and insisted, notwithstanding his stout reluctance, on opening a bank account for him so he could sign all checks.

How could she please her debonair amorist? She bought him shirts, suits, and six traveling bags which he did not require, as he told her he had no intention of making a single journey except to her arms and bed. His modesty and refusal to accept any more presents from her only increased her desire to do something unusual for him. Hearing of a bread that was made of beans and rice flour that was a depilatory, she could not wait until she had purchased a crucible and sundry Paracelsian utensils. One night, after returning unexpectedly early from a wrestling match he had won, he watched her unobserved soaking a loaf in whisky and garnishing it with precious pearls. Her kitchen had become a Faustian laboratory.

Finally, he interrupted her and asked her what she was doing.

"Oh, my beloved husband," she cried, "you have married a hairy crone. I am small, stumpy, and brown as a walnut, and if I cannot be Aphrodite for my Priapus the least I can do is give you a lip without down on it."

Taken aback by her apology he expostulated: "I detest beautiful damsels. They never gaze at a man if a looking glass is handy. Though you complain you are not tall as Andromache, you are not short of what I need. Boor that I am, I should have guessed your needless uneasiness. Maybe you think you have the complexion of a nut or even of sandpaper, but do you realize what happiness it is for me to scratch myself against your darling rough cheek? Were you smooth as marble I would be a good-for-nothing husband."

And he knelt down and importuned her: "Please, for the sake of our revolutionary cause, be as you are. Should you change you might be another woman, and each night I could not lie in your bed and enjoy you without feeling I had committed adultery. I am a loyal serf."

He rubbed his passionate strong chap against hers, and in nine months he played Chopin for her, and she pressed her fur-clad upper lip against his columnar neck, and their bliss was boundless.

17

First of all the gods she con-
trived Eros.

—Parmenides

For well-nigh a year I lived entirely by myself, in a woman-
less world desolate as the northern regions of Hudson Bay
and its surrounding snow ponds. I had no luck with the
damsels on the campus. William Carlos Williams wrote in
"Jacataqua" that our finely molded dames favored grocery
boys and butchers. During the reign of the French Valois
the ladies at court pined away for a freckled pageboy.

In one mood I was no better than the polypus that will
lay its eggs among the sherds; in a black humor I fleered
at any girl who refused me, and shouted after her: "Chastity
is plagiarism." Was I ever to be more than a prentice in passion? At the same time I was unreasonably stung, and suffered from infamies I had not committed or had imagined
in my sleep, that sea of Sodom upon which every carcass
floats.

I met Kate Carla and we had a virgin relationship. Tall
Kate Carla was long as a dolphin; her hair shone as the gold
of Ophir. She had a waggish nose, perspicacious rather than

Dionysiac, and when I told her the remedy of my life was Heraclitus she showed me her teeth, each one a white apothegm cut by a lapidary.

"My friend," she said, "your receipt is the uterus."

Our excursions were gamy, but never sensual. She wrapped her legs in the grogram of Cocytus and wore walking shoes. Holofernes would never have lost his head over Kate's flat shoes. Was she doing her utmost to allay my wantonness? Making ready to go out with me she appeared in dudgeon woolens; her thick stockings clogged my boisterous tumults.

Sauntering is for cogitation, as the Aristotelian peripatetics inform us, and it dawned upon me that she who demands you walk with her is insisting that you better not believe you will lie by her. From that moment I loathed strolling with a female.

Kate and I had opposing conceptions of our companionship. She insisted that I employ my vertebrae and ever be upright, and I deemed there was no other way of becoming her bosom friend than by being recumbent. In a waspish humor I said: "We shall sit or I'll be quit of you."

"On your hunkers," she calmly responded.

We were seated, and I said nothing, a morose occupation. Kate endeavored to comfort me: "A pair of billowy trim legs would physic you."

"Sure," I said. "I see them oftentimes, and have set birdlime on a twig to catch a jillflirt, but every one has escaped me. Why is an udder so important? A man is fagging all day at his studies in order to have brighter prospects; all a woman requires is two rosy plump hams. When it comes to the venereal meal she has the longest moans and swinish sighs. A man has only his shortcomings."

Kate placed her teasing bookish hand on my resigned knee. "Since you can't capture a trollop, why not get a wife?"

"Would that I could step into a department store and purchase a woman on credit, making the usual small down payment. And what then? Shall I say to the first he-vulture we encounter, 'Meet my wife,' and right off declare she has a lien on my genitals? Soon as I have been so imprudent be sure my closest foe will ask when I am likely to go out for a brace of pensive hours, and how long do I expect this cogitation to endure? After I have begged, knelt and wept for this spouse I don't want her to give me a cuckold's cross for all my grim efforts."

Kate showed me her dialectical smile. "Why, Edward," she exclaimed, "you have no scruples at all."

"Man cannot live by precepts alone. You have already robbed me of sixpence worth of self-assurance, a stone of understanding and a farthing of wit."

Musing upon what I had said I noticed one thigh leaning against her tweed skirt, and I fell into half a pleurisy of venery. I say half rather than the whole because tweeds do not have such a cunning and raving influence upon me as cotton, and cotton is not so crafty and taunting as silk, which is salacious and slippery. In August, linen breaks me up and I am a patch of veins and cankerworm heat. As for wool, I don't make much of it. When I see a woman garbed in drugget I show all my axiomatic morals and am in the pulpit preaching the Sermon on the Mount.

Apparently Kate had no intention of leaving off her prate about marital quibbles. "Since you don't get along with yourself," she said, "why not marry a woman who is your opposite? As you are fire, seek snow, or being a volcano of absurdity, wed prudent rationalism. Or since you are always flying in the face of fortune, unite your follies to a sensible kitchen pan, skillet, saucer, and have a sober, housely scone, tea, milk and butter *ewige weibe*. That is really right for you, though it is wrong for your quicksilver madding senses."

This did not go down my craw: "I am no pedagogue of the boudoir," I retorted. "Are you such a brach as to ask me to go out and actually search for an opponent when you admit I am my own stout and valiant adversary? I don't want a mildewed spinster; I don't desire to be a celibate, either."

"But you hate a virgin," said Kate.

"Should I drown, to cite Herman Melville, it won't be in shoals, and as for a maidenhead, like Lucretius I would rather see another lose his manhood in a shallow crimped vagina while I stand offshore."

Now she gave me the knout. "You don't like women."

"Alas, every one of them. But the choicest feminine confection soon waxes rotten."

"Maybe you keep poor hours," Kate said thoughtfully. "Anaxagoras awoke at dawn. Do you subscribe to early rising?"

"Well, early or late, so long as I rise."

Once more I could detect her loins pulsing against her tweed. I lusted to exchange a germ or two with her, for this is the dearest contagion man can catch, besides stupidity which makes each one a member of society. Had I not been so timorous I would have suggested a barter with her, that I borrow her legs and she mine and our skins could then join in such a merry festival. But she gave no hint she would be willing and I feared such a proposal would end our antiseptic friendship.

By now I was undone, and in my spleen I muttered: "Nobody will victual a man unless he has a full stomach. What is more precious to those who possess everything than failure which they cannot achieve?"

Kate listened quietly while I continued: "I propose to take my own legendary way, and to do this I cannot chew facts, statistics, average incidents. I shall dig into my burial site for a relic, a pylon, a suffering Amoritish ancestor. Were it not that one rots, who would think? Somehow it is the dirt in me that is my redemption."

Kate turned to me. "Why should you desire to woo indigence and obscurity?"

"The patron of authors is penury," I replied sullenly. "Whichever way I may go I am doomed to gather losses. Besides, I have not the slightest regard for the porkers of our modern Hellas who consider themselves originals. Who wrote the aphorisms of Solomon? The age, for books write themselves, but the gimcrack author, glutted with hubris, alleges he did it. The greatest sage of any century is Anonymity. We are God's maggots and as we crawl we scrawl."

"But why do you wish to write?" persisted Kate. "Poor already, is it not a tautology for you to take the vow of poverty? Or is it your belief that writing is a biological necessity?"

"You give me a delirium," I cried. "Is the invention of the alphabet any less essential to the anatomy than eating, dunging, sniveling or wriggling in bed with a jill?"

With no benison from Kate Carla I decided to give over pining for the wimple and the crisping pins. All I received from Kate was the worst part of her body, her mind, and I longed for the song of the dolphins, and to hymn praises to the olive yards by the river Alpheus.

Not averse to the lullaby of venery, should I pretend I mislike being cribbed in the matrix at night or on a mizzling afternoon? It is a dear place to sink one's despondency, especially should a creditor be at my heels or the usurer knock at my door. Am I deceived? Were I not, think of the lorn feminine crevice and pity that woman who must nail a sign on her front porch: "Unfurnished. Bachelors only."

Naturally I claimed I was an archeologist of all female parts, and viewed myself as the artists who painted diverse portions of the bosom of Lais.

Having nothing to do I thought about the Creator, and

saw He was as much of a cully as I; otherwise, He would not have spawned me. Then I reconsidered erudition, for I could not exhaust myself doting on distempered carpets, mute chairs and cobwebbed stairs. Nor could I be rid of stupidity that never seemed to weary of me, though it must be admitted that stupidity can be profound and learning shallow. As for all the babbling about knowledge, each one is a cento of someone else's emptiness. Tell a friend that and the blood runs out of his face.

Since nothing occurred, I began to be on the lookout for bad luck. I had lost all delight in speaking to groves, glens, glades, and trees.

What saddens me is that I am taken for a solemn cemetery fellow. Forget it; every hour hangs on the thread of Ariadne and since our losses are our gains the end may be that I shall be shaking hands with myself.

Would that be amiss? Meantime let us call for a mug of ale. I'm a roisterer in English, and before I go back to my flea'd room, attend, O patient reader, to this little chant of the Logos.

18

> *But all this language gotten, and augmented by Adam and his posterity, was again lost at the tower of* Babel, *when by the hand of God every man was stricken for his rebellion, with an oblivion of his former language.*
>
> —Thomas Hobbes

This is St. English day. Weep not for Thammuz, but cry unto the Fallen Word: "Holy Logos is dead." Homer catalogued the ships of the Argives, but who can count the deceased words that lie in the books of Langland, Chaucer, Gower, Sir Thomas Wyatt, Philemon Holland, Thomas Dekker? Unhouseled English is in the minds of a small knot of the learned. Thousands upon thousands of words of good odor are sore decayed, and few have the bravery to re-edify them.

Amerce the spoiler of the Word, haul his neologies to the Spittle or to Bedlam, and heap the billingsgate of mealy-mouthed Thersites upon Houndes Ditch. May a million fleas nest in his fundament.

Be wary of the newfangled scrawl; take heed of sluttish

discourse as inedible as a carrion trot. Modern jargon is a whore; fillip the disemboweled pornographer and confine him until Doomsday to the close-stool. Inscribe on each copy of venereal fustian the Boar's Head, the sign of the stews in ancient London.

No prig, I say in the beginning was the Word, but who gelded it? Isis still searches for the genitals of an Osirian poem. By Zeus, debile diction signifies feeble ballocks, and the sciolist. Blessed be Rabelais, who put the Psalter in his codpiece.

The ink-fools don't kneel before Sophia, the goddess of wisdom, lip the peplum of Isis, or before commencing a boke pray to the Muse, Chance.

Heed not the mungrill scribbler who firks the tradition of Gower, Thomas Nash, Ben Jonson, Robert Greene. Olden works gravel his throat, and at the mention of Virgil's *Georgics* or Milton's *Areopagitica* he fleers and wipes his piked didactic nose.

Words of good worship re-create the mind and their dissolution lards foolery. I do not seek what is old because I dote upon ruins, but only purpose to attend to Anglo-Saxon once spoke by husbandmen, drapers, fullers, mercers. Nor do I look for hard, burial expressions. This is a liturgy; Pan has lost his reedy pipe, and the everyday mouthings of an eighteenth-century lubber are no longer extant.

What martyrs have suffered as much as the Sacred Logoi, put in the stocks, roasted on the gridiron or quartered? How many Grub Street mawworms have put to the torture bourn, highte, frith, bight, kelp geese, roadstead? Windlestraw has not been given a Christian burial. I speak of halfpenny utterances that fell out of the glad lips of tinkers, greengrocers, cordwainers.

I address the wretched brethren of letters who dwell in hapless kinless rooms; give the indigents a lusty meal of similes savory as truffles or gorbellied tunnies hard by Cadiz. A single phrase that has died in George Chapman's *Bussy d'Ambois* is a balsam for hurt souls in asphaltic coffin towns. The monosyllable, swad, will heal the wounds of an entire hour.

When the language dwindles the sorrows grow, where is the pissing conduit to relieve broken men? There is scarce a dark niche in a soke for the poor to urine though the rich jet up and down in costly gawds or furnish a lawn sleeve for a bishop.

The roynish pedagogue pockets up barbarisms and says his mammon matins in the college sewers. Plain, angelic speech is not for the pedant. As Chaucer holds: "I am a rude man, I kan not gloze." What's left except bedridden clauses and ulcerated tropes, and the suppurated vocabulary of malice?

Harsh language provokes hatred, claims Ovid; the brain lags and fails when it is emptied of Wycliffe's *Potiphar, Pharao's gelding.*

Do virgin words remain? Where are graith, brabble, the scalding-house, or a cantle of cheese? When we bid farewell to the tanner, the pewterer, the kiln, the livery stable, the people lose Ben Jonson's *The Alchemist.* Cockloft, gallipot, pottle, croft, gulligut have grown out of memory. Phial, pot-house, cony, malkin, pursy, pestle, squab are covered with a threadbare coat, and nowhere to go.

Ye who mourn, hear the ram's horn; Gavin Douglas's *Aeneid* has been laid to rest.

The right use and memory of English is the praxis of the soul. Break the gods of the vulgus. Hellebore for those that pester a volume until it has lost its wits. Either we venerate Ben Jonson or trumpery wares surfeiting upon the slops of pleonasms, or are slack and frowsy like Dekker's "nine or tenne drowsie Malt-men, that lye nodding over their Sackes."

Basil comfort those who sigh for the mother tongue. Plow under the fallow aura, equation, creativity, imbalance, stance, normalcy, dichotomy, sociological, ambient, viable, escalate. What a hailstone of torment, and a stroke of misery are existential, confrontation, infiltrate, rationalize, sorted out, and activate. Purge the unlearned mouth with a "combe of corn." Sing a benedictus praising colewort, pillicock, jill-flirt. Our books are the dropping of starlings and the putrid blubber of seals lying on the wet shingle of Tierra del Fuego.

I study with the masters; what I learn I know not. My faculties fail me every page, worse, each phrase; and not a clench I make that does not provide me qualms. I sigh as I err. The labor is too much, and may my blushes salve my tired conscience.

My language is hoveled in the sorriest clouts, but may I wear the tatters of Odysseus returning to Ithaca and Penelope. If some of my passages be relics of a gone English I make no apologies; one old galliard word is a ravishing fume of Storax.

And if a damp has fallen upon you dig up the hedge-towns with Venerable Bede, or pause before a monument of a baker-miller called to our attention by Stow. Though what's left of our English be no more than the reliquary toe of St. Edward the Confessor deposited in the vault of Westminster Abbey, I purpose to reverence it best I can.

Thus I bring this orison to a close. May Saints Wyatt, Surrey, Gower, Walter Raleigh, Philip Sidney, John Lyly, and Ben Jonson shrive my soul and my beggarly and mean-bodied Letters.

19

Dear delicate mistress, I am your
slave,
Your little worm, that loves you;
your fine monkey,
Your dog, your Jack, your Pug,
that longs to be
Styled, o'your pleasures.
—Ben Jonson

I had a rather flimsy relationship with Charles Malamuth, in the Slavic department, and his wife, the daughter of Jack London. At once I was torn piecemeal by her. Not wishing to jar a marital household I harbored the wan suspicion that the two who were living together were quite apart. This eased my wild guilt. Her bust meant more to me than Chekhov's tales. That Jack London's books were nothing to me was of no moment; I was ready to believe *Martin Eden* and *The Iron Heel* were classics.

Besides, Malamuth was a protegé of Upton Sinclair and this made her even more desirable. I didn't appreciate Sinclair's dull muckraking pages, but this did not disturb me unduly. *The Jungle* had sickened me, though it may have put a few manufacturers of sausages out of business.

Now I had two signal honors: I was acquainted with one who had touched the sleeve of St. Sinclair and my hands were starved for the lunar knees of Jack London's daughter. Could I press my fingers against her buxom anatomy I felt I would be close to the father. Had not Rozanov married Dostoevsky's mistress so that he might possess all the details of the master's underclothing life?

For a pair of months I had the most incontinent rages. Of course, a drumbling ninny, I failed. Instead I invented a couple of aphorisms: Man is a disorderly animal; ecstasy is a highly flavored torment; love is a disease, a pest begotten by Scratch, and a total madness. The emperor Caligula, of ancient Rome, beseeched the moon when she was full to come down and lie with him.

Attacked by monstrous lusts, which Philemon Holland calls spinistrae, I considered wooing her would be decorous, for was not courtship the hors d'oeuvre of marriage? Should she marry me and be faithless I would be renowned; the cuckold is a more wondrous rumor than Helen of Troy, for he is famous everywhere. Maybe I would grow tired of her. Does not the bored husband just help himself to his wife?

Then I thought how I had forgotten to compliment her. A man who does not extol a woman is certain to have a poor snack in her bed.

I had one dinner with her, alone, and I was so overwhelmed I said nothing. I gaped at her mouth and adored her motions. After I said good-bye I muttered to myself that a pair of mutes at table would be two tombs in the boudoir.

I was in the rutting season every instant. Utterly dazed, I thought perhaps I had been avoiding her. The cuttlefish when pursued discharges his ink and so hides himself. Lost, I importuned my ancestral maggots to assist me in my lewd

insanity. Whenever I was near her I snuffed up her odor-
iferous raiment; I was ready to quaff her footprints.

There is a story narrated by a remarkable author who was
at the court during the reign of the French Valois. He tells
that when Pope Clement came to Marseilles the maid-in-
waiting of the Queen Regent's Majesty took one of the pillows from His Holiness's bed and wiped herself with it. His
Holiness would not allow the pillow to be laundered. Every
night when he lay his head upon it he turned so that he
could poke his nose into it and retain the smell of her.

Meantime at the university I mused upon false studies.
Education can be no better than the caitiff products of the
country; when nylon is a substitute for cotton and wool one
can expect poisonous courses in pedagogy.

All I got from lectures by a botanist is that the sap rises
in plants and then declines. Years later I fed upon the pages
of Theophrastus, Marcus Porcius Cato, Buffon, but still
cannot recognize a gillyflower, a cherry tree or a maple.

I heard lectures by the eminent anthropologist Kroeber,
who forced the students to read H. G. Wells's vulgarian
Outline of History.

There was a great deal of chatter about the Greek theater and Shakespeare, but I cannot sit like a costive grammarian on his close-stool, and listen to a clown reduce *Lear*
to tedious elocution. For what motive I am unable to fathom
I enrolled in a class in drama under the tutelage of a woman
best described as a lean-witted termagant. We had to recite
aloud a banal one-act play by Susan Glaspell.

Impetuous I hurried to the teacher's office to complain:
was trash a Jacob's ladder to the apprehension of Aristophanes' *The Clouds?* Should I be phlebotomized by such
dross I would be thoroughly uneducated by the time I re-

ceived a Bachelor of Arts. The brangle with her was futile. Flayed by arguments which I continued long afterward, I had as a result of this one many emaciated weeks.

I began to have faith in the ignoramous provided he never learned to read and write. I also felt the intimations of non-existence, and suspected *that* all Things were No-Things. Had anything ever happened, I wondered? Does one really believe Moses saw the hinder parts of God, that Christ crossed the brook Kidron, or Hannibal took firebrands and tied them to the tails of kine and by this stratagem routed the Romans?

My emptiness could never be filled, and books too were wraiths. But ghosts also rot; masterpieces have their seasons and centuries. Should one go to Gautier when the roots of trees are parched? Will not a snowfall embitter the pages of Apulieus' *The Golden Ass?* What worth is Baudelaire's *Les Fleurs du Mal* when one's soul is tormented by Getic winds, and is April better for understanding Flaubert's *L'Éducation Sentimentale?*

I still revered Tolstoy although he taught me that books are wicked and I craved to belong to this well-nigh dissolved priory of pariahs. Then I shed tears because Andreyev was a worm, and so was I.

There was the old vexation: how soon would my privy members be graved? Already I saw the day when I should have to repair to the cemetery, attired in black cloth, and lay a branch of cypress on the marble covering my deceased phallus. In the dumps I admired Caligula, who never permitted anybody to visit him unless he knew the passwords, either Priapus or Venus.

None of these vexations prevented me believing that I would be "a Dionysus tamed and clothed in his right mind." It was a glorious reference, but it didn't help me; for besides being the prey of everybody I fell into the tyranny of myself. By chance I had come upon the herbalist, Dioscorides, in a secondhand bookshop. This ancient writer counsels the hypochondriac to cure himself by using a sponge in which lachryma is gathered, drying it, and then interring it in a fictile vase.

On days when I saw no students I was hurled about in my sleep by hurricanes, downpours and tornadoes. Zero produces one and one is snow, hail, wormwood, and all are nothing. And all was my fault though nothing was, because nothing is. I was determined to arrange the most congenial meetings with people. Prepared to be meek when I was to see a humble man I was startled to discover he was overbearing. After this humiliation I invented an adage: "He who says he is your equal is making ready to be your despot." The next occasion I resolved to be a wag, but I encountered such a dullard that in less than an hour with him I proved to be a greater dunce than he.

Little by little I became more dismayed; how could I earn enough from literature for bed, gout and latrine?

What did all these vagaries come to? As I sit at my used deal table, my gibbet, at 64 Rivington Street, going over a sentence I conjecture is a virgin, I am as incoherent as I ever was. Were I not would I bother about the rueful attempt to be lucid? All I can do is consider the January dying bark of myself and affirm I would not go back to those cruel doldrums in order to scent the vernal equinox with avid nostrils.

Does it matter? I am grateful to the stout thighs of my mother and her strong back; otherwise, I would not be passionate. But everything is important to me. Should I ask for fog I return to Amiel's *Journal:* "What have I drawn from my soul? Thousands of sincere pages that are but a collection of dry leaves."

One afternoon a student accused me of being bitter; he

expected me to be crestfallen, but I surprised him, replying that each one is entitled to his jeremiads, essential as eating, thinking, sleeping, and not eating, thinking and sleeping. He fled.

However, each day is a new apocalypse; when my head was inert I relied upon Nietzsche's chant: "Out of thy poisons breweth thou balsams for thyself."

20

> *I perceive that love is not unlike
> the fig-tree, whose fruit is sweet,
> whose root is more bitter than
> the claw of a bitter; or like the
> apple in Persia, whose blossom
> savoureth like honey, whose bud
> is more sour than gall.*
>
> —John Lyly

Before leaving San Francisco for New York I forsook a tender aspen amour, a gone love I must sorrily pipe.

This is a tale of desire and of the ballocks, a ruined moan of winter that has left me clothed in my unkind bark. It is a stave of remorse for which there is no remedy except more cruel smart. Were it only the ragged fires of lust the blaze would have long since gone out. For years I have sucked up the draff of regret, but am still pinched for want of her.

My image of her is feeble, and waste and years have blasted her flowers—bituminous buds growing on the marge of the Dead Sea. Suppose heaven vouchsafed me a new green youth would I pass through the flames of another trance? My mind falters, and I stumble in the shallows of wan remembrance. Oblivion clogs my unkindled lakes.

Whatever were the frailties of G. mine were far worse;

for I have as many faults as the hairs on the head of Abraham.

It was a blowy, brine-fed day in San Francisco. I took the ferry going by Goat's Island. At the Embarcadero I walked briskly up Market Street. On Post Street I stepped in Newbegin's bookshop and I was shortly fingering Turgenev's *Smoke*. With the book in hand I approached the saleslady, a virgin of twenty. By then I had given my sharkskin suit extreme unction, and in its place I wore another suit of indigence. She showed chaste pity for my worn-out presence more productive than any love potion. Nor did she hesitate to grant my entreaty.

That evening I was introduced to her mother, who liked me. That I could not understand, but since she was prepared to care for me I could not help cherishing her. I appeared to be a sensible young man, perhaps foolhardy in that I was poor, but this was never mentioned to me although obviously discussed.

Very soon I was the thrall of G., her black flowing hair, and her fair polite body, rich in round graces.

> *Hir manners might no man amend;*
> *Of tong she was trew and renable,*
> *And of her semblant soft and stable.*
> —Chaucer

My eyes furnished her with all the panegyrics a maid needs, nor could one doubt my cheeks pale with undernourished sleeplessness.

Our romance was the wine of acacia and wild broom and soft stemmy April rain. On Sunday when I was at liberty from my studies at the university we went by ferry to Sausalito. She had packed a lunch which we ate in the woods, seated on moss hard by a eucalyptus that perfumed my sighs. I was twenty-two, my habits torn, and my passions untutored. I had nothing to offer her. But I was in the horse latitudes, certain that a mild trade wind would bring me the windfall I needed to support a marriage, for we were betrothed to one another.

What I did not suspect was that I had gained a modest position in the world. I learned of this when G. and I spent a Sunday in Marin County with a married couple and I heard the wife say with gorged respect that her husband was college-bred.

I foolishly presume everything would have gone well but for the mother's obscure role. She was a stout widow with heavy plain legs and a solid but not unpleasant face; her mouth had perhaps grown wider with the years. She had the same traits as the furnishings in her home, which were ordinary but not mean: the oak table was phlegmatic, the tablecloth on it well-laundered, and the five chairs sat around the dining room table in a civil aloof manner.

She continued to wear black long after her husband had died. She seldom spoke of him beyond saying he was a genteel lawyer, and she regretted he could no longer fill the rooms as her couch and settee did. He had left a very moderate amount of money which spared his widow and daughter the stigma of low-class poverty.

On Saturday afternoons when I was at the apartment with G. her mother after several remarks would complain of fatigue and retire to her bedroom to lie down. I had the impression that her heart was not strong. In those days a weak heart was considered in good taste but hard-working people could seldom afford it.

Somewhat later I learned G. had a sister, married to a well-to-do lawyer, and they were expected shortly. This troubled me somewhat, for although my love had increased I had an unquiet presage. There had been no plans for a wedlock. Timorously I had suggested to G. that what with her wages at the bookstore and my weekly stipend from my mother we could be married, rent a little cottage in the Berkeley Hills for twenty-five dollars a month, and I could write and study and not lie rusting in my moans. No wiles could I discern in G., but no clear answer either.

No ravisher of her scarce-born summer, I wondered was this to be a vigil and I a Benedict burning for years. G., the lodestar of my life, was to become my raging uproaring woe. Was my sole gratification to be inside the girdle and shift of a book? "I was young and ful of ragerys," and meek as my aconited blood would let me.

One Saturday afternoon we exchanged two or three slender kisses, and the mother came in and upbraided us. What morsel of G. could I have, could I put the venereal tooth into the wastel-bread of her flesh? My soul was in my hands that rushed headlong up beneath her dress. I bruised her nipples and quaffed the Pierian fountain of her breasts. Yet I would not spoil the dainty prime of her virginity. She was my mortification and my orison. Guilt I had and more than I could cast down my gullet.

My frenzy and my sins grew amain. I would have drunk serpent's dust could it have slaked my lust. Oh, could I freeze my vile aches at the poles where no April sings, or could I hymn, all is dead, and forget the unquenched bed, maybe yet I would be shriven by God's lambish morn.

How oft in my Berkeley room I lay my bereft head on my arm, for I was all grief, and mire. The next time I saw her would I not again poke and pudder about her skirts?

Matters waxed worse. How hard was my lot, becrazed as I was by her stint of kisses and the spare ration of caresses she allowed. My feelings were so mixed, my shame so huge, that I considered a tittle of desire for her a swarm of fatted fleas.

One whole year I guarded myself best I could, content to

cherish her shoes and her half-tasted dresses. I cursed her sabbath logic skirt where I could not victual. Was she a grammarian of love? Did she expect to clause, adverb and adjective our amour? Wreathed in wormy pain I exclaimed: "Let me be a whirlwind under your saintly clothes."

Often we parted, each enclosed in a cenotaph of silence. On one occasion I sent her a scribbled note: Did she give me leave to quench my agony by guzzling an ugglesome dug? A bladder of ungovernable penance, I rushed to her on my sinking knees to bless all the hours of my unrequited pulses.

Late one morning, after we had danced on the roof of the Fairmount Hotel in San Francisco we sat huddled together on a neighbor's empty wooden steps. She was tightly harnessed in my seething arms. I touched the vestal, and for an angelic second I had a heady return, when a secular couple passed by. Then she sat, apart from me, a shriveled heap of shame, and I a heap of maggots.   .

I castigated her. "Let me be, thou uncooked chink. Jehovah bless the virgin prig. What's the price of your occult wares? Shall we wait until you've lost your noonday blush and I've earned my degree of impotency? Even then how shall I house and apparel thee?"

What was to become of my Maid Prude? Let her win a basilisk's day, I refused to see her. She had transformed the nuptial couch that never was into a dungeon of satiety never earned. In the gentlest breast of a damsel lurks the cunning shrew.

I could no longer crawl and beg. Better to go with the unsure step of the aged and fume no more.

She called me, and I shouted: "My surd fingers are worn thin; when the cerecloth is near and the weevil sings, come back to me. Begone, I'm an oven of profligacy."

In the mean space my dark thicket groaned, and my dismal mere chattered. Gravel clogged my long unsated hours.

What more could I have done? Utterly deface her vestal glories I could not. Already I lay in the muddy slime of concupiscence.

Again she sent me hurried word and I telephoned; her voice was an ossuary. Her brother-in-law and sister were going to Lake George and desired she accompany them. Should she go? she pleaded.

I could bear no more punishment from this hard nubile damsel. God forbid! He hardened Pharaoh's neck, why mine against her who was my Holy Writ. "I despise your wiles," I raved. "Leave me. Let my embers die, thou snudge who gave me a monk's fast."

What were our short annals of prentice love? I touseled her shamefast tongue and dabbled her lips and received a mite of her precious saliva. 'Tis long ago, but not erased. Yet is there more than a breath betwixt my ribald unrinsed infamy and my beloved's chaste grace?

Two letters from her at Lake George came to me, imbrued in the blood of the lamb of her youth but I, steeped in the vomit of soured love, could not reply.

The best evidence of my love is the long, unremitting anguish, and my bootless sighs. "Dole on my ruine feeds, and with sucking smarte."

2 I

---

*O Metaphysics! We are now
just as advanced as in the time
of the first Druids.*

— Voltaire

Always expecting to do better elsewhere, I had followed
my books to New York. I had matriculated at Rabble University and sought asylum for my bereaved wits at St.
Pragma.

It was June 1925, and no more of that can I say except
I don't think such a year existed.

How could I have foreseen that St. Pragma would be a
boreal textbook priory? Again I had erred. Now a beggarly
Odysseus, with no Penelope or dog to greet or recognize me,
I sat on a stone bench in the university quadrangle, my
baccalaureate and my university learning packed in a scrip
that lay at my feet.

To the rear of me was the Augean Stable of Pragmatic
Thought, as well as a statue of St. Pragma holding a polypus close to his chest. There was this inscription chiseled
into the sculpture: "The Seer is he who adapts himself to
his age"—Cicero John Dewey.

Over against the Augean Stable was the School of Pecula-

159

tion, Barter, Cavil, Cheat and Cabal, where thousands of
students were enrolled for the study of commerce and juris-
prudence. This was an august colossus deified by a statue
of a huge and noble cormorant. Hard by was the Institute
of Ologies for pupils preparing for their doctorates in human
association, syllogism, enthymeme, and the Aristotelian
grammar of political economy.

I had studied with Anathon Aall, the eminent scholar of
the doctrine of the Logos. A visiting professor from the
University of Oslo, Norway, he was a sunken, damp man
with the complexion of brown porridge; he had a few poor
hairs on his head, and a triangular nose which would have
commanded a hecatomb to Zeus from Pythagoras.

The class began at eight o'clock of the morning; the students, wild asses, chewed the thistles of knowledge. All
lubbers, they slouched in their seats, their filthy trousers
rolled up to their thighs, so that Anathon Aall was ashamed
to lift his eyes. While he spoke about the origin of Logos,
going back to Heraclitus, the Nous of Anaxagoras, Philo, St.
John, Clement of Alexandria, and Tatian, they snored,
belched and ate cracknel.

The Logos was as much of an enigma to me as the Sphinx
at Gizeh; besides, I suffered from an obscure academic disease, gargantuism, for like Rabelais' heroic pupil, Gar-
gantua, the more I studied the more stupid I became. The
lectures emptied my pate and belly. I sucked my teeth and
gums, chewed my lips, and all I had was a snack of Nous
and assorted hors d'oeuvres of brute abstractions not even
dressed with oil and a few lettuce leaves.

Nous had to be gotten rid of. If he turned out to be a
timber god I intended to chop him up, as Diagoras did the
wooden Hercules, which he used for kindling to boil his
turnips. One morning I made my speech: "Sir, I'm sore
graveled. Tell me, once for all, who's Nous? Is he Father-

Mind seated in his vasty, gaseous pleroma excogitating in-
numerable planets? Who's Logos the Word? The issue of
the Father who enjoined him to be the Carnal Bread and
associate with a troop of bestial, warring dolts called mor-
tals? But if God told his son, Logos, to go ahead and beget
the World, why didn't he do it Himself instead of palming
off the job on Demiurgus and forcing him to make Day and
Night?

"The Gnostics claim the World never became social
spermal Bread, leaving Aether to mingle with shameless
men, and that there was no embodied Messiah the people
were looking for when the vernal equinox enters the sign
of Aquarius.

"Puzzled, but not irreverent, I don't believe Logos has
the bowels of a spider, or the pericranium of a flea. And
what about those felting clouds, shaped by God, the hat-
maker? Are they first causes, too?

"I'll never find out who framed the Universe. That's too
much for the wayward mind of man. Besides, I'm starved;
I've been chewing the Logos for two semesters. It's useless.
Couldn't you relent a little just as Theophrastus, who alleges
that man was originally filet of sole, hake or flounder? What
an appetite that gives me! Oh, I have an Orcus of confusions
in my stomach for a cucumber. Couldn't you steep fossil
Nous and Logos in a barrel of brine? How can I moisten
my soul? Explain how dropsical Heraclitus says a dry soul
is the wisest, though he wrapped himself up in cow dung
and was so parched he died of thirst. When a man is dying
of thirst is it metaphysics to say it's best to be dry?

"What do I do for food? I hear that Sophia, that Primor-
dial Chit, said to be She-Wisdom, has replaced the good-
for-nothing male gods, and that she's sensible, too, refusing
to be wise unless she was furnished with that dark velvety
chink which all deities and men covet. How is it nobody

knew that a plain tiny crevice could take care of every mortal complexity? Nor did any metaphysical clod catch on to her lubricious nature; there's none so lascivious as she. There was Isis going about crazily in a wicker boat on the river Nile searching for Osiris' shameful parts which she couldn't find because a scambling fish, the sea bream, got there first and devoured it. Who needs Nous when he's got Sophia and Isis?

"I simply can't afford to subsist on stale clumps of epistemology and scraps of aetiology. Even Pythagoras wasn't forever bolting down theorems, cubes and triangles. He was either munching a sucking pig, a tender kid, or bent over a plate of lima beans. Let's have done with it. Allow me to sit with Xenophanes and eat chick-peas and drink sweet wine while I nibble on a peel of Isis' peplum."

The students were restless, the color of Aall's nose was puce, it was eight twenty-five. The pupils could ascertain the pigment of his nose to the minute. When the damp flanks were of an emerald hue it was nine ten. Close to the hour of dismissal the wings of his nostrils were the shade of saffron.

On another occasion I could not repress this query: "Professor Aall, can you separate will from intellect and mind from feeling? Is lust seated near the inflammatory liver, whilst velleity can be located in the coward feet? How many meters of skin does ignorance require?"

Anathon Aall gave me a pained, wry face. Then he provided me with his remote, ontological smile. "You're a naïve primitive," he said, "and you are looking for anthropomorphic gods. Do you wish the deities to have human jaws and necks?"

"Why not, sir?" I replied. "Plato said the world was a great animal, and Pythagoras, of like mind, claimed it had legs, arms and feet."

Aall was hardly to be the victim of a juvenile Socratic

elenchus. He had furnished us with a course in divine indifference, for he had locked up in his brave, dialectical
heart that honeycomb, his holy Logos.

A graduate course in Jamesian Platonic epistemology,
with a Deweyan exegesis, was offered by Professor Montague. A classroom metaphysician, he had a three-cornered
face, and parted his snowy hair clean down the middle with
a laboratory knife. He had a malady described as St. Pragma
dryness and his lecture notes had long since been parched
by the Dog Star.

I was forced to trifle out my time with the theory of Ness,
that is, the study of the universals deskness, tableness, chairness, houseness. With Anathon Aall I was fuddled with
Nous and Logos; now I had Ness as well.

Professor Montague went to the blackboard and with a
pedagogic piece of chalk listed the profane things—chair,
table, footstool—on one side, and the holy Platonic universals—chairness, tableness, footstoolness—on the other.

After sitting on my hunkers like a hare on its scut for a
month I objected: "Sir, my mind is a gravid rabbit though
I can only bring forth Ness. Tell me, please, why is chair
less angelic than chairness? Why can't we be content with
earthen particulars?"

"We must rise above the particular to the universal," said
Professor Montague, "in order to apprentice ourselves to the
meditative life."

"But can't you wrap Ness with summer grass, a lettuce
leaf, or colewort?" I protested. "These universals give me
pains in my two ears. My ankle rings, and my mouth
chimes; my head's been tolling for seven hours. I just haven't
the strength to raise my smarting arm and reach for chan-
delierness. Matter is such a grief. We live with it and die
of it; it's hard, but that's our portion. It is impossible to
avoid dying things. Corrupt, we cannot perceive unless we

partake of original sin. According to St. Augustine (and one of his pagan preceptors, Marcus Terentius Varro) the word carcass derives from cado, to fall. Man thinks, because he is a fallen angel. Does not Augustine imply the vanity of all philosophy when he declares that whereas Plato's flesh putrefies, the peacock's doesn't?"

"A pretty whim, but scarce scientific," said Professor Montague. "It would be courteous to the students would you permit us to return to Ness."

"Sir, please, I make full conscience of the predicament, and am not entirely confuting you."

Montague arranged a philosophic smile for the benefit of the class. "Are you setting up the boundaries beyond which the Mind cannot pass?"

"I've grown old and wrinkled as the cockle thinking of the Mind," I said.

Montague was about to reply when I interrupted. "I can't even get the small beer of pleasure from Ness. If I may say so, you demand we atone for villainous things by taking a cowardly flight to Ness. I adore the furniture of the cosmos, and believe that table is more heroic than your spado, table-ness. All knowledge is corporeal, and when it deteriorates into terminology it is a pedantical dunce. Lucian tells us that pots, kettles, ladles, were originally called Prometheus, who was the first philosopher. Anaxagoras held that man was the wisest of animals, not because he has a better sort of Nous—intelligence—but simply because he has hands."

"Well, my boy, you've trapped yourself," crowed Montague. "You, too, lean on Nous."

"Sir, please allow me the oil and grace of error. I was citing Anaxagoras, and only employing a word. Anyway, I'll cross myself before Ness if you'll provide him with hands, legs, feet and arms."

"Are you serious? You insist that a chair should have a . . ." he paused, blushing.

"Yes, sir, a seat and legs and the sacrum of Osiris. A study lamp has the lissom neck of Pallas and a woman the figure of an Etruscan vase."

"Just to cocker your extravagant conceit," Montague said, "are you claiming doors, ceilings and houses are simply different sorts of animals, some male, others female? In your froward head I suppose a couch is a woman."

"Wasn't she made for a man to lie on? Who except a simpleton will do no more than cover her with a blanket?"

"Then I suppose things—a footstool, a pebble, a marsh plant—have joys and pains."

"Yea," I avowed, "all things suffer. Matter itself grieves until it is form."

"Fine, excellent. Doubtless a chair is a sanguine breathing brute."

"Indeed. How often when I'm tired do I need a reposeful chair. And if I'm put out with the world, and sit on that chair, it won't reproach me. When I'm forsaken, it won't let me down or borrow money from me, for it will always stand on its own legs. May I say that since Alcibiades cut off the phalloi of the gods man has not produced a single table with generative properties."

"No, you may not say it." Montague set his foot down hard on the pedantic floor. "This is no course in the lechery of objects. Never have I heard such arrant nonsense."

"Sir," I protested, "is there any other kind of sense?"

I left Montague's class and attended two lectures on pedagogy, and then I cast this menstruous cloth of education down the lavatory bowl. Following this I took a semester of Behaviourism described in the catalogue as the Golden Mean of Grammar, with asides on Aristotle's Rhetoric.

I recalled best I could scraps of eloquent orations on the rhetoric of behavior and political economy grounded on the Aristotelian Golden Mean, offered by Dr. However Pointless. Dr. Pointless was an albino. He had a nose thin as a needle and his general expression was worse than my outlook. His acute intellect was not so close a companion to him as his umbrella which he always carried into the classroom. Sometimes he used the metal edge for writing on the blackboard, forgetting it was not a piece of chalk. Again, when he was absorbed in his penetrating analysis of our glowing social organism, he would chew the cotton cloth of the umbrella and scatter the ribs on the academic floor. When the windows were open, and there was a northwesterly wind, the pieces looked like black swallows flying everywhere about the room.

His lectures commenced thus: "Gentlemen, we are not concerned with the ideal but the real, with what is, with the more or less, the less always exceeding the more. To prove it let us example the Stagirite who says 'less evil compared with the greater becomes the good.' In short, our interest is in the preservation of a cash society and its paying citizens. Settlements were originally planned for the quick rather than the dead.

"To achieve this men must dwell in the closest association with one another. Those who decline to mingle with others are morbid dissidents, and are *sub specie aeternitatis*, a losing proposition to the corporate nation. Let me instance the following: each commoner has his distinct social and economic position, as the rules of grammar provide; the verb should nuzzle the noun, and the adjective that shows the results of the national resources should take its vigilant place before the substantive. Grammatical disorder of the economy cannot be tolerated lest there be strife, riot, discord; each word, or citizen, is a logician; otherwise the words in disarray may be said to be living illegally together within the social framework of the sentence.

"Money is the ineluctable consequence of social adjustment. As the Spanish poet Quevedo so rightly remarks, he who is out of pocket is out of this world. The pauper as well as the prodigal is the economic foe of more or less. Dismiss at the outset indolent utopian vagaries, for we must concentrate upon the possibilities of man as a radiant usurious animal who must perforce enjoy his fellow men to the fullest extent. As Aristotle reminds us in the *Ethics*, the lion does not take pleasure in hearing the ox, but in eating him."

Dr. However Pointless now took his umbrella and pointing with it explained: "Here on one side we have excess, the wealth of the state, and on the other the deficit, the lower classes. Let it be clearly understood, those who pay lose; we shall take this up apace. Therefore only the rich man can afford to buy; whilst he is making his purchases Nature refects him, for as he spends the interest is growing in both his pockets. The poor man can only rid himself of his character. He has nothing else to spend since it is his sole property.

"Obviously, the lower classes are conspicuous unthrifts, easily tempted by witless goods, and stupid baubles, radios, automobiles, television sets, or a gloomy gallimaufry of new furniture. The easy prey of gross and cankered advertisements, he is always a bankrupt. He is a giddy ambulatory paralogism. Whatever he buys is a loan he receives from the rich as a token of confidence. Once he betrays his trust following an economic panic or unemployment he then can be said to have wholly consumed himself. At this point he is like the Locrians described by an ancient as the cigalas who so devastated themselves that they had not a branch to sit upon. In all periods of the glowing social adventure is the amphibology of the loser, his whining shibboleths—justice, benevolence, charity, compassion—but only the milksop believes in these dreggy words.

"Everything is based upon the more or less of what was,

which is what is, that is, more or less. The cause of seeming disharmony in a polity of sociable and agreeable emotions is the gluttony of the wage earner. He ceaselessly covets his wealthy neighbor's wife, house, garden and money. He is the economic adulterer who is found in bed with the rich man's wife, and like a hungry ass who, when beaten, will not leave the pasture.

"We have sufficiently proven that to be poor is to err; it is a moral defect in character. Therefore to pity the poor wretches in the nation is a stigma of weak-mindedness. Let us not overlook the fact that the loser is an asset to the cash corporate commonality. This is Hegelian dialectics, but allow me to cite the greatest economic philosopher since Aristotle, Dr. Pangloss, who rightly observes: 'Private misfortunes are public benefits so that the more private misfortunes there are, the greater is the general good.'

"Point two. There is enough condescension in the ephors of the public weal to inculcate good feelings among those who offend against the laws. As one among multifarious examples: a senseless man, starving to death, steals a loaf of bread and is arraigned in our noble areopagus. The magistrate, though austere, is not morose; instead of mentioning bread, milk, cheese, anchovies and cakes, and whetting the appetite of the hungry culprit, he nicely states that the prisoner has violated ordinance 764538. This is the majesty of the law, and the cash grace of the nation.

"Once more let me emphasize that those idealistic theorists who prate over justice, and the equitable distribution of goods are economic diviners who are basting a bawd in a chancel. At the risk of being repetitious I must needs assert that those who purchase what they cannot afford are no better than a parcel of cuckolds. Let me illustrate further. The grubby pleb cannot wait until he has received his Saturday night's wages. The money, not yet in his hand, teases and tickles his skin, itches and burns like a raw scab that he deliriously wishes to remove when he espies a washing machine his slut of a wife can well do without. He gapes until he is wounded with joy; his pain becrazes him and he's furious and intractable as if he were having carnal commerce with a round delicious tart. This excruciating throb is at the same time an intolerable pleasure. See how Euripides expresses the ecstasy of pain: the wound of Telephus, he says, was 'soothed by the filings ground from the same spear.' The rabble will stick at nothing to get a parasitic toy; to quote Sallust, 'The Commons' . . . inherent disposition to novelties.'

"To spend is the main recreation of the petit-bourgeois workman; as Aristotle holds, the worker's mind is 'cheated into a persuasion.' Only the rich are frugal, content as Diogenes with a dilapidated leek, a sprat, some antique greens, the relic of a potato the shape of one of St. Francis' ankles deposited at Tours. The Cato of the Commonwealth, the rich man, abides by Cicero's exhortation: 'Unguents with an earthly taste are better than the flavor of saffron.'

"To conclude our dissertation for the day: The basis of society is sacred robbery, or the subtlest craft of the imperial transaction. Likewise, guile and plunder are the Scripture of the nation. Truth, under all conditions, is a scourge, an economic anachronism. Were there no hypocrites everybody would be worn out before they were eighteen years of age."

Needless to say, I was so entranced with the Professor's style of delivery I never interrupted him. Nor did I ever forget the political economy of more or less, or his golden maxim, that the worse is the better because it isn't really that bad.

22

It may be said that there is an abecedarian ignorance that goes before learning; another that comes after learning; an ignorance which learning makes and engenders.

—Montaigne

That I recollect well-nigh nothing is not to be scorned; it may be that if we study, what we forget is what we remember. Our bodies seldom fail us. We are automatic, far more so than Pascal believed.

In the twenty-fourth year of my rugged and barren life I had pored over *The Stromata* and *Exhortations to the Greeks* by Clement of Alexandria, lipped pages here and there of Tatian, Tertullian, St. Jerome, and fallen into a madness over St. Augustine's *The City of God*. Much of this was a mumble to me, but character rules man's morning and dusk, and no one may deprive himself of his portion. To misunderstand what one is doing is also to learn; it was, as it had to be, and I can only cry out: "My cup runneth over with self-delusion."

My constellation is Sagittarius, Contemplation, as Giordano Bruno said. I am the dust of Ovid, Horace, Plotinus, Thucydides; my viaticum is the booke. I'll study until my face is a pallid winding sheet. As John Lyly relates: "What scholar is he that is so zealous of his book as Chrysippus, who had not his maid Melissa thrust meat into his mouth, had perished with famine, being always studying?"

Give me an onion of Propertius, a bunch of the watercress of Euripides, and the English of Dekker's *Plague Pamphlets*. Read as if the casket were near, and then you may understand a tittle of the *Iliads*.

Still sitting in St. Pragma's quadrangle, I bent over to caress my scrip bulging with Nous, Ness and More or Less. My mind, weakened by countless digressions, was hard to bring to a stop. In a little while I saw the image of Father Cornelius Clifford, a Jesuit priest who gave a weekly seminar in the primitive church fathers. Father Clifford had a thin, humble parish at Whippany, New Jersey. The most eminent scholar of St. Augustine, he once opened his heart to me, confiding that there was no advancement in the church for a learned man. He was the familiar of Lord Balfour, the statesman who had written the most pessimistic book on philosophy I had read, Henri Bergson, and a whole galaxy of metaphysicians now extinct. He had Celtic eyes, the hue of an Iberian sky, his head was covered with heavy albic down and his rosy cheeks were washed in the blood of the paschal lamb.

Under Father Clifford's tutelage I misread scraps of Origen, Saints Anselm, Boniface, Thomas Aquinas and Augustine. However, it is better to misunderstand profound works than to comprehend trash. Little do I recall of his easy, informal divagations. A military Jesuit, he inveighed against the meacock pacifism of Bertrand Russell.

I would wait to accompany him at the close of the class and as the elevator rose to our floor, before stepping into it, it was his wont to say: "If it please God may we avoid foul Styx as we descend."

One afternoon Father Clifford gave a lecture on Augustine's *Confessions* at the mansion of Clarence Mackay, the president of Postal Telegraph. The priest, my sole companion of those blighted days, informed me that were Mackay to know that a Jew was under his roof, he would scarce deem it a venial sin on his part. Chance is a wily god, for Mackay's daughter was to elope with Irving Berlin, the Jewish Tin Pan Alley composer of "Alexander's Ragtime Band."

With the exception of Rabbi Martin of San Francisco and Father Clifford, I never had much palate for the deceit of the clerical cloth. When I was thirty, and on my way to visit Alfred Stieglitz at An American Place, an aged man shambled along Madison Avenue and I thought he paused. His footsteps were flaccid, his eyes dim twilight, his cheeks lapt in their final sunset. It was Father Clifford. "My son," he said, "are you successful?"

I lowered my eyes. "Father," I replied, "I have published a book, and have drunk the water of gall, *Marah*."

In a small while I heard that Father Clifford had died. He was the one warm mammal, the Lord's Elect, the Thinking Lamb of St. Pragma.

The students at St. Pragma were no less aloof and spectral than the pedagogues. Nobody pestered me, which was a great nuisance. What companions had Prometheus save the elements? Then and now I could envisage no other course except to be trimmed, shaved, polled, and divided as if I were Christ's garment. Were the alternatives, assuming one had any, to be a man of genius or to be average? The mediocre squanders his brief eructations beneath the stars. I walked alone. Go then to Parnassus, ye who long for nothing.

Had St. Pragma undone me? For a while longer I re-

mained in the university quadrangle, wasting and limbeck-
ing my brain. Then I chanced to push my foot against my
gulligut scrip filled with Nous, Logos, Ness and More or
Less, and faint with nausea rushed to the closest pharmacy.

"What's wrong?" said the chemist in dismay.

"Sir, I just gave up Ness, and I think Sophia, too. What
do you think I've got? Will I die of it?"

"Don't worry," he reassured me. "You've been dying all
your life."

"But what can one take for such a mortal sickness as
life?" I asked.

"Swallow eight grams of niter with calcined charcoal
and lixivium," he advised.

"I forgot to tell you a bedbug sucked up a pint of my
blood a week ago, when my mind was on More or Less."

"Cook a pot of lentils with the bitumen of Judea said to
have been used by the ancient Egyptians for embalming."

"Then, too," I said, "I sit too much. It's very hard on
virtue."

"Three scruples of powdered nightingale, with a course
of hellebore, and a pint of old muscadine should relieve you
of any complaint. Be sure to avoid all sly lecherous conceptions that might involuntarily creep into your head."

"I also had a fit of vanity," I confessed.

"That's bad," said the chemist. "Not even humility will
cure it."

"What do I do for bedlam miseries, long uninterrupted
aches of insanity?"

"Avoid anybody who considers himself sensible."

"But why is it," I persisted, "I don't have my mind on
anything?"

"You think too much."

"Hmm. I never thought of that. Is there a remedy for stiff-
ness of the brain? The other night my wit took ill."

"For God's sake, man, what is the matter?" asked the chemist.

"My bowels."

"What's the trouble with your bowels?"

"Though I stand still, they move. Then there's my insomnia."

"Sleep will fix you up. It never fails."

After paying the chemist all my gramercies for his goodness I stood outside his shop for a while. An old man loaded with something very heavy came by. Minded to help him, as I drew closer I saw he was carrying himself. "That's a heavy load," I grieved. He had a long, slack paunch which he held in his hands. Noticing my pitying glance, he spoke: "Gentleman, any old bottles, newspapers? A suit hanging in the closet is worse than a sorrow or debt hanging around one's neck." When I did not reply, for I was collecting a pile of unfinished meditations, he persisted: "Do you have a dozen or so of used shoes, or years of gone socks with not too many holes? Rusty underwear? I pay spot cash."

Younger than I supposed, he was fingering the lapel of my jacket. I was already obliged to him; bowing, I requested that he come upstairs to my monastic kennel in the St. Pragma dormitory, and promised him he could take whatever was in my wardrobe I was not using.

"Good boy," he said. "I can see you're highly educated. One doesn't come across such politeness in these rude times. It is an honor to meet you. My name is Samuel Kindly. Really a privilege to meet a diploma man."

He gingerly rubbed the palm of his hand against the wool of my coat. His color changed a little; still, he accompanied me, although he was not so overflowing and I missed his compliments.

He bent over and examined the frayed cuffs of my trousers. "Who beat your pants?" He put the best face on this he could, and laughing unnaturally continued: "I guess your trousers are like a well-read book, hungry and worn to the thread. But I'd buy the pants for a quarter. Throw in the jacket and I'll make it thirty-five cents."

Reaching my room I opened the door to the clothes closet. "Here's a pillowcase full of two left-over sour summers," I said. "I nearly forgot a brand-new month of June I hardly wore. June makes me quite nervous; by the time it's gone, I never needed it."

I crawled under the bed and tossed out some shirttails and several unlaundered spiritless shirts that had had a bad effect on my health. Then catching a glimpse of the rag-picker, who looked bewildered and slightly hostile, I took his hand in mine. He stepped back with a show of contempt.

I had so much desire to do something for this good man, I said: "I see last autumn. Rather frowsy, but it's yours. Unless I'm mistaken there ought to be two hundred pounds of indifference beneath my mattress. My back's been troubling me of late and I like to sleep on something hard." I lifted the mattress, and the ragpicker scrutinized it and me.

"Mister," he said, "my time isn't exactly yours. I'm in a hurry."

Not hearing, as one always grasps what one has not listened to, I remarked: "One afternoon I couldn't find my-self. I stopped every passer-by and requested, 'Please, sir, do you happen to know where Mr. Anybody's Miserable Chagrin lives?' What a relief it is to be lost when I'm weary of myself, for who can endure speaking to the same person every livelong day, getting the usual trite replies? All my acts are so miasmal. When the ghost of one of these deeds closely hovers over me I reverently tiptoe to the bureau drawer where I keep my treasures, my mother's letters, and all my anguishes, and I pick up each one and fondle it. All my regrets are old as I am. No matter how long ago I had a remorse it still stings me. Odd, one cannot hold onto pleasure but pain stays with you until it has given up its last breath. Then, too, one never loses a single emotion. Whatever I am saying at this moment happened long ago."

I looked up and around me. The ragpicker was gone. I sat down in a chair, my eyes bleary, and muttered: "Why is it that nothing has ever happened to me?" I was certain he had never been there.

23

Commerce is Satanic, because it is the basest and vilest form of egoism.

—Baudelaire

On a piscatorial Friday, when there was a mild consoling breeze blowing from the gray ruffled Hudson, and a rising of the Crab, I felt it was propitious to make a decision. With twenty-five dollars moldering in my pocket I entered the house of the moneychangers.

Gingerly I tiptoed into the august ossuary of lucre. The sign in the window had eased me: "We trust you—You are our sole interest—Come in and deposit yourself." Yet I tottered a little and captured the attention of the guards. Mistaking me for a drunkard, two of them seized my arms as if about to eject me from the tabernacle. My best suit had lost faith in me. In such attire I had expected to give off the delightful odor of a man in very good circumstances.

Oblivious of my sickly impecunious look I shouted, "Unhand me. The jaundice in my cheek is not marcasite but the pure yellow of gold." A vice-president, seated in his monetary sanctuary and reviewing a pile of sacred fiscal papers, raised the cold ashes of his hair and beckoned me to enter the altar. I took a seat next his desk and gazed at his double-breasted stole.

He scowled. "Are you a vagabond? There's a confidence man in every beggar. Far as I can see, you're a pestilence blown in from the gutters; something's amiss. Know by the grace of the Lord's Security Savings Bank that money is St. Paul's Epistle to the Romans. Be soft, say what you want, and be off. You've already spent two minutes of my eyesight and brains."

"Sir," I said, "accept my kindest apologies, but I've come to lay my entire fortune in your crypt. Are there as many relics in your canonized iron cellar as in Toulouse?"

His frown was hard. "How religious are you? To the extent of at least $10,000? We can invest that in U.S. Steel at seven percent; if you bring the incense of $25,000, you can be a shareholder in Texas Oil. Be vigilant, praise your Creator, and never keep money lazy. A habit of that sort distresses the colon.

"Have you any proof your fortune is yours?" he continued. "We're friendly, but not foolish; it's our experience a man is bad as he was, and as he grows a day older worse. What a palpitating fellow you are; are you ailing? If stricken with poverty you should go to the hospital for incurable joint diseases."

"I'm sorry, sir," I apologized. "I've had a black storm of rotten feelings, and swallowed a poor day."

"Apparently you're in no condition to be investigated," said the vice-president. "Perhaps you've been fleeced or deceived. It's not our policy to attract simpletons; they hurt our reputation and usually arrive in slushy weather and dirty the premises. I doubt we can afford you. Are you on probation, or just released, or overskilled in calligraphy? You're on trial, you realize. How much of my face do you expect me to waste upon a total stranger? We don't want

EDWARD DAHLBERG

trash off the streets. Be frank: have you changed wives
recently? An unstable husband can provide us with a tumor
of nuisances. Have you mislaid a parent in some obscure
cemetery? What about your death taxes? Might as well admit it, I don't like you. I always rely on first impressions;
soon as I get used to a man I fail to see his evil traits. Taking a chance is all right for the young for they have nothing
to renounce but their future which I've already had and,
thank God, lost . . ."

"Pardon me for interrupting you," I begged. "You worry
me. Allow me to ask, should I leave my wealth in your bank
for the wet months? Or would it fester and attract spiders
or ants? Would it be better to plant riches during the spring
equinox?"

The vice-president was exasperated. "Come now, get on
with your business. I fail to detect the expensive midtown
scent about you. Have you a respiratory complaint? All a
potential client has to do is blow his nose, and we can ascertain his social standing. To be plain, don't seek refuge
in the Lord's Security Savings Bank. Is it bootless to inform
you these are robber times? No depositor can be accepted
until he is fingerprinted, photographed and fluoroscoped. Our
trustees insist that petitioners wear top hats and tails and
be disinfected before going through our portals."

"Mr. Vice-President, there's enough niter to be had from
pens or stalls where cattle make water to purge every customer, and enough salt in urine to furnish the doddering
dollar with more stamina."

"I forbid you," he rasped, "to employ impolite words or
base references in this hallowed pantheon. Be respectful or
leave. For ten minutes you've been raving, and I still know
nothing of your character; either you're concealing it or don't
have one. From the beginning I suspected you. Will Sears,
Roebuck or Montgomery Ward vouch for you?"

179

Gleefully I replied: "No, sir, I owe them nothing. I'm indebted to no one except the Creator and I don't propose to repay him for the unkindness he has offered me."

"Aha, that's where you're mistaken," exclaimed the vice-president. "One who is incapable of acquiring many debts has no credit. Why, a man afflicted with bronchial bankruptcy is less of a peril than you. You're more of a risk than a bedridden depositor who's overdrawn."

He lifted his head and rearranged his entire face. "The bank keeps index cards," he explained. "One shows that a certain customer has a papal thumb, or a slinking small finger. In a way we are fortunetellers. We examine a man's palm quite strictly to observe his life line, or whether he's a profligate or a pest who demands weekly bank statements. That's very hard on our machines. High time people began to recognize that a computer has feelings, too. Then there's another kind of undesirable businessman: the small grocer or fruiterer who starts a savings account on Monday and withdraws it on Thursday. Such accounts are described by us as departed souls. Often these penny scullions come back, but we place their names on a waiting list. Though we may not have a whit of evidence, we can detect an arsonist, or one likely to skip town. At the top of the list are bachelors; they're not given to excessive use of Venus and don't stumble about the teller's counter. Most of the females we deal with are spinsters dry as pumice stone, no bother at all."

At this moment I was more illogical than usual, which is the kind of emotion I enjoy most of all. Having no intention of allowing him to ramble on, since I had more belief in my monologue than in his, I said, "Although I do not claim to have your boudoir erudition, nevertheless I offer you a bit of an exhortation. Do you have a daughter? Then do not let her go on a sea voyage alone; the ocean is sterile, but she is not. Keep her indoors during rainy weather; a storm can have baleful effects upon modest teats. As for your son, advise him, should he be courting a lady, not to read a poem to her on his first or second visit lest she receive the dingy impression that he's all mind and no body. Well, I have nothing to say although I'm glad I said it since I've nothing better to do with my life."

The vice-president rose, his nose three leagues of indignation, then sat down again. "Don't care to underestimate a stranger," he said. "Do you have any homeless money with you? You look pale, and a man in poor health could cause a bank to fail."

I stopped him. "When you awaken, before you brush your teeth, may this be your prayer: 'Give me this day my daily mistake.' It's too hard on one's digestion to be in the right. Should you make a practice of it you won't have a friend in the world."

"You need a holiday," he responded dismally. "We could furnish you with a vacation loan to Tortuga, the Virgin Islands or the Argentines."

I was overwhelmed by his generous offer. "I'm a pessimist," I confessed. "I thought human goodness had become a collector's item. As it is, I have enough trouble keeping my mind on what I'm doing, it's such an excessive traveler. Come to think of it, the apute juba has green wings and feet that are cinereous, and never leaves Guiana. Be frank, has this bird ever asked for a loan?"

His craw was bugling, but I let that pass. Eying me shrewdly he said: "We have a number of rich eccentrics. Maybe you're one of those sneaky stockholders."

"As a matter of fact," I admitted, "I own forty thousand shares of self-deception, inconstancy and insults. The other day an inimical acquaintance who wants to get closer to me presented me with a large bundle of bonds of human coldness."

As I viewed the vice-president's bent grasping beak of the eagle, it seemed to me he was weighing my investments with puzzled seriousness. Now he showed his entire unshriven face, more jaw than visage. He was obviously interested.

"You're entitled to our special checking account," he offered. "Just what color would suit your apartment? A harsh pigment might distress you. How would you take to deep puce checks to match your drapes? What about our mild fallow to mate with your upholstery? Or a strong vermilion? Too suggestive, I own, and an eyestrain. I have it! We could make an exception for you and request a mahogany design, provided you're the oak and not the maple type. I just remembered: one of our vestals, aged eighty, just passed away. We could dig her up; she was a pure jasper. She left me her shawl—same tone, of course."

Pensive myself, I petitioned him to overlook my behavior. "You're a fine person and I've sinned against you. I have bad nights going over all my encounters; I wish I'd never met anybody so I wouldn't worry so much. One has to swallow almost everything. Yesterday I was sure a passer-by in the street gave me a horrible grimace. And what for? I wept for hours on the Mount of Olives over that."

He had fallen into a scholarly vein, though he continued to study me. "A man who's a peril to himself is no security for us," he said. "Doubt that you'll last till evening. We'd have to close the account, which means overtime and extra pay for the cashier. On the other hand, there may be more hazards than you."

"How deeply I respect you, sir. Early today I had a difference of opinion with a man bold enough to say he was my friend. I don't really like friends—a hostile lot."

He stopped me short. "Let's get back to business. What do you do for a living?"

"Sir, little as possible. I don't really understand why I care to go on living. Far as I can determine, there's nothing much to it."

The vice-president's Adam's apple appeared. There's something very lewd about an Adam's apple, the remnant of our original sin.

"I'm a collector," I rambled on. "I pick other people's despair, and sell nineteenth-century obituary notices to people who are afraid they're going to die. You'd be surprised what self-assurance a cardiac gets from an article about a woolen manufacturer who suffered from a heart ailment for years and expired at the age of ninety."

The vice-president pressed his right hand against his heart. "You puzzle me," he said. "Can't make you out at all. I've got a heavy lump in my lower abdomen, thanks to your making me think."

By now I cared for him, and fervently. Each one is the portrait painter of the other man, depicting his character to suit himself. When somebody gives me his confidence I'm done in, positively giddy. Without thinking, if it would have done me any good to think, I asked him in the most formal manner whether he would not have lunch with me. Without ado he consulted his watch, framed a busied mouth, and told me gruffly he could not spare the time.

As everything is pointless—and I'm willing to allow anybody to give me evidence there is a point to anything one can do—I blustered: "It is very inhospitable of you not to accept an invitation offered with enthusiasm."

He sat shrouded in silence, his shoulders inert, wrapping one finger about another and waiting for me to collect myself and go. I fell into one of my endless chagrins. Although I had despised him from the start, how could I prognosticate that this would turn out to be a foul incident? Naturally, I would erase the entire affair within the hour, and then redigest it a week later. In a month I would examine this trifling defeat, forget it, and then it would pop up at another time to plague me.

By mistake I offered him my hand, which he declined even to see. My ire was boisterous: "Do you intend to be rude to me? Are you so parsimonious you won't lend me your hand, or are you first demanding interest on this loan before you make it?"

He glowered. I was sure I did not like his face, yet a minute ago I could only perceive an abundance of benevolence in it. He was a usurer, but I was willing to make the best of that. Why did he not show me the same tolerance?

"We don't shake hands during business hours," he snapped. "This is not a social gathering. Go to a recreational center, a gymnasium, or your neighborhood club."

My wrinkled suit sagged, and I endeavored to straighten myself out. It was quite evident the interview had come to a close. The vice-president rose to his fiscal height, but my mind was meandering. "I wouldn't dream of asking you to trust me," I said, "for I have no confidence in myself. Besides, that's the ruse of a rogue. I get dizzy when I meet people; I am unstable and hilarious the whole day after that and am not fit to do anything. I did not believe it proper to show you the most mellow and congenial aspect of myself, for I did not come here to take advantage of you. I admit I'm taking up your time and wasting myself, but it's a universal custom. Couldn't we part on a kindly basis? Any unpleasant meeting crucifies me. Either take my deposit or let us forget it. I'll still esteem you and will always remember you. Money makes a rascal out of a man who otherwise might have stayed at home, watered his parsnips, taken up the study of kelp as a pastime. No matter, it's all over. Just say good-bye to your spouse for me.

"Would that there were a trade wind to give me a bracing

gale of self-assurance. You're a moneylender, but do you know that salt is the third part of the pristine essence of gold, and that tears are composed of salt, rosebuds and lilies?

"Engage in a civil occupation," I admonished him. "Do something useful. Be a cabinetmaker—Ben Jonson was a bricklayer—or a pewterer. Why such a grim mien? Have I done something bad? All right, so I'm ridiculous, a piece of mirth. The average person thinks that laughter is a great joke. Let me paraphrase the bard: a man can laugh and laugh and suffer. Once and for all, which are better investments, long or short visages? Would you risk a depositor with a feeble chin?"

Awakening from my vapours I realized the two guards of the Lord's Security Savings Bank were holding me by my arms. In another moment they had pushed me through the door. Outside on the pavement I stood there holding the twenty-five dollars in my hand. The sky was a great swell of the sea, and the clouds were full udders.

11

Paris and London:
"From the Alone
to Alone"

24

*Why! Should he studie, and
make himselve wood,
Upon a book in cloystre always
to pore.*

—Chaucer

For the etiological poet there is no time, and I allude to the Julian calendar for the sake of convenience. I came to Paris in 1926.

At that time a shoal of authors, seldom mentioned, were appearing in a quarterly magazine that was issued every two years or so, whenever the pair of editors, Ernest Walsh and Ethel Moorhead, had gathered together their ecstatic errors or truths.

Among those printed in *This Quarter* were Kay Boyle, Ernest Walsh, Emanuel Carnevali, Robert McAlmon, Ezra Pound, James Joyce, John Herrmann and Ernest Hemingway. Most of these contributors were mumpers. Thinkers frequently come from the gutters of the earth. The poet of the *Thebaid* was called Statius, a common slave's name in Rome; Proclus, the disciple of Plotinus, was a porter; Epictetus, the philosopher, was freed by his master; and Plautus, the waggish Latin playwright, hired himself out to a baker. Antisthenes, the cynic, and contemporary of Socrates, looked upon the barest walls as warm tunics, and any roof as a thick blanket.

Those who left the States for Europe in the twenties have been described as deracinated exiles. The Greeks regarded ostracism as the cruelest punishment, and there was no reason any one of us should go abroad to be more homeless than we were. Besides there is never any place for the waifs of the Muses to go, for as Josephine Herbst said of the writer, "Our fate is desertion." Charles Baudelaire, altogether lost when away from Paris, spoke of the "grandeur of the pariahs."

Unable to secure refuge for his verse and energetic judgments, Ernest Walsh was living in bizarre poverty at the Ritz Hotel, when he happened to meet with Ethel Moorhead. Enchanted by his Irish braggadocio she suggested they start a magazine to be called *This Quarter*.

Ethel Moorhead had studied painting under Whistler. She was a dogmatic feminist, had marched to Whitehall with a battalion of suffragettes, and whenever this procession of Irish and London Furies came upon a man they cried out, "Shame."

Walsh, a dying tubercular, wanted to roam Europe, so he and Moorhead edited *This Quarter* at Milano, Nice, Monte Carlo, and Roquebrune on the Riviera, where I had gone to see him; but he had died. There I first encountered Miss Moorhead. Alone, she was fuming away the empty hours gambling at the casino in Monte Carlo to cover her grief. I was too young to understand the debauch of solitude. Even buzzards go in pairs on the desolate island of Peruvian Titicaca. However, she continued to issue the magazine in a villa hanging over the Mediterranean Sea. Her three or four rooms were cluttered with the manuscripts of the small commune of illuminati.

Ethel Moorhead had a lean, stiff figure, a long theoretical nose, an acrimonious mouth, and wore thick lenses over which she darted her suspicious glances.

She despised the Calibans of the bookish world: Arnold Bennett, Chesterton, Van Wyck Brooks, Waldo Frank, Gorham B. Munson, and Ernest Hemingway, whose first short story she had published. Walsh, no less waspish, had called the well-known hackneys whose creed was self-service, "dilettantes of passion."

Something about Ernest Walsh's life should be mentioned. He had been a pilot in the First World War, had fallen in a plane at a Texas airfield, and been discharged from the military hospital as an incurable invalid. He looked so ill that strangers often avoided him. Once "a fat healthy gentleman," upset by Walsh's appearance, asked the *patron* of a French hotel to tell the consumptive to leave so that he could enjoy his meal. "I hope he is guarding his health well enough to enter the army of the next war," Walsh said afterward; but usually he accepted his illness without sulking about it. "Like other beds the bed of a sick man has its conventions."

He loathed the muckworms who conceal truthful writers with whose ideas they lard their own haggard and hungry pages. They are "picking their teeth after a cheap lunch on other peoples' notions," Walsh said. And again, they "remind me of gentlemen who advertise in the London *Times*, 'Intentions respectable.'"

In spite of the wild friendship the marvelous youths of *This Quarter* had for one another, each was a solitary. But who can dissolve the wall between himself and other spectral persons? "The hills are nearer to me than to themselves," Walsh remarked.

Absolutely disinterested, and highly intelligent, Ethel Moorhead emptied her purse, not obese by any means, to her juvenescent geniuses, particularly for Walsh and Emanuel Carnevali, and opened her pages to me.

I was supposed to be co-editor of *This Quarter*, number 4, but I could not accept her anti-Semitism. She declared that if the great Hebrew prophets could not redeem the stiff-necked Jews they were indeed a hopeless lot. O indignant droll, did you not realize that no seer has ever healed a nation—according to Giordano Bruno and John Ruskin, always a mob.

On the occasions when we were making ready to go to Monte Carlo there was the inevitable search for her keys; beside herself because she could not find them she scarcely failed to give me a flensed and untrusting look accompanied by, "You're a Jew, have you been rummaging through my papers? Where are my keys?" Bewildered I did not know how to reply. Once James Joyce gave a party in honor of Paul Valéry, who was to be seated in the chair at the head of the table. The late Humbert Wolfe, arriving and seeing the chair was vacant, sat down in it, but could not decipher the glowering face of Joyce until he heard him say: "You're a Jew, aren't you?" To which the English poet answered, "You're a writer, aren't you?" However, Ethel Moorhead misplaced her keys too often for our friendship to endure.

Before we separated I showed her a covey of disconnected words supposed to be a tale. She read it, and said, "Why don't you write a novel?" and so I did. She printed a heavy parcel of "The Beginnings and Continuations of Lorry Gilchrist" in *This Quarter*, which later became part of my first book, *Bottom Dogs*.

It was a dull litany of revulsions—sick ink. Determined to expunge sky, grass, sea and trees the robber giants had stolen from the American people, what I failed to realize was that I was also starving their exieic eyes. There was not a drop of water in the novel. Thinkers are salty, olden hulls, and so are their books. What is Thales except the cry of the sea? It is fabled that water was: God sat shrouded in the ocean, which is His tear-bottle, for sorrow is the cause of immortal conceptions. The Beginner, garbed in water, framed such books as Heaven, Earth, Darkness and Evening. Gulp down a chalice of the great seas and ye also shall be as the Lord.

How had I purposed to compose an energetic novel in the corrupt language of inertia? Wherefore had I renounced Heraclitus, Xenophanes and Empedocles for a stunted, dry jargon? I had been affected by James Joyce, and had absorbed the dregs of Robert McAlmon, John Herrmann, and the flunkeys of Baal Peor, the Fact.

Although I had no intention of going to the salon of that squab Buddha, Gertrude Stein, I had read her gibberish, *Melanctha* and *The Making of Americans* with rapturous vacuity. Miserable foibles are no accidents; they are a part of one's spectral life absolutely essential to the writer. Whatever self-knowledge is, it is not a continuous experience. It was necessary for me to reflect the stinks of this age though I defied it.

I detest my second and third novels no less than my first. One is humiliated by nature, then by the world, and afterward by his books.

Ethel Moorhead was far clearer about her idolatry of the American scene than I. Her mistakes were those of a vigorous bigot, mine an enervated trance. To understand those embittered children of the New one must bear in mind that all were placeless. When persons are greedy for a past or a country they cannot forsake, innovation is supposed to be the remedy. Novelty was as much the insignia of the troop of satyrs on the Left Bank as the scrip and the staff of the Stoa.

They came to Paris not to be expatriates but to fornicate wantonly and to drink the entire river Scamander of alcohol on a cheap franc.

They were sincere charlatans. Can one doubt the honesty of Lincoln Gillespie, an earnest Montparnasse rhapsode who talked joyceisms. He spouted his *Ulysses* in the vein of a becrazed Grecian vestal: "Iambus, strophe, the Liffey, Prometheus' liver, gammon your gammer, a crone, a bone of Ignatius Loyola, O my fiction, my ineluctable diction, he stood upon his punctilio, O, O, don't guffaw, there's a collop of a saw, can't remember, collop, no matter, flitch the bitch, a stich of verse is a short solace for the hearse, don't grieve while you read the Venerable Bede, no matter, I scatter the leaves of James Joyce Homer's poltfoot idiot."

Bile flowed freely at the cafés. Malice, like Cacotopia, is everywhere, in Paris or New York. Scandals were rife; Kay Boyle had taken Walsh away from Ethel Moorhead. The perishable triumph was Kay Boyle's; she possessed the prize both coveted. Moorhead continued to print the work of her foe, who published a novel, *Year before Last*, and could not cease hating her in that fiction.

In 1927 the café litterateurs at the Rotonde and the Dome were in an uproar over the feud between Ethel Moorhead and Ezra Pound. After dedicating one issue of *This Quarter* to Pound, she withdrew the tribute in the next. He had refused to eulogize the Americanese-Chaucerian poems of the deceased Walsh. Pound had been wrong so frequently he could not have been less infatuated with himself had he committed a chivalrous error.

There had been strife between Pound and Moorhead earlier. For a short poem he had contributed to the magazine Pound demanded about two hundred dollars. Actually *This Quarter* was published in the Elysian fields where lucre is unknown, although Moorhead insisted on paying for the work of writers. Moorhead was a she-Savonarola, and a literary fanatic is guileless; she had not asked Pound beforehand how much he wished for his verse. Who can know the quicksilver of human character, or explain how Pound, who had anathematized the usuria of Jews, could be so shrewd?

Whatever may be said of the poetasters of the Left Bank, they were not the shopkeepers of *belles lettres*. There was Ludwig Lewisohn, a quack Bohemian with a chic automobile and a chauffeur, neither of which he used on the sabbath. This was also the heyday of the recherché mystagogue; another mystic, Rabindranath Tagore, rode about Berlin with two uniformed attendants in the front seat.

Lewisohn had caused a great stir, not so much for his novel, *The Case of Mr. Crump*, published by Edward Titus, as for the bizarre inscription on the flyleaf of the book: "Dedicated to the amatory powers of Thelma." The arts were a source of prodigious confusion to the United States customs officials. Waldo Frank had given his novel the title *The Bridegroom Cometh*, and the book was seized at the docks by our platoon of purists. Only after Frank had appealed to a prominent minister were the guardians of our national phalloi convinced that the title came out of the Gospels. Then after the dust of D. H. Lawrence, deposited in an urn burial, arrived, the same connoisseurs decided it was a work of art. It took awhile for them to appraise the remains, and ultimately to release them to Lawrence's widow, Frieda.

Transition, our surrealistic Hellas of Paris, took up the cause of Charles Chaplin, who was being tried on the charge of having impregnated a young woman. Very shortly an article defending the right of the American citizen to sow and seed where he willeth, particularly in any vulva that was available, was featured on the cover of *transition* under the title "Hands Off Love." The vigilant customs officials, believing in the laying on of hands, seized most of the copies that were taken off the ship and inspected on our U.S.A. Jonah's wharves.

Emanuel Carnevali, mortally ill with encephalitis, was in a sanatorium at Bazzano, Italy. I resolved to visit this picaro who could have been delineated by Quevedo. A sixpenny palmer, I journeyed to Bologna and there went to hilly, medieval Bazzano for I was an enthusiast of Carnevali's *The Villa Rubazziana*, and I desired to see the author. The blinds of his windows were drawn as he could not suffer the light. Who can? After the pain had abated a youth, very bent and with a nose and mouth of much feeling and a sloping, cogitative forehead, saluted me. I had brought him cartons of cigarettes and Italian pastries, and we had dinner, wine and laughter in the piazza.

My own pockets were wailing but I asked Ethel Moorhead to send him whatever she owed me for divers contributions to *This Quarter*. It was eighty dollars, a pauper's el dorado.

Rumors about Carnevali followed me when I returned to the States; he had died, had quit Italy, or was playing the organ in the Vatican. In 1950 I stepped inside a vast loft loaded with books bought from the Merchant Marine. One volume I purchased was the Florio translation of Montaigne; originally it had been in Andrew Carnegie's library. I noticed the name of the bookseller, Carnevali, and nearly quaked. Did he know Emanuel? Yes, he was his nephew. Where was he? His whereabouts were unknown to him. Was he alive? He did not know.

Ethel Moorhead sold *This Quarter* to Edward Titus, former husband of Helena Rubinstein, and fell into a darkling eclipse. *Transition* was soon discontinued by the editors. Harry Crosby, who had printed the first edition of Hart Crane's "The Bridge" in his Black Sun Press, committed suicide. Robert McAlmon had returned to the States.

At Santa Monica in 1953 I was told that McAlmon, entirely forgotten by his friends—and who else has the imperial privilege of ignoring us?—was an eremite on a sand dune, Desert Hot Springs. In Paris he had published in his Contact Editions a brood of obscurians. There were pages of James Joyce's *Work in Progress*, Carnevali's *The Hurried Man*, John Herrmann's *What Happens*, Gertrude Stein's *The Making of Americans*, Mary Butts's *Ashe of Rings*, Robert Coates's *Eater of Darkness*, the writings of Marsden Hartley, the painter, and of William Carlos Williams. Now the hailstone of oblivion had fallen on his head.

William Carlos Williams, in his autobiography, a sough of gossip, said that McAlmon "had slipped." Williams was a chameleon; he could be coarse and unpredictably kind. Embittered, McAlmon resented Williams and had no more to say of Joyce or Pound except neither had more than "efficient intelligence."

On his return to the U.S. McAlmon had sold trusses and surgical underwear for his brother in El Paso, Texas, and with his savings had purchased a diminutive stucco cottage on the burning sands. A consumptive, he drank and toiled over a sequel to his *Being Geniuses Together*, the dregs of addle chatter of the "Exiles." Although I did not care what Marianne Moore had to say to Ezra Pound, I implored James Laughlin to publish it but he declined, it is plain I was moved by compassion rather than judgment.

McAlmon's obscurity hurt me. In his prime his *The Distinguished Air* was esoterica; the principal figures in the narrative are James Joyce and Marsden Hartley. Presently the book is sold as pornography under the title, *There Was a Rustle of Silk Stockings*, in one of the most obscene streets in the world, Times Square. Written in a clean brutal style it is a book about pederasts and lesbians in Berlin after the First World War.

Full of bilge and wild disappointment, and ruttish to the

end, McAlmon lamented his shrunken testicles. I suggested I might publish his book privately and asked if he would lend me the English edition of *Being Geniuses Together* and his unpublished manuscripts. He was uneasy. What could I pilfer from the fermented lees of his brain?

Long after McAlmon's death *Being Geniuses Together* was imprinted in New York under the surveillance of Kay Boyle. The junk dealers in recondite Americana were enthusiastic. Sir Thomas More held: "I wyll be bounden to eate it though the booke be bounded in bordes."

Kay Boyle cannot relinquish her past. She was the first lady of verse in *This Quarter*, the companion of Joyce, McAlmon, Ernest Walsh, Ethel Moorhead, Carnevali, Hart Crane, Harry and Caresse Crosby and William Carlos Williams. All that is irrevocably gone. Every woman grieves for the aspen vernal leaf she was. A man, moldering, is also rueful, but more likely to dismiss that hagridden trance, his youth. One French writer said, "Had I to live my life over again I would shoot myself." As an author, Kay Boyle can no longer afford to ache for what cannot be lest her reminiscences be a dead pillar of salt. These are the tears we spend at the cost of our understanding. The affliction of the "exiles," common to the American, is perennial boyism.

Take as another instance Ezra Pound's primer bombast, his apotheosis of George Antheil's symphonic howl. In 1927 Antheil's *Ballet Mécanique* was performed, with twelve pianos, in Carnegie Hall. Naturally one of his advocates was William Carlos Williams, a fellow student of Pound's at the University of Pennsylvania.

The noise at Carnegie Hall was not so unusual then as it might appear. During that period a lavatory bowl was presented as abstract art at the Armory Show. Years ago an abstractionist showed me one of his canvases. I looked at a telegraph pole, infinite flat tableland of sallow weeds, and a mouse trap. A while later a toilet was flushed off stage in a Broadway play, which was deemed *non plus ultra* realism. Ordure and modern art are now kindred.

After the furor over Antheil's machine-shop music was forgotten, an unknown youth wrote a column for a Boston paper: "Advice to the Lovelorn." He was the son of a Polish cobbler in New Jersey and his name was George Antheil. From New England Antheil went to Hollywood to mimic the sounds of the quadruped for pictures.

25

*Will you be an ass, despite your
  Aristotle?
Or a cuckold, contrary to your
  Ephemerides
Which shows you under what
  smiling planet you
Were first swaddled?*
                                    —Webster

There had been a great pother over a pothouse fiction, *The Sun Also Rises* by Ernest Hemingway. It is a small novel about the musty liaisons of left-bank mault-wormes. At the time of Langland's *Piers the Plowman*, a fraudulent miller was pilloried for giving customers a false assize of grain, also a condign punishment for one who cobbles up muckhill books. Shakespeare is nobler than his varlets; Hemingway is as vicious. A plain prose style is not the same as a mean one. A few jolly words joined together justly is Shakespeare. The following is from *The Merry Wives of Windsor:* "And given to fornications, and to taverns, and sack, and wine, and metheglins, starings, pribbles and prabbles."

In Roquebrune, Ethel Moorhead showed me notes of Ernest Walsh and I lingered over one in particular: "Don't trust Hemingway." I was to recall this many years later when I came across Hemingway's roynish reference to the man who had befriended him—Ford Madox Ford.

In the thirties I was asked to speak at the New School for Social Research in New York on behalf of the proposed federal project for writers and artists. On the same platform with me was a tall gorbellied man with silver hairs, the dove-gray eyes of the Shulamite (D. H. Lawrence's description of Ford Madox Ford), a triune chin and a dense asthmatic lisp. At first not favorably impressed with this fat old boy, I shortly began to alter my impressions of authors.

E. E. Cummings, in a tone of exasperation, told me he could not understand how Sherwood Anderson had so neglected his face. Nature is not in the cosmetics business, I thought as I regarded Cummings' lean-witted nose and the parsimonious surfaces of his visage. A face is the looking glass of the spectator; if the latter is mediocre he will only be satisfied with a dunce. Greenwich Village rumor had painted Theodore Dreiser as an ugly Thersites; I thought he was Apollo. A reflective head is always a glorious one. Alfred Stieglitz had photographed a younger Sherwood Anderson, the populist poet, with a spatial rural forehead, a moiety of it covered with a warm shock of hair. Read the books of authors and then you will be the dragoman of their faces.

Suddenly as he was addressing the audience Ford Madox Ford turned toward me and complimented my books. This venerable gentleman of letters became my patron saint. One day William Carlos Williams and I were with him in his sparse apartment opposite the old Brevoort Hotel, and Ford suggested: "Why don't we start a group to get Bill's books published? What about calling it the Friends of William Carlos Williams?" I fervently agreed; I had peddled Wil-

liams' manuscripts and thought I had arranged matters with
Charles A. Pearce to publish them, but I don't know what
occurred.

Ford's genius, and almost his insanity, was his kindness.
He was never ruffled by my iconoclasms; both he and Dreiser,
gourmets of the intellect, relished them. Whenever he was
preparing for one of his Thursday afternoon teas he made
sure I was to be there; he was not interested in having an
assortment of corpses making effete chatter.

The Friends of William Carlos Williams met once a
month in the Downtown Art Gallery. I was asked to read
some passages from my novels and a segment of *Can These
Bones Live*. I was seated next to Williams and I began
searching crazily for something in my books to read, perhaps a page or less if need be, for I was extremely nervous and did not want to bore my auditors or myself. I
could not find anything I did not abhor. Williams, who could
be enchanting or flinty, glared at me and hissed fiercely:
"For Christ's sake, are you going to read all three novels?"

Ford's frugal apartment consisted of two rooms holding
some used and stricken furniture and a pile of marvelous
debts, his own books. Ford had a generous kneeling heart.
He was also famous for his falsehoods. Both Sherwood Anderson and William Carlos Williams said he was a gargantuan liar. True, Ford had such a tender nature that he gave
away what he never possessed; he invited poor authors to be
guests at his mansion in the south, which did not exist. As
the tongue wags one way or the other, a man is entitled to
harmless lies. Quite confidentially Ford told me he never had
to look up a single quotation that was in his tome, *The
March of Literature*. With what bawdy glee he mentioned
that the swift copulates on the wing. But he did not say that
this observation came from White's *Selborne*.

He never tired of repeating his admiration for Ernest

Hemingway, Elizabeth Madox Ford, Ezra Pound, Allen Tate, E. E. Cummings, Williams and myself. He persuaded Unwin to publish Williams' *White Mule* in England, and wrote the introduction to *Farewell to Arms* when Hemingway deeply needed his encomium. He also printed D. H. Lawrence's earliest verse in the *Transatlantic Review* which he edited in a London cock-loft, and later was his advocate although he did not like Lawrence.

His sole faith was in the aristocracy of the intellect. One had to have two prerequisites to be of this noble lineage: be an experimentalist in prose style and as poor as he. Ford was a renowned elder of international letters, and his last few books were remaindered.

Those he aided never even read his rare memoirs—*Reminiscences of Joseph Conrad, Portraits from Life, Return to Yesterday*, which has exceptional insights into the character of Oscar Wilde.

Ford was the most splendid busybody of our era. He was a speculative dealer in American geniuses. He was an occult spendthrift like Gérard de Nerval, who returned to Paris penniless but with four thousand francs' worth of marble chimney pieces. Engaged in the most unprofitable business imaginable, the business of friendship, he always ended as a bankrupt. I was to inherit this idyllic malaise, and naïvely wondered why writers I helped became my enemies. The difficulty is that apprentice authors grow older, and shrewd.

Ford would meet me on Eighth Street and reproach me for not having brought him my novels. A raw youth, what could I know about an older man seasoned with centuries of imponderable liabilities?

After he had gone through my manuscript of *Can These Bones Live*, he adopted me. Could he be my literary agent? What a glorious query. We were seated at a table in the sidewalk café of the Brevoort. Then he hurled this caveat at me: "You keep away from all publishers. Let me handle everything. You've not got a pinch of prudence. Soon as I win a friendly publisher for you you're certain to deride him, tell him how corrupt he is."

Concerned with myself, the principal occupation of obtuse flesh, I did not realize that Ford was suffering from a grave heart ailment. Saying he would be proud to write a foreword to *Can These Bones Live*, he took the manuscript to Deauville. I was summering at Westport in Connecticut when I saw in the *Herald Tribune* that he had died in France. I wept; yea, tears are easy, good acts are hard. I had lost my only defender, and after he was gone I was to be forgotten for many years.

One afternoon Ford and I were in the throes of a crapulous harangue. I denied that America was a household of geniuses. Ford suggested that Jews were a negative people. My ire rose: "Thucydides allows that the Greeks were born to trouble others. What of that Athenian gadfly, Socrates, the gloom of Euripides, the pessimism of Schopenhauer? And was Nietzsche, the icon-breaker, a Semite? Don't expect me to be the whimsical dear who can't find his way to his own door at night." I did not know that his wife, Biala, was Jewish.

Ford was determined to pester me, but good-naturedly. "What about Hemingway?" he said. "What do you think of him?"

I gave him a short reply: "I refuse to think of him."

Ford had no intimation that he was espousing the cause of a furtive adversary. Hemingway, a disciple of Sherwood Anderson, had parodied him in *Torrents of Spring*. He was to be Ford's meacock epitapher. Uneasiness is foreknowledge; I have the long, oracular nose of Tiresias and can predict who stinks. A brace of years before Hemingway's own end he was to assure his readers that Ford gave off a fetid scent. It is boorish to remark that I had sat next to Ford and not noticed this at all. Everyone smells at one time or another; so does the sweaty sea, and that briny fellow the seal, who has the broad thoughtful brow of Ford Madox Ford.

Ultimately one cannot blame anybody for what he is. A man with a spiteful character is unlucky, and so are his friends. An ancient scholiast informs us: "Plato never once asked Destiny why she created Thersites contemptible and Patroclus noble."

26

I also strive to suck the honey which once comforted me, but it palls on my palate.

—Tolstoy

Those who hackneyed English offered in its room nothing except *Opulentia Sordida*. Drained by disappointments, bilge, the café proser had "set up a hot liquor shop in his breast," as Plautus said.

Although my wits had begun to waste away I had enough natural hauteur to remain apart from the flock. Nearly always wrong, I was for once right. I accepted solitude, for I felt my spectral life was the essential one. Even as a novice I desired to personate the lonely mythic figures in literature, since man can only know himself as a fable.

Most of the day I walked through Montparnasse in a hilly slumber, and the marge of my watery sleep was covered with the toxic weeds of tedium. Momentarily I roused myself, and standing on the Boulevard Raspail with its charred bony plane trees I whispered: "O life, you are all my ills."

What had the ruffian café logodaedalus taught me? They had one dictum from Mallarmé, who had exorcised the word *comme*, like, and another from Marinetti, the futurist prose

machinist, who had stated that the adjective was the impedi-
ment of the velocity of the sentence. Speed, the father of
Fascism, was the fetish of Marinetti, Mussolini's Minister
of Education. He was the old raving child of Henry Ford,
who abominated the intellect and whose automobile destroyed
any thinker thoughtless enough to cross an avenue lost in
thought. Gone was the peripatetic of Hellas who conceived
as he walked. The flag carrier of vulgarity was *il condottiero
della letteratura*, the streetcar conductor of literature.

The children of the arts of billingsgate were orphans.
They had torn up their filial roots and had shed the blood
of a father or mother by pretending they did not exist. Authors of kinless verses and stories, they were intellectual par-
ricides. Dante says: *"Bestemiavano Iddio e lor parenti,
l'umana specie . . . e i'l seme di lor semenza"*—They blas-
phemed God and their parents; the human kind . . . and the
origin of their seed.

More, they disowned most of ancient literature; they
trucked Horace, Martial, Virgil, Lucretius, Lucian, Lucan,
Juvenal, George Chapman, Shakespeare, Ben Jonson, Sir
Thomas Browne, Robert Burton, Robert Herrick for Sté-
phane Mallarmé, Guillaume Apollinaire, Laforgue, Louis
Aragon, André Breton, James Joyce, Ezra Pound, T. S. Eliot
and Gertrude Stein. The noble manes of Spenser and Milton
merited their profane wind.

The pains of my imagination sucked up shrunken sepul-
chres, smoky ponds, and the brackish depths of Lake Titicaca, water of our indigenous remembrance.

Since childhood I had been overwhelmed with the swelt-
ered dumb rage of ennui. Was I an inlet, a headland, gravel
or a gully, suffering ground and water, and what relief was
there? I muttered: "The tombs that sleep within me are my
poems."

I was in Baudelaire's Paris, his "orgy of silence." My

force had perished, and the will is the angelic thunder and lightning of the mind. I had rejected the grass, the bliss of flowers, and the forgiving orchards. Woe was me; sky, earth, and rivers were God's ruse. At twenty-eight I felt aged as the pylons of ancient Heliopolis. The Tolstoyan mice were gnawing at the branch of my being.

Late afternoons I sat at the cafés du Dome or the Rotonde, gazing with a groveling appetite at the gibbet faces I detested. How similar were la Bruyère's own experiences: "We meet at Paris . . . without appointment, as if it were some publick Assignation; punctual every evening at the Cours and Tuileries, to observe Faces there, and dislike one another. We can't forbear even the Company of those we hate and deride."

One has to recover or live dead. I spoke to my specter: "Tell me, O Lord, what is my physic?" And I was answered: "Words, O fallen one, words." For a moment I saw the Seraphim, with the Logoi beneath their wings.

My convalescence lasted no more than seconds. A black snow of Tartarus began to fall thick upon my tombs, and again I stalked the ancient cobbles of Paris, where François Villon had left his footprints.

Then I mused upon a broken amour. My paramour was the near kin of a Cleveland industrialist, a professor of greed, who could not fill his paunch with enough pelf. He was inhibited as King Ahab unless he could devour one more Vineyard of Naboth; like Achilles, he was a people-eater. That a viper lurked in the azury eyes of Aphrodite I could not guess. Casanova reveals: "I was the dupe of every woman I ever knew." She had the double face of Janus; one cheek was tender, the other a serpent.

I was blameworthy, too. My profligacy was unrelieved agony. Stricken with the pleurisy of pleasure I could not abandon it, though I cried for an ounce of gutwort that I might remedy my lecherous pangs. Oh, the body is a load of grief from which we expect joy.

I adored her skirts but was insanely hindered, with no prospects but my dunghill fiction, *Bottom Dogs*. So I sought oblivion in that mock Orphic cave where I sank my force until none was left for my Angelic Logos. Wholly defeated, I was always to be shaken by the slightest mischance, and bleed without cause. How often, because I am peevish, and a damp has fallen upon me and I know not why, have I seen drops of Abel's gore on my shirt, jacket, shoes or a button.

I was determined never to be struck again by those crazy siroccos of passion, and all I accomplished was the difficulty to utter the word, love. I then realized I was forced to live in a humid latitude, with no faculty to handle lukewarm people.

I am ashamed of this, for I have all the rot of original sin in my skin. This revulsion is Hebraic and Christian, and is clearly expressed by the Goncourt brothers: "One week of love disgusts us for a month. We emerge . . . with dejected souls and sickened hearts, dead to desire, and possessed of a vague, shapeless, endless gloom."

How refractory is libidinous blood, since I must declare I could not bear to lose her. "If I succumbed to her dear looks and lovely deceits, of such sweet treachery that they pierce my heart," wrote Villon, "they have now left me well in the lurch, forlorn in my greatest need."

We were in Brussels, where I was completing my novel. She was making ready, in hugger-mugger, to leave me. We were staying at a modest hotel and one day the chamber-maid entered to rearrange the crumpled wanton sheets. My nostrils were feral and I heard a titter that cut me to pieces. It came from my bed companion. A wild ass I snuffed up every odor of the maidservant. No ancient Israelite yearned for the leeks, the melons and the cucumbers of Egypt as I ached for her mouth, her arms and loins.

The prey of hapless venery, I was also the victim of my companion's suspicions. She thought I coveted the lucre she was to inherit. But I've never gone to bed with money; what a dreary piece of lead is a coin, no substitute for the Moabitess. I was starved, not for mammon, not even for a lecherous hour or so; I was just starved.

She offered some makeshift excuse that she had to go to Paris. Crushed, I waited, utterly impatient. In this anguish I was alone in the bedroom the day she left when the Belgian servant came in. Before I realized what I was doing I threw my sullen broiling arms around her, crying: "*Je t'adore, je t'adore.*"

I am still bitten by this tawdry incident and to this day am unable to laugh about it. In wry moments I hear a street vendor bawling: "Stale loaves, a batch of tresses of one who has forsaken you. Buy secondhand maidenheads."

The liaison was finished. I tarried in Paris, and my blood mournfully tolled.

27

After dry bread, and no cakes,
he washes down his guts with
lashings of water.

—François Villon

I met Arabella York, the second wife of Richard Aldington.
She was one of the characters in D. H. Lawrence's *Aaron's
Rod*, a novel I zealously endeavored to enjoy, but with no
luck. Wholly unknown, I was more than delighted to meet
the spouse of a renowned author and one who had been the
friend of the Italian artist, Modigliani. It would be hypo-
critical to relate that although I condemned modern literature I was not very impressed when I met those who were
responsible for it. It would require at least a generation for
me to deem acts of mine issuing from an entire person.

Arabella York was separated from Aldington, who was
then an important figure in the whirlpool of Anglo-American
letters. They had been living on the island of Bandol and
were neighbors of Lawrence and his wife, Frieda. At that
time Aldington had as his mistress Brigit Patmore, of the
poetry family of Patmores. She, too, wrote, and as Arabella
divulged, brought her novel to Lawrence, who read it and
told her: "Brigit, you can't write, but you'd make a very

good whore." Brigit Patmore's son arrived with his wife, Netta, a young and pretty woman whose father was prominent in the Scottish Labor Party. Stocky and virile, and foaming with amative desires, Aldington ran off with her.

Arabella and I had a ten-franc lunch, worth about twenty cents, at a restaurant not far from Les Deux Magots, including palatable food and a carafe of *vin ordinaire*. She asked me what I did, and I stumbled into a few broken phrases: "Oh, I try to write; it's the universal disease today." She asked that I bring the manuscript to her at our next luncheon together.

Arabella was not only a fine looking woman but kind. Goodness and beauty are seldom companions. As it fell out she was extremely interested in my unpublished fiction. That I was exhilarated may surprise the reader, but no author who disbelieves in what he has done fails to feel rapturous when somebody cares for it. Authors are congenital liars; otherwise, how could they invent anything, including their lives, which otherwise would be tiresome.

Arabella suggested she send the manuscript to Lawrence. Would I mind? I was jubilant. Meantime I attempted to venerate another book of Lawrence's, *Women in Love*, and I must disclose that this famous author was making it exceedingly difficult for me to admire him.

About a week later Arabella had a letter from Lawrence. He had read half the manuscript and said if I kept up my "bony Spartanism" throughout the latter portion of the narrative I would have a book. My excitement was boundless. Surely there must be a volume of this author's I could adore. My perplexity was to become prodigious, and was to be a stumbling block for me as a writer. I don't want to intimate that flocks of people are peacocking my genius. Nevertheless, I was to find myself in severe straits because I could not laurel a man who had just told me what a remarkable *homme de lettres* I was.

I seldom lost the opportunity of reproaching an adherent by suggesting that he was foolish in exaggerating the importance of a short story or verse of mine. Actually I thought a display of such sincere modesty would bring my advocate and me closer together. On the contrary, he found this a real annoy, and took little time in becoming my enemy. That I destroyed his self-esteem by attacking his literary values had not occurred to me. So I was to be a loser in the humility game.

Later Joseph Freeman, author of *An American Testament*, had perused with immense enthusiasm my book of essays on our literature, *Can These Bones Live*. At that time I knew Sherwood Anderson, for whose works I had great affection, and adopting his midwestern Ohio drawl I said to Freeman: "Aw, it's not that good," and mentioned Charles Olson's *Call Me Ishmael*, a progeny of my book, whereupon Freeman read *Ishmael* and forsook me.

It should be added that I took a few chances in the maturity gamble also, and had no less ill hap in this than in my fugitive mood as the very modest man. I even failed when I posed as an arrogant person. Having so many mixed conceits about human behavior, I don't know how I came to any stout conclusions. I only wish I could let the entire nonsense drop, and be kind when I can, puerile if I must, an adult by chance, and generally a dunce. This also may sound as if I were in an agony of self-abasement. Maybe, I don't know, and I am not going to investigate this deportment of mine just now.

Soon a lengthy epistle came from D. H. Lawrence to me. I took the channel boat and the train and arrived in London with twelve dollars and Lawrence's letter in my pocket. Arabella York was in London with her mother, and she introduced me to F. S. Flint, poet and polymath, who had translated the love poems of Émile Verhaeren, the Belgian poet, and was a reader for G. P. Putnam's in London.

Frank Flint had a strong rectangular physiognomy, and a squat amber-colored nose. He was one of the founders of the imagist movement in verse; Ezra Pound had supplied the word, *image*, and he had added *ist*. We had a good deal in common. He was the son of a barber and was a working-class author; there was ease between us from the start. He read and liked my manuscript very much, but expressed sorrow that I had not allowed the protagonist, Lorry Gilchrist, any erotical relief. For me, America was a ramshackle hovel for the blighted poor; it was my intent to show that a young man without a roof, food or coal would not find feminine flesh to heat him either. The average woman flees a discouraged man, and trouble is not generally virile, or so she presumes.

Meantime I lay in diggings somewhere in Chelsea. I had the upstairs room in one of those London dwellings that has the grime and desperation of a collier's life. As a matter of fact, I was the tenant of a mailcarrier and his wife.

Soon I could no longer afford the one meal a day I indulged in about three o'clock of the afternoon, when I dined in a pub on roast beef, potatoes, Yorkshire pudding, and a tall glass of beer that I imagined was the beverage which flowed out of the Temple Jupiter Ammon.

My mother could send me only twenty-five dollars a month, and shortly I had to relinquish my joy, a hot meal and beer. I became a customer of meat wagons and filled myself with tuppenny pies.

I was haggard as the winds. There were the long nights in my frozen, peeled room. I bought a tenpenny bag of coal when I could spare the pence, and dropped each coal into the puny hearth, hoarding best I could every ember and tiny spark, and scribbled verses and half-bits of lines, while the fire glowed like Minerva's lamp of wisdom.

I wrote how Poverty loved, clothed and fed me, but my

belly was a wrinkled washboard. In another vein I chanted: "Thou made me a harper of words, lutist of phrases," and I was so proud of the vesture of my sentence, and so vain of the cottons and linens and all the cloths of my language that I hung upon my words like Absalom suspended from the branch of a tree by the locks he doted on.

When next I saw Flint he took a sharp glance at my vanishing face and dagger chin and my hair looking as needy as want. He went to see Constant Huntington, president of G. P. Putnam's in London, who had been a friend of Henry James, and demanded that he give me a contract for the book.

A day later Huntington arrived at my diggings. He said he would publish the book, but considered my fiction somewhat dirty, and I asked him if he thought poverty well laundered. He anticipated some difficulty—the censors might ban the book in England—and advanced an idea that made me extremely uncomfortable. Why did I not write to D. H. Lawrence and ask him to do an introduction? Despite my protest he insisted.

Lawrence had been very kind, and sent me exhortatory epistles bullying me: Did I have no more brains than to eat one meal a day? What ailed me? Nobody had the right to be a drumbling ass in this world. Except Lawrence; his own books in America brought him oblivion and ridiculous royalties. I sent him a crippled letter and he responded graciously; he would write a preface for my book.

The end of this feverish perplexity was not yet in sight. Years after the publication of *Bottom Dogs* I heard that a certain poet had spread the evil report that when Lawrence was dying I had stood over his wretched frame and commanded him to write the introduction. I had never set eyes upon Lawrence until I returned to Paris months afterward.

When my second novel, *From Flushing to Calvary*, was

published another well-wisher of mine said I had hired a ghost writer to make the book. What a wry moment this mendacious gossip gave me. Considering the ferine defects in that book, I thought had I done this at least I would have employed a more intelligent author to perform the task. *From Flushing to Calvary* was a heap of pleonasms, misconceived metaphors, outrageous similes, and "new" conceits. Most volumes of our "costermonger age" are joyless industrial products.

Lawrence and I continued to correspond. I still had no title for the novel and when I mentioned this bafflement to him he wrote: "What about, 'Bark, You Dogs.'" Well, I didn't relish that; finally Lawrence or Huntington, or was it I, decided to name it *Bottom Dogs*.

I was to alter my mind a great deal about Lawrence's works, but it never occurred to me that there was a strain of spite in him, or that he could be so oblivious of his own miseries. Above a year ago I came upon a thick volume containing multifarious scraps about him, and also his own remarks. I fell down when I came upon this: "Dahlberg asked me to write an introduction to *Bottom Dogs*. Nothing like asking." He had omitted to mention his own mishaps; how often he had importuned Middleton Murry, Richard Aldington or Aldous Huxley to come to his rescue. His books were either corpses or lying behind other books in shops, entirely ignored or assailed by reviewers. Horace is correct; writers are a cantankerous lot, go very low when mendicants, and haughty if they prevail with the disgusting literary horde. Neither Lawrence nor I was ever to be anything except drudges of the Muse. With rare exceptions this has been the portion of authors.

Actually, Lawrence's preface to *Bottom Dogs* was a long, hectic and cerebrated invective and I was the cony of the attack. Why did Lawrence, who wished to help an unknown and poverty-stricken author, make him the victim of his own theoretical malice? In the Goncourt journals it is stated: "The greatest and most malignant conversational wit that Saint-Beuve possesses consists of tearing a man to pieces in the guise of defending him. A poisoner of eulogies."

Lawrence considered the waifs in that Jewish Lazar-house, the orphan home in Cleveland, almost unborn. Those gray puking gnomes, their necks covered with impostumes and their heads pestered with ringworm, were all belly and no feeling, so hungry were they for a plate of porridge they could eat, or for that other sop they were never given, affection. What did Lawrence, the son of a poor drunken Derbyshire collier, expect?

It is not irrelevant to assert how much in need he was. I had to ask Huntington to pay him for the introduction, and also to request that Simon and Schuster, in the U.S., do the same, and the famous Lawrence received a hundred dollars for his work. When I was in New York he wrote to ask if I would not go to the Holiday bookshop (no longer extant) and ask for money. Ted Holiday, a fervid admirer, had been selling the pirated edition of *Lady Chatterley's Lover* and the author had not received a penny. God save us from our admirers! However, following my very civil importunity, Mr. Holiday sent Lawrence a check for three hundred and fifty dollars.

With every resolve to assist me, Lawrence at all costs had to have his apocalyptic thesis, his dark intuition. In the introduction he claims that the American cannot endure the sight of ordure, and that when he sees it he is a bedlamite. Lawrence gives one the impression that when a sensible Englishman inadvertently steps into a puddle of human tripe, the plucky fellow just takes the pocky muck in his stride.

Erasmus, the great humanist, alleged that each man thinks his own excrement smells good, but he never stipulated that one must put up with somebody else's.

Making what use he could of *Bottom Dogs* he was still not quite ready to be as darkly intuitive as he was to be in *Pornography and Obscenity*. In this renowned chapbook, he decided that Jonathan Swift was insane, because he did not have the same aplomb while defecating as did D. H. Lawrence, who had had a malevolent experience with one of Swift's poems, in which the Dean grieves because Celia shits. We all know Lawrence's wry reply: What a pity she didn't. He was preparing to be the vehement Pauline defender of four-letter words and the jocular close-stool.

Each one couples and dungs best he can, and that is a very privy affair. Harrington spent a whole volume on human droppings, much to the disgust of his sixteenth-century critics. This scatophagous Elizabethan suggests that the word jakes derives from the hulking Greek dolt, Ajax. Later, Baudelaire was to remark: "It is indeed a proof of the degradation of men of this century that several have been capable of falling in love with this latrine."

The Essene had a shovel suspended from his girdle when he used to carry his bowels beyond the confines of the village. This is a clean moral custom which is likely to raise the qualms of many a modern man. Shakespeare can manage this nimbly: "Falstaffe, you carried your guts away," but Lawrence couldn't. Once you start thinking about what you're doing, you won't do it naturally.

Each man is entitled to do with his body what he must; the body is a nuisance anyway, so each one to his own jakes. That Lawrence snared me cannot be questioned; he got me into a great deal of attitudinarian trouble.

Then there is the thesis about the pudendum. As I look back upon this remarkable fragile man I realize that *Lady*

EDWARD DAHLBERG

Chatterley's Lover is a flaccid prepuce. There is no real carnal mischief in Lawrence's novel. Nonetheless he set up a phallic shop, though he had none of the ritualistic erudition for this sort of erotica. With puerile glee Lawrence informs us that Renoir painted with his penis. Rozanov, disciple of Dostoevsky, said he held his private parts in one hand while he wrote with the other, a somewhat occult performance, it would seem. But Rozanov was merely imitating the rites of the priests at Coptus where the statue of Horus could be observed holding fast in one hand the privates of Typhon. Plutarch declares that Osiris' statue was in the shape of a man with his secret member erect.

Authors will always be concerned with the worm of concupiscence. "There is no passion," Laurence Sterne says, "so serious as lust." Sterne was a far greater prose stylist than Lawrence and hence more serious. Unlike the English cleric, who obviously had no difficulty in being sensual, Lawrence did not have the appetite for it. The Derbyshire boy, bred in provincial Christian tenets, wanted to be a heathen. He was a sort of St. Jerome of the Pudendum, "whipt by the Divell in a Lenten dream for reading Cicero," as John Milton said.

That Lawrence is the father of the riggish feculent fry, the twentieth-century venal pornographer, cannot be argued. All such fiction from the odious de Sade on is a disgusting fly-gall upon our palate. No prude, I joy in the hymeneal sheets stained with olives, figs, watercresses, endives and the strength of Priapus. But I am not minded to ease the parched Dog Star of my flesh by scrawling a whorehouse book. Who with a dram of sensual sanity wants to stew over a novel, or open its pages as if one were parting the legs of a strumpet of Tyre? He who expects the raptures of Aspasia out of four-letter words is insane.

I confess that *Can These Bones Live* could not have been conceived without a literary parent, Lawrence's *Studies in*

Classic American Literature. What has always astonished me is the fear that the American author has of being influenced. A writer who comes only under the spell of himself is a madman; he is also too feeble to include Propertius, Apuleius, Quevedo, Le Sage, and Rabelais. Instead his work shows the mark of Cain, or the anite scribblings of James, Hemingway and Faulkner. As for my own work, it is seamed together with a thousand ghosts of the past. All of Russian literature is said to have come out of Gogol's *Overcoat* and who can ever omit or diminish Dostoevsky's cry: "Go down in the dust before Corneille." The tragedy of the writer is that he might only be himself.

28

The flesh is bruckle, the Feynd
is she.

—Dunbar

Constant Huntington took me, and my few wearied clothes stung by winter nights, and my shoal of books, to a Quaker House on Sydenham Hill in the outskirts of London.

The meals were sparse, but clean, and there was a common table for about fifteen persons. The hostess was a large woman with sectarian curdled breasts. Had she any odor at all it was of the pew. The abundance of the nipples and the cry of the mouth for a man's embrace are not to be found in a feminist, be she a Quaker, a Socialist, spiritualist, vegetarian, Shaker or Communist.

Edith Sitwell invited me to tea. She was a spidery creature with acerb fingernails the color of potassium permanganate. She was taken with my "barbaric American energy," and so enthralled with my remarks about Emanuel Carnevali's *The Hurried Man* that she beseeched me to bring a copy of his book the next day, which I did.

Pleased that I had found an enthusiastic reader for Carnevali I was startled to get a note from the Dame demanding that I collect the book without delay. Evidently she had not touched the book. I had mentioned that Carnevali suffered from encephalitis. Had she feared she would be infected with sleeping sickness?

Frank Flint asked if I would like to lunch with T. S. Eliot, T. M. Ragg, an enchanting Irishman, Frank Morley, and Herbert Read, whose poems, *Mutations of Phoenix*, had just been published. Flint informed me that Eliot did not care for Jews. Genteel anti-Semitism had been a strain in English literature since Christopher Marlowe's *The Jew of Malta*, and this affectation was taken up by Wyndham Lewis (although I believe he recanted) and Ezra Pound.

To my amazement the literary figures who gathered weekly at the Chelsea pub showed me unusual respect. The Lawrence letter had obviously affected them, yet I continued to be a mute. I had nothing to say and was clever enough not to say it. As was my wont, I desired to admire Eliot. I did not care for that dull tractate on Lancelot Andrewes, but I did wish to please though I sought no advantage of him.

Don't listen to anybody who seriously alludes to scientific literary criticism, for it is an idle blab. The best advice to be given the reader is to abide by this sentence in one of Chekhov's letters: "I divide literary works into two classes: those I like and those I do not like." Go through Aristotle's *Poetics*, Horace, Dryden's essays, La Bruyère's *The Characters* and Coleridge's *Biographia Literaria*. Imbibe what is useful to you, and you will forget the rest anyway.

At one of the luncheons Eliot engaged Frank Flint in a discourse on Matthew Arnold and Walt Whitman. To pundits this may appear absurd, but writing is writing whether it be a poem, novel or a dissertation. Saint-Beuve did not hesitate to refer to Rabelais and Montaigne as poets. Eliot turned to me abruptly and asked, "Which one do you think is more important, Matthew Arnold or Walt Whitman?" I hadn't the slightest idea, but I had caught his drift, and he got no sluggish reply. "Without ambiguity, I would elect Matthew Arnold." To this day I am not positive, and surely do not know how good or ill is Whitman.

Eliot was delighted. An avid reader, I didn't know much about Matthew Arnold except his poem on Empedocles, a chapter dealing with Heinrich Heine and the three nineteenth-century Romantic poets of England. But there is no method in reading; getting educated is going from one master to another. A sophister will demand that his pupil ransack a given period, but I prefer to go here and there, ambling from the *Georgics* of Virgil to the *Spectator Papers*, and then perhaps picking up the *Journal to Stella*. In this regard I have the assistance of Gibbon. To cite d'Israeli: "Thus in the midst of Homer he read Longinus; a chapter of Longinus led to an epistle of Pliny." Petrarch writes of learning in a similar vein: "The *Academics* of Cicero made Marcus Varro dear to me; it was in the *Office* that I first heard the name of Ennius; through the treatise on *Old Age* I became acquainted with Cato's *Origins*."

To return for a moment to T. S. Eliot, I know of no better description of him than the following I've culled from the *Memoirs* of Saint-Simon: "He was a humble down-looking man, whose physiognomy promised nothing."

Meanwhile I tarried at Sydenham Hill. The galleys came from Putnam and I read them enraptured with the cold cuts of my jargon garnished with a few greens and a mingle-mangle of sickly tropes. Then the dust of ennui descended upon me. I had nothing to do, and that was a purgatory. The wormwood impotence between books is unbearable.

The making of a book is an oath taken by the river Styx. I have never begun a novel or a task of any kind that did not so persecute me that by the time I was past the middle of it I hated every word, considered writing utterly point-less, yet went on because I was afraid that if I didn't my life would be worse than it was. There is henbane in every volume. A writer is no better than the mare that pastures on the plains by the river Astaces and suckles her young with black milk.

Late afternoons I walked in the garden in the rear of the refectory. There was a fleeting encounter between me and an eighteen-year-old Quaker girl. Today she is a wraith without a name. When I first set eyes upon her I bolted down all her beauty with one glance. What enrages the pre-puce seldom touches the heart, and certainly not a virgin one. A night before I left for the continent I went to her bed, but made no attempt to remove her chaste cestus. Accord-ing to Hors Apollo, the Egyptian God Ptah holds the *"penis manu compressa,"* denoting restraint and continence in a man.

I relinquished a rare delight, but after a while pleasure cloys the bruckle flesh. How soon the potable breast is a dried-up kitchen oracle. I was never to find a woman who deeply gratified me. What a banal phrase is the "grand passion."

Once I believed a waitress with sturdy legs, a touch of aristocracy about the mouth and the nostrils would be all that I needed. When I courted a maid and she crossed her legs I was in a frenzy, and should she then disclose a fringe of her petticoat I blessed Zeus, God and Lucifer, and was sure I had found the one woman. After possessing her I wondered why she sat in such a salacious manner; could she not modestly close her knees? I dislike too much rouge and fucus, and I don't care for a naked face. Sexual tastes are erratic, not what the bourgeois Tartuffe pretends.

Baudelaire admits: "I used to confuse the smell of women with the smell of furs." Childhood experiences can never be

224

replaced by erotical conventions, if for no other reason than that one would rather part with a friend than a habit. I despise the slut and am more appeased by a woman dressed than by one without a shift. I never ached for a woman with songless hands, long morbid feet, ignorant teeth, sullen flat hair, splenetic ankles, or a vascular neck.

Tolstoy says no man should marry until he is positively good for nothing. I had not yet reached that point, but no doubt I would develop.

The London episode was finished. Flint had advised me to return to the United States. I considered going to Oxford, but Eliot said this would be too sterile for a novelist. Without any clear motive I returned to Paris, still dogged by Pecunia, "the shake-rag goddess."

At the Shakespeare shop on the Place de l'Odeon, in whose attic James Joyce had written *Ulysses* on brown wrapping paper, I was looking over the heap of squitter-books when my eyes found a reedy figure of a man speaking to Sylvia Beach, the proprietor of the store. From photographs I had seen I knew it was D. H. Lawrence and I introduced myself to him.

Again I must say I was enormously impressed with rumors of this man. I had heard that he sat on the ground, cross-legged, when he commenced to write a novel, and never stopped until he blundered into one of his intuitions (about page 200, with luck). I had heard, too, that he was ill-tempered, and in an argument with Harry Crosby had thrown a hot poker on the floor. But then I've always suspected the congenial man, wondering why he was so relentlessly pleasant. Don't people have anything better to do with their faces than to paint them with smiles and intolerable whimsical charm?

Women were said to be Lawrence's flock of disciples.

This was puzzling since his short stories, "The Prussian Soldier" and "The Woman Who Rode Away," confute his interest in women. In the latter tale she is unclothed, not for coition but to be flayed by Indians. I tried *The Plumed Serpent*, but with ill success; those endless hymns to the Mexican god, Quetzalcoatl, were a farrago of nonsense. People said Lawrence was prolific, but he was simply verbose. Then there is that humbug of size that obtains now as it did then. Apparently nobody can be a genius in a novella; a book has to be long, high, broad, seemingly endless.

One should not forget that Lawrence went around the world twice before accepting the invitation of Mabel Dodge to settle at Taos, New Mexico. I don't blame him; I met Mabel Dodge.

I went to see the Derbyshire idolator of the prepuce. That he was a remarkable nature cannot be doubted. He was so frail I dreaded he shortly would be dust. He was staying at the Grand Versailles Hotel, a plushy name for a hostel on the Boulevard Montparnasse.

He was reclining on the bed, and I sat in a chair close to him. His thick plumes of hair resembled a cluster of red peppers; oddly enough, he represented to me one of the Aztec gods, whose teeth are composed of pumpkin seeds, and eyes of black beans. Soon after I arrived Frieda issued from the other room. She made some reference to their pecuniary circumstances, which prompted Lawrence to say: "Don't mention that devil, money, to me." It was evident that the Lawrences were poor. Little wonder he could not stop writing. He is probably making novels in his grave.

During our talk he dismissed Eliot and Joyce and was incensed with Proust. Then he asked my opinion of Proust's works. Was I always to be bitten by the sharp tooth of ignorance? I had not read one line of *Remembrance of Things*

Past, but I agreed with Lawrence. That I devoured nearly all of Marcel Proust's books later does not alter the situation. Suppose somebody asked me today how I regarded this author. I would be in the same condition I was when I lied to Lawrence only to please him. Our weak minds make liars of us all. John Donne relates that after he had read 525 pages of a book all he recalled was that he had turned 525 leaves.

Another day Lawrence discussed with me *Lady Chatterley's Lover*. This book was originally printed in Italy by Oriolo. More or less a clandestine publication, the first edition consisted of one thousand copies and the second of five hundred. Spurred by the prick of indigence Lawrence was considering a large trade issue to be published by Edward Titus. He solicited my advice. I had been in Titus's bookshop on the Rue Delambre, and thought him quite gross. It was my feeling that Lawrence would be harmed by Titus. He listened attentively to me—and shortly thereafter Titus brought out *Lady Chatterley's Lover*.

Hart Crane had read *Bottom Dogs* in manuscript and liked it—a little, much, or not, I can't say. He asked me to read his unpublished "The Bridge." I read it with purblind admiration. It is just as easy to be put off by Dr. Johnson's epigrams as to be enticed by them. To the point: I went through "The Bridge" with diligent obtuseness, and told Crane quite sincerely that I deeply cared for the poem. Only much later did I grasp his major intention. However, in matters of literary taste sincerity only counts when one is as awake as the poet, for the poem is the distillation of his inward strength which the reader or critic seldom possesses; usually he lacks it altogether. Bear in mind that we are not dealing with sidereal trash; seldom do I bother to read the contemporary rubbish I attack. Besides, should one impugn a book the critic himself cannot write? Most of the time we are impenitent readers and should adopt the practice of the Aztecs who pierced their tongues in the middle with a maguey thorn whenever they sinned. I deeply respected Hart Crane's lyrical blood, and my high estimate of "The Bridge" was merely a splendid guess.

Crane did what few Americans comprehend is their duty. He selected several masters—Donne, Blake, Melville, Whitman, Nietzsche, the water poet Michael Drayton—to guide him. Unless an author consults old, revered poets and essayists he is defeated at the beginning. But Crane could not cure his suffering; the aches of the imaginative faculty, when inert, are insupportable. None understand this except the poet himself. The reason is simple; it is a special sickness that is beyond the outsider, the critic. When Crane was not a volcano, shooting forth his fiery lava, he was convinced he was absolutely extinct. But the mountain, Popocatepetl, regarded as a Mexican god, has long sabbaths between eruptions. Miserable during his dead seasons, Crane drank the waters of Lethe; he also swallowed hundreds of bottles of gin, and rioted without stint. In his thirty-first year he leaped into the Caribbean Sea and vanished.

Did the poet die too young? It cannot be known just what is the ripe year for a man to cease to be Hart Crane.

29

*But Age, allas! that al wole
envenyme,
Hath me biraft my beautee and
my pith.*

—Chaucer

So much of me has departed. Long ago I left massy tufts of
my hair in boxcars, and in cheap, profligate hotel rooms in
the Mexican quarter of Los Angeles, and all for a pence of
a thought. How hard and usurious is the Muse, exacting the
cruelest payment for the mite she gives.

My youth is clean gone, and for a cock of prose thin and
dwarfed as the lichen in the Barren Grounds. I sigh for
vision, and know not what shirt I wore that day. I examine
my hands and wonder whose they are; my nose is a stranger
to my face. When I think I know I do not know. If I am
quiet, impatience were better; if choleric, it is a caggy
day. That's how it is with me.

I've got no theories to peddle, for I hawk parables, or
chew my moldy weather, and that's good, too. That's how
it is with me.

I swallow people's scoffs, and that's not a dirty meal

229

either; in the long run, I like what I've got to bolt down. That's how it is with me.

When I don't tremble, I am full of multitude. Would you be prophetic or sink into the dotage of the Many? Touch me, and you'll be soothsayers. You don't think so, I do. That's how it is with me.

O hungry ones, I am starved, and I drink the rains and the heavens. When I'm empty, and there are freezing steppes in my spirit, I disgorge my Muse, the Void. What a constellation is Nothing. Still what have I gotten out of it? But everything matters. That's how it is with me.

Wherever I am I wish to be elsewhere. I leave my unfriended steps in last year's snow, and give my confidence to a sharper in today's rain. That's how it is with me.

I try to mend my lot, though I am my portion. I endeavor to pick myself up when I fall, but it is better there. Truth has given me nothing, yet that nothing I require. That's how it is with me.

As I write this I'm seated at a kitchen table in Geneva, in a sallow bald room of an old manor house where Voltaire once lived and wrote. My bones shake, and my pulses scarce murmur, yet I hope, poor fool that I am, to get off a line that flames like tow. And after that, what? I wait for the morrow, another guillotine morning. That's how it is with me.

But it is better to gnaw my secondhand sour sighs, and eat old groans, and suck up the foul drizzle of hackneyed disappointments—better to be pinheaded François Villon, with his long-knived nose, and chew my days that are bread "black as a malkin"—than to nuzzle at the slops of other people's opinions. The real sacrilege is the low farce, everyday life. That's how it is with me.

Jesus was a nervous man and just as unsure of himself as I am, and though nothing can be proved I have all the evidence in my vest pocket. Who understands the divine man who begged the world to smite him on the other cheek? Long ago I found out that only he who requires love most of all is absolutely crestfallen when nobody even bothers to do him the slightest mischief.

The poor Holy Ghost appeared before the disciples, and although he had been absent for the shortest while, they didn't know him. They had eaten together day after day, gone on foot to Capernaum, walked about the sea of Galilee together and discussed various stiff-necked infidel towns, yet the twelve looked at him without a tithe of recognition. He had to tell them to handle him and *see*. Be plain, is there any other way of seeing except by touching? I am that sort of specter, and though profane a distant kin of his, for every friend I ever had has been a blundering stranger who did not know me. How many times they cogged me, or stabbed me with a simper; just a passing leer grieves my entrails. Still, if I were sharp as they it would be bad for me. That's how it is with me.

When someone strokes my shoulder or caresses my coat lapel, I'm lost. Once a rogue grinned at me, and though I don't care for a smile that is no more than cosmetics on the mouth, could I turn my back on him and step on his feelings? I admit it: Christ is my sort of poet. Once you decline to turn the other cheek you're ignominious. So while I bent my neck toward him he picked my purse. Suppose I had ignored him, I would have been spiteful, and malice is lust. Of course my wallet sorrowed for many weeks and even now it hasn't gotten over that wicked experience. But if I hadn't been deceived could I possess what belongs to me?

Then a former convict came to my apartment. I knew he was a confidence man, and he realized right away I could be taken. But didn't he know me? And is that evil? When he asked me for twenty-five dollars could I refuse him? He said he had a ring at the pawnbroker's which he would redeem and would return the money the next day. I knew he would not come back. That was his greatest unkindness, for we could have talked some more and exchanged the cruelties in our lives. I never saw him again. Yet why should he imagine I would not receive or embrace him? I always forgive my enemies, they're so close to me. That's how it is with me.

How hard it is to know what to do with one's self. The shoe knows it must be worn, otherwise it's been abandoned. A button understands that it hangs by a thread to a coat. A rock knows what to do in the fog or a mean mizzte. A headland is just as calm in foul weather as it is in a mild sun. The shingle at Tierra del Fuego doesn't show any disgust with carrion whale washed up on it. A pebble knows how to handle a pack of wolvish winds that beat it all day long. But I'm thrown down by a trifling slight. I offer affection to people who mean nothing to me, and am courteous to one who has done his best to hinder me; shrewd as he is he doesn't know that's my lot and he's served me. A passerby roughly jostles me, and though I beg his pardon for doing it his silence cuts me. That's how it is with me.

What bothers me more than anything else is a day of zero. When nothing happens I cry out for an event, an unlooked-for pain, a stitch in my side, or I moan for long-standing scums of water; I boil over everything. Aristotle says worms are born in snow. Would that I were a frosty maggot, but that would be bad for my nature. That's how it is with me.

Suppose Christ had not drunk his cup of affliction, or that the cruel Roman Titus had not slaughtered a million Jews in ancient Jerusalem, what could I now do with a so-called life that had not made everyone suffer? That's how it is with me.

III

The Thirties:
Penultimate Judgments

30

There mark what ills the
Scholar's life assail:
Toil, envy, want, the Patron,
and the Jail.
—Samuel Johnson

Now approaching my thirtieth year and in New York once
more, I mourned for my mother still barbering on Eighth
Street underneath the viaduct in Kansas City. Would I be
able to provide her with bread by champing crabbed dusty
words? I was only a sorry piece of a writer.

Had my mother been nature's simpleton? There was the
water-stained photograph of her when she had a tender
ovaline face and a long nose as pointed as feeling; her soft
walnut-colored hair was jagged and thin after typhoid fever,
and her skin since then brown and wrinkled as a used paper
bag.

The inclement doubt returned. Why had she prayed every
day solely to have bitter losses? Where was that great pensive bird, with hands just as a pentagram and myrrh in his
mouth, who was supposed to succor the poor? Unlike my
mother I was resolved not to fawn upon the All-Destroyer.

A man of my age, I am too embarrassed to chatter about God.

There was the carcass of my own miserable childhood. My body is still harrowed up whenever I hear the gibbering rats in the room to the rear of my mother's shop; I groan for mercy when I hear them.

I had returned to a country that was on the eve of an economic plague. The morrow would bring the seven lean years of Pharaoh's dream, when humble people would be without the loaves and the gudgeons, or a roof, or a scurvy job. Misery and fear would soon lay siege to the city.

One evening I found myself at a Bohemian radical party in Greenwich Village and for the first time set eyes on Mike Gold, the minion of the *Daily Worker* and the Communist Party. He had a cigar in his mouth and his arms around the bodices of two young women. Roughly made in body and mind, he had the handsome unskilled face of a navvy and a head of heavy sensual hair. Nature had not taken the trouble to refine his visage or to furnish him with intellectual subtlety.

Later in the evening Joseph Freeman arrived. The son of a rabbi, he was one of the elite revolutionaries; he had been to Moscow several times and knew Stalin and Litvinov and other luminaries in the Kremlin. He was a good-looking youth, quite swarthy and soundly built, but later had a flaccid oleaginous face. He had just married one of the prettiest women I ever encountered. I had met her before leaving for Paris; she was a novice painter who was making her living selling cubistic furniture and ceramics. She had the delicately featured countenance of the Virgin Mary, and a peasant body. Powerfully agitated by her, I had seen her perhaps twice at her apartment in the Village, but was too timorous to make overtures to her lest she give me a sharp repulse.

The marriage was of short duration. After their nuptials she went to Mexico City while her husband remained in New York. Why people get married in order to live apart is an egalitarian riddle for petit-bourgeois Bohemians. Hearing that his wife was studying under Diego Rivera, the Mexican muralist, Freeman wrote a lengthy acrimonious article in the *New Masses* alleging Rivera was a Trotskyite.

Despite the considerable attention I had received in the press, the revenue from *Bottom Dogs* was meager. In England there was a limited edition of this fiction and a tribute from Arnold Bennett that appeared in about sixty English papers.

The introduction by D. H. Lawrence was no venal help; his own books had only a middling sale in England and no better in America, and so it was one pauper trying to rescue another. Lawrence, a wry one, indeed, had taken some pains to counsel me not to make a financial holocaust of my life. I listened diligently to his words and managed to do worse than he had. Again I did my best only to succeed in being unfortunate.

Was I stupid? Doubtless, but patch up ignorance any way one can, and title it intelligence, I could not resolve the predicament. I was still in tatters.

It was 1930, a viperish year. Handshakes were nearly out of date, or were the leftovers of somebody else's skin. I didn't know whether it was Wednesday, the carcass of Tuesday; it didn't matter, it was a hungry yesterday. I had inherited my mother's genius for poverty, Panurge's purse always ailing of a flux.

I was invited to the MacDowell Colony for artists as the guest of the widow of the American composer Edward Mac-Dowell.

She was an erect, spare woman, her hair the color of granite, and with a face as sharp as her measure of people.

I thought her eyeglasses were waspish. Past her middle sixties she was given to a few stony words. Although I was born in Boston I never knew how to handle New Englanders, but that does not mean she had a similar lack of skill with me.

The MacDowell plantation for authors, composers, sculptors and painters covered several hundred wooded acres at Peterborough, New Hampshire. Each artist was provided with a lovely wooden cottage containing a fireplace, and he was expected to start work at eight o'clock in the morning. To make sure he was no idler at one o'clock a pair of sandwiches, salubrious and appetizing, was brought to his door.

Mrs. MacDowell was as austere a lawgiver as Lycurgus; she viewed the artist as a celibate, a kind of MacDowell Essene, and did not approve of members of her tribe wandering about and gaping at a birch, or strolling with one of the female practitioners at the colony. There were no overt laws that forbade meandering during eight hours of the sun, or squandering the time of a woman in the midst of her masterpiece, but if one did either of these things he knew he would have to muster up courage enough to stand before the reticent obsidian face of Mrs. MacDowell.

Restless, with a throbbing side, and a void pericranium, I did not know how to scrawl a second novel. I fretted and was devoured by the interminable day, spent tedious hours looking for a simile, or *le mot juste*, which was a gibbet. I had not learned to let the feelings take care of the words, but hoped that with luck the book would be all right. But I was to be maimed by innovations, a farrago of misbegotten brand-new words. We are given the language, the olden mulled words, on trust, and it is a heresy to ruin or deny them.

At no time in a literary man's life can he do better than he does. Not even the hack compromises or stoops; he does what he is, and as people are frequently bad, or mediocre, so is the work. No matter what his intentions are, should he adopt a simple prose style he is likely to be affected, or excessively humble. The book takes command of him, for writing is a trance, and the author at noon a noctambulist. One resolves to keep the vigil, but sleep is the scribe.

After a few miserable weeks I hesitantly approached Mrs. MacDowell and asked her if she would not let me move to quarters closer to the other colonists. Her eyes darted glances, sharp-edged as a javelin. How much work was I doing? I quoted Felltham: "The idle man is the barrenest piece of Earth in the Orbe," but apparently I was in her disfavor. She wanted rebel artists who were disciplined Laconians. I was garrulous, and I wandered.

Mrs. MacDowell had founded the colony with money she got as a concert pianist and she had no intention of allowing her Spartan commune to decay into a free-love society. There had been a few scandals, and the colonists still spoke of Louis Untermeyer's virile outrage; he had run off with a female poet.

I was given a single room next to the eminent poet, Edwin Arlington Robinson. The novel I was working on was such a pest that I soon became aware of the sound of the floor creaking outside my door. I went out to look and saw Robinson walking up and down to exercise his bruised arches. He said nothing to me nor I to him. Bored and vexed with my drudgery, I was glad to be the spectator of this ordinary activity of a man who was positively not average. He usually took his exercise about midday, and I was a little grateful to his poor arches as they relieved my ennui.

Robinson was the elite artist at the colony, and long before the sun began to dwindle I would see him seated in a chair, rocking back and forth. He, too, was overcome by satiety, and I conjectured he was moaning: "My God, must I write another poem?"

A dour man, with much hidden feeling, he once watched

a couple who had just gotten married step into a carriage, and he said, "Were I that happy I'd never make a single verse." It is said, and quite justly, that poets are never happy, and few readers who love their books are sensible enough to prize their misery. Writing is a cruel occupation, and often a tiresome one, and there are so few incidents in an author's life that one wonders if he is entitled to an autobiography. There are hardly any events in George Moore's *Confessions of a Young Man*. Meditation is clandestine; little wonder that the *Intimate Journals* of Charles Baudelaire is still a secret to the public at large. La Bruyère divulges the habits and preoccupation of a contemplative man which deprive him of the bustling existence of the active empty gadabout: "If my Friend should ask you how I employ myself . . . You may tell him having my Head filled with a Thousand Glorious Projects. I lead a tedious disagreeable life." An author is about the only man who has much to do but is never busy.

At rare intervals I spoke to Mrs. MacDowell. What a flinty visage she had! Once I heard her laugh, and I believed I had heard a rock laugh, and wondered whether this gallant Puritan were not a sensual woman.

One evening Robinson had no billiard partner and he asked me to join him in a game. He could not have chosen a worse billiard opponent in the country. Half an hour after we started I was beating him although the ball kept bouncing off the table and leaping to various parts of the floor. Robinson was incensed. How could such a freakish player as I be winning? Fortunately he was the victor, and I was glad of it. He had had enough defeats and hardly required such a paltry one.

He had been a drunkard, and in very woeful years had worked in a subway change booth until President Theodore Roosevelt, a relative of his, heard of his plight, and did something to relieve him.

A friend once accused him of being savagely abstemious, charging that he had never lain with a woman, and Robinson irascibly pounded the table, shouting, "How do you know?"

A woman painter of real talent, who was a close friend of mine, had been in love with him for years. Each year she went to the colony to be near him. When he dropped his cane, and she bent to pick it up for him, he nervously snatched up the cane lest their fingers should tangle. He was too moral a man to entice a woman unless he meant business.

I had somehow finished about two hundred typewritten pages of a novel later to be titled *From Flushing to Calvary*. The fiction was ailing and so was I. The pangs of hunger in London and tuppenny meat wagons had their evil effects upon me; I was stricken with acute appendicitis. Mrs. Mac-Dowell saw to it I had hospital care in Peterborough. Whenever this lady visited me I never failed to kiss her hand and to express my gratitude to her. Behind that rigid pillar was a noble human being. I had quite fallen in love with the wonderful old lady.

Was I a trial to her, and did I in some way oppose her conservative code? A writer is a preposterous person. Bear in mind she was very much the artist herself and superior to most of those to whom she gave refuge. Doubtless she had some real inkling of my nature, but was resolved to rule the colony as she saw fit.

The following year I came to see her in New York, where during the winter months she would occasionally stay at a small midtown hotel. Her sight was commencing to fail and quite badly, but she saw me, more than I knew. I was utterly taken aback when she asked me if I wanted to return to Peterborough the next summer. "Oh, no, Mrs. Mac-

Dowell," I replied, "but please do not think I am a bad person, or ungracious. You know I love and respect every particle of your rigorous nature." Again I heard that passionate rocklike laugh, and remembered that in her prime she had sat in a buggy and with a whip in one hand wildly drove the pair of horses harnessed to it.

I went on: "Tell me, Mrs. MacDowell, why have you spent so much of your strength as a concert pianist to provide utopian shelter and food for so many mediocrities?" Her reply was finely carved and prompt: "If more than twenty-five percent of the people were geniuses they would disrupt the entire colony." She then asked me what I desired to do, and I said I was contemplating going to a seaside town where I could write, and she gave me the money.

Later, she became totally blind, and then I began to see she always *saw*. Mrs. MacDowell did more for the American artist than anyone else. She had a deep religious feeling for the arts, and as I now finish this all too small portrait of a great person I bow and kiss her hand again.

3 1

Saint-Marc Girardin has uttered
one phrase which will endure:
"Let us be mediocre."*

—Baudelaire

Waldo Frank, a divine popinjay who wrote in an exalted falsetto style, informed me that he was a great man, and since I was impressionable I believed him. People know what they are, and few are mistaken, but Frank was. He had published a vasty novel, *The Birth and Death of David Markand*, and Edwin Seaver had dismissed it in the *New Masses*. Frank was positive he was a genius and Seaver was just as sure he was not. All Frank had done was to evacuate several slices of Stalinist precepts; the fiction was Left-wing frippery. Nevertheless I listened to his feverish rantings; Seaver, he said, was another one of his turncoat disciples. Frank was a crazy rag-picker who went about collecting followers who declined to pursue him.

Resolved to carry his grievous crucifix, I stoutly defended his book in the *New Masses*. One cannot slay a remarkable book or keep a bad one alive for long. *The Birth and Death of David Markand* has justly "sunk into waste paper and oblivion," to use Swift's words.

Waldo Frank regarded himself as a virgin Adam of eroticism. Alfred Stieglitz photographed him eating the Mandrake apple, and Frank looked as if he were the first one who had ever partaken of the forbidden fruit. How simple it is for a man to cozen himself; it terrifies me. Frank was not an ordinary motley; he was a special museum fool with tender sensibilities, who supposed he levitated as he created. He worked with a word brush instead of a typewriter, fuming away the hours over a touchy and excitable teacup. He was such an overwrought person that when you expected him to express some primy feeling he simply sneezed. He was crazy about words and was positive he was the sublime artificer of language.

At this point I cannot refrain from referring to La Bruyère's sobering maxim: "A man of moderate Understanding thinks he writes divinely. A man of good Understanding thinks he writes reasonably."

Waldo Frank and Paul Rosenfeld were thick friends, but Waldo couldn't let a word alone and this got on Rosenfeld's nerves; he attacked his friend in *The Dial*. Stieglitz told me that when Rosenfeld was writing one of his immaculate essays, "Deliberations," he did not know what to do with the word "horse." How could he keep on repeating "horse" without crucifying the reader's ears? He had not been altogether unlucky; he had used stallion, charger, courser, but now he was at the end of his resources. He was ready to give his kingdom for a reader but not for a horse!

Waldo Frank and Paul Rosenfeld fancied themselves two Ariels of the thirties. Recalling them, I cannot repress Chekhov's derisive opinion of the ballerina word-caperers: "There go a pair of artists." Stieglitz said he didn't mind a man even if he was a writer. An author should discourse with as much truth as his head will allow, neither being careless, nor overnice, fussing too much about every word, nor falling into the worst of all errors, profligate beauty-mongering.

Sherwood Anderson revealed to me that when he and Waldo Frank were one day engaged in intimate conversation Waldo burst forth: "The three greatest writers of this century are James Joyce, Sherwood Anderson and Waldo Frank."

Anderson chided him, and swore he would relinquish his friendship if Frank ever talked that way to him again. Waldo was contrite, the mother welling up in his circular virgin eyes, and he assured Anderson that henceforth he would be a humble man.

As the two men went out into the streets a short time later, Waldo bubbled over. "Sherwood," he said, "Europe is waiting for us."

Now let us go to Homer's grapeless sea. Would that I could, but I must indite other matters.

I met Edmund Wilson, the St. John the Baptist of our *literati mediocriter*, when he was the book review editor of *The New Republic*. Were there a pile of maggoty books he had no intention of sending out to be noticed, he would fill a pair of suitcases with them for me to sell to the secondhand bookseller, Schulte, on Fourth Avenue. In 1930 Greenwich Village was an Elysium for a lackpenny poet, and I was content with my portion, deeming "frugality a handsome income." As Chaucer holds, "povrete is hateful good."

Wilson had thin, leafy hair of a rusty-colored hue, a lisp, a caustic chin, and a mouth too niggardly clothed for his vocation, literature. I had the utmost faith in his faculties, and was sure he would be a Boileau or a La Bruyère of letters, but had uneasy feelings about his physiognomy. It is the age of the Grubean face, and I am reminded of Pascal's assertion that ancient history depended upon the shape of Cleopatra's nose. The thought comes to me that American Literature might be different had Edmund Wilson had carnal lips.

He never ceased to show me kindnesses. He was recalcitrant, unwilling to be governed by a better idea than his own, and quite ready to help a writer provided he felt he was superior to him.

About this time Henry Allen Moe, secretary of the Guggenheim Foundation, and I became quite friendly, and I informed him that the persons selected by him to award authors and painters of unusual ability were a crew of milk-livered dotards. Much to my surprise he asked Wilson, whose name I had suggested to him, to serve on the committee.

Not long afterward I received a notice from the Guggenheim committee asking how much money I required to study and write abroad for one year. I was elated and so was my spiritless purse. Within a short space of time I heard that the money to be given to Hart Crane and Katherine Anne Porter was withheld from me and that Wilson was outraged by what he deemed an injustice. A man about eighty was my opponent. He had gone through some pages of *Bottom Dogs* and was aghast. There are no evil or obscene words in the novel. Yet . . . ? *Mea culpa!* He was correct, and how could that be? Had I set out to paint America as a Gehenna for the poor and become a pornographer? It is a bleak, inhuman and unkind book, and who needs more pitilessness? Human feeling is so protean that an author may have the most ethical intentions when he commences a novel and yet have little else for his travail than didactic billingsgate.

I may declare I am not opinionated, cunning, or hostile to people, and still bend my back too low, be uncommonly overflowing, or unexpectedly overcome by spleen. A man is never what he thinks he is, and that is one of nature's rare civilities to him.

Naturally I was mortified to be undone by *Bottom Dogs*. In 1960 when Ferlinghetti offered to reissue *Bottom Dogs* under his City Lights imprint, I told him I would consent provided I could write a brief foreword attacking such mephitic diction. I began with Tolstoy's caveat: "Many men write books but very few are ashamed of them afterwards."

Tolstoy did not know what he was doing either, for toward the fag-end of his tormented life he wished to destroy all his works save one religious short story. This was a fanatical desire, but if a writer does not distrust himself at all who will ever have confidence in him?

Pondering my own dreggy inceptions it occurs to me that the seer, St. Augustine, whose *Confessions* I consult when my blood flags or is depraved, has libidinous defects in his pages. The *Confessions* are pure as flesh will allow them to be. Although Augustine discloses little of his turpitudes it is sufficient to arouse a virile youth pining for the arms of a maid or craving her chaste bed strewn with the frankincense of her body. I cite one of Augustine's sentences: "With what companions I walked the streets of Babylon, and wallowed in the mire thereof, as if in a bed of spices and precious ointments."

One asks, is man so easily tempted? He boils until every pore of the skin has a devil in it. Origen, one of the primitive church fathers, was so weary of the battle against lust that he castrated himself. But it is reported that eunuchs burn! Were man not a perverse animal Augustine would have had no need to confess. Let the sacred author speak further: "Yet I insisted to thieve, and did it, compelled by no hunger, nor poverty, but through a cloyedness . . . and a pamperedness of iniquity."

That I am doomed to sin on many pages I have no doubt; if I did not err I would not have a single thought. Could books cure me I'd be a bore. What troubles me is that I may be worse but never better. Voltaire says, "Man is neither an angel nor a brute, and the misfortune is that he who attempts to act the angel plays the brute."

I had a congenial connection with the deceased Eduard Lindemann, a contributing editor of *The New Republic:* he was a member of the Willard Straight Foundation which furnished the money for the existence of the magazine. Lindemann, urged by Edmund Wilson, got a stipend for me from the foundation, and with that I went to Provincetown to go on with my second novel. During the winter this Cape Cod Bohemia, emptied of the arts and letters trash, is a bracing, fishy town. In the harsh months one has all the quiet the snowy heart requires for reflection.

Wilson had suggested I call on John Dos Passos, whose house was next to the studio I had rented on the garbaged bay. My first meeting with Dos Passos was at a party. Looking for a heretic and an icon-breaker I was surprised to be in the presence of a pleasant unoriginal man, quite myopic, and with a levantine bald-looking face. I made a grave mistake: I tried to talk to him about *belles lettres.*

The writing and painting roisterers seated at the table looked at me with hostility. Earnest conversation had died long ago, and what clearer proof is there than the fiction of these ephebes. Seldom is a tedious man an entertaining author. Many years afterward Francis Brown, Book Review editor of the New York *Times*, told me his mother knew George Washington Cable and considered him an implacable bore and the rereading of *Old Creole Days* and *The Grandissimes* was ample evidence of her acuity.

I realized nobody was supposed to do anything at these bibulous soirées except vomit, fall on the floor or insult somebody. Incensed, I later wrote Dos Passos a waspish letter which became the *scandale* of the Provincetown Bohemians. One day he came to my studio and informed me he was far more interested in what a grocer had to say than in the conceptions of a novelist. In the thirties the fisherman at Provincetown was the mystic pleb. It was not uncommon for a wife tired of her husband who was an artist to run off with a fisherman with whom she lived out her idyllic days babbling about hake, mackerel, halibut, clams and oysters.

Were Dos Passos' work superior to everyday palaver I could appreciate his contempt for mungrill American writers. Aside from Theodore Dreiser I never met with one of the members of this tribe who could heal a half-hour of my ennui with some wondrous observation. Suppose one wants to speak of Plutarch, Suetonius, Cassius Dio, Plotinus, Polybius, or Montaigne, more intestinal than even cerebral for me, where will he go for such a colloquy? Aside from Nathaniel Hawthorne, Melville had no other pensive companion.

After that I saw Dos Passos several times, and I liked him. He did not lack probity; he spoke out of his shallows because he was mediocre, and he could do nothing else unless he were a hypocrite. I think he feared putting on airs. What a pity; a man can be honest and be affected. Is it not curious that one is afraid to be sincere lest he be taken for a lofty braggart. Felltham has this in his long-forgotten *Resolves:* "The world is so much Knave, that 'tis growne a vice to be honest."

32

*Criticism consists in saying
whatever comes into one's head.*
—Saint-Beuve

After six months at Provincetown I repaired to Martha's Vineyard, where I finished the novel in a little cottage that sat upon the dunes neighboring a colony of Indians and Negroes.

My second abysmal failure, *From Flushing to Calvary,* published by Harcourt, Brace, was a triumph in literary circles. Upton Sinclair, whom I had visited at Pasadena, wrote a glowing statement for it; so did Edmund Wilson and William Soskin, book review editor of the New York *Post,* who had been a Socialist newspaperman on the *Globe.* Soskin, a short, burly man with a beige complexion, permitted me to do a weekly review for which I earned fifteen dollars: I considered him my benefactor. Charles A. Pearce, then editor of Harcourt, told me Carl Sandburg claimed that *Flushing* had the authentic *stink* of American realism, and *Contempo,* a gamy literary sheet published at Chapel Hill, North Carolina, devoted a whole issue to the novel.

Meanwhile, I contributed verse and short stories to *Pagany,* one of the brave little magazines, whose editor was

Richard Johns. He was able to support *Pagany* with the allowance provided by his father, proprietor of two burlesque houses in Boston. This is in the gaudy American vein; William Marion Reedy, a St. Louis publisher, obtained the money to bring out Harris Merton Lyon's *Graphics*, and other books, from his wife, a madam of a brothel. Dreiser, a friend of Reedy, had encouraged Merton Lyon, and Reedy himself became the staunch defender of an obscure novel, *Sister Carrie*. The wife of the publisher, a social worker and Dreiser's cockatrice, had buried *Sister Carrie* in the basement, considering its author a menace to humanity.

There is a droll portrait of William Marion Reedy, huge fleshy rake, cartoonist and connoisseur of art, jade and women in Dreiser's *Twelve Men*. One of his other apostles, a fallen one, was Harris Merton Lyon. Dreiser calls him de Maupassant, Jr. In *Twelve Men* he depicts Lyon as the young intransigent author who detests the literary money grubs, but who after a few seizures of impecuniosity becomes a scenario writer in Hollywood.

My friendly relations with Wilson continued after I had published a third novel, *Those Who Perish*, the first anti-Nazi fiction to appear in America. By then I was a desperado, doing what I could to rid myself of scatophagous naturalism, morose jargon and debile metaphors. I regard the word *technique* a pusillanimous evasion; when one has no emotion he prattles about his clauses, his craft, or his critical faculties. Saint-Beuve remarks that criticism is what comes out of a man's head, and so is a novel.

Edmund Wilson saw the galleys of *Those Who Perish*, and he compared me with the nineteenth-century French writer, Huysmans. Now I was *un homme de lettres!* But was I? I was to abjure every book I ever wrote for the ideas of yesterday wax moldy before one has inhumed a sigh.

One afternoon Wilson asked me to accompany him to

Grand Central Station, and I thanked him profusely for his
tribute, for I deeply esteemed Huysmans. He replied he had
made the statement to advance the sale of my novel. What
wounds and rime gathered around my calcined spirit. Suddenly I realized that Edmund Wilson was Everyman's Opinion, and that he had no conceptions of his own that one
cannot come by in twenty-five other drumbling critics. I
mention the spurious panegyric because this is a common
practice of the Grub Street litterateur, and I should also add
I don't care a whit about the novel. A man who will tell a
lie about one book is sure to be false about another; this is
the "miching malicho," the patchery, in our bookish agora.
Wilson never pardoned me for misliking his corrupt encomium of *Those Who Perish*.

At the time I was stung. Overcome by another defeat,
I picked myself up from the dust and with a granitic resolve promised myself I would yet be a writer. At the close
of a later tribulation I had as my guerdon *Can These Bones
Live*. Had I toiled in Laban's field for a radiant Rachel or a
dim-eyed Leah?

After I had separated from Edmund Wilson I realized I
had left the herd, and according to Kierkegaard, "The Crowd
is Untruth." By then I was alluded to as a hard, craggy
man. The passion for Truth is unsociable.

My loneliness was impermeable; a Prometheus I was
shackled to my blizzards. I had not one friend brave enough
to stand alongside me except Alone. The flock of Laodicea
who were neither hot nor cold and who had feigned to be
my admirers—Edmund Wilson, Waldo Frank, Lionel Tril-
ling, Horace Gregory, James T. Farrell, whom when obscure and hungry I had fed and helped, Kenneth Fearing,
neglected and mourned by none, whom I aided to get published, Harvey Breit, to whom I furnished the hearth of

friendship and nursed in his cruel illness, Charles Olson, who had looked upon me as father and mentor—all eschewed me. They forsook me to huddle together in the sheepcote of dungy comfort.

What was my fault? I refused to be memorably average; I denounced the cult of the same, and was to refuse the fatal hellebore of political doctrines.

Go, I cried to my darkness, into the forests forty days and nights lest you be tempted by one shibboleth.

Banished by the merchant pack, I was the apostate who, as Shestov says, is never forgiven. They pretended to affirm the cant creed of equality, but the greatest destroyer is the leveler. Only the lion has honey in his carcass.

To return to Edmund Wilson, and to my remembrance of him, let me say it is a pain to do what I must perforce do. Memory, Nietzsche taught me, is a "gathering of wounds." So I must gibbet Wilson as he has others. Dr. Johnson relates it is a benefaction to the commonwealth to attack a bad book. Wilson had told me he found it awkward to associate with writers who were his inferiors, and he never has.

Years after our rupture, he sent me the galleys of his work on the Dead Sea Scrolls, which I read with a civil ear. In his sixth decade he had discovered the Old Testament. However, his exuberance was bathetic, and I sent him a lenitive reproach for this brimborion: "Oh, isn't Genesis wonderful." He didn't reply. Had he mistaken me for the raw parvenu of letters he knew in the thirties?

He had a house at Wellfleet, a village on Cape Cod where I spent six years as a frozen eremite. In 1947 I taught Enlish at Boston University three days a week, and the rest of the time I studied and wrote in Wellfleet. Once at his home Wilson made such pygmean assertions about literature that I admonished him: "Socrates opined that it is easy for a Greek to panegyrize the Athenians. You are praising the driest sherds in our Sinai; let me show you where are the manna and the quail."

This was a pachydermatous affront, and he did not invite me to his home again, preferring to guzzle and chatter with Frank Shay, Waldo Frank, Dos Passos and others of our bookish larvae. On rare occasions we met in the village, and this doughty pertinacious man would ask me to join him for several paces which I gladly did.

After the despot Franco had vanquished the Spanish Republic, I asked Wilson whether he was not enthralled by Miguel de Unamuno's *The Tragic Sense of Life* and the *Soliloquies and Conversations of Don Quixote*. It was believed that Unamuno was poisoned by Franco's epigones. Wilson had not heard of him.

What troubles me about his judgments of poems and novels is not that he is so often wrong but that his mistakes are so shrewd. He is one of the canniest forecasters of books likely to sell. Since the twenties he has had an aprioristic curiosity about poverty, but a quick salt nose for the fetid smell of success. Homer can name all the towns in ancient Hellas more easily than I can recall the scrofulous hackneys Wilson has laureled. Posing as a book Rhadamanthus, by nefandous suasion he endeavors to convince the reader torn to pieces by a society grounded upon "the lechery of money" that the vulgarians who have defamed the populace to lard their own pockets are our savants.

Does a reader have to consult the Sibylline Oracles to interpret his title, *Classics and Commercials*, a whorehouse directory of stage dolts and scullion prosers that includes Houdini, Michael Arlen, Fannie Hurst, Compton Mackenzie, Alexander Woollcott, P. G. Wodehouse, Harold Bell Wright, Florenz Ziegfeld, James Durante, Joseph Hergesheimer, Ring Lardner, Louis Bromfield, Dorothy Parker, John Barrymore, Maxwell Anderson, Arthur Conan Doyle, Jim Tully, Marlene Dietrich, Anita Loos, Greta Garbo, Budd Schulberg, George Kaufman, and J. B. Priestley?

Edmund Wilson, along with other shallow feuilletonists of his kidney, has the habit of merely naming authors without any comment, which implies a favorable critical judgment. This kind of quackery is common; the merchant writer, who has only slubbered over the pages of Pliny the Elder, Dioscorides, Columella, Theophrastus, Statius, or Philostratus, creates the impression that he is a scholar.

Occasionally Wilson has a leaf of parsley for Aeschylus, Euripides, and Tolstoy, and hemlock observation on such wights as Montaigne and Robert Burton and their "garrulous works." He informed me he could not read Sir Thomas Browne, but he who is incapable of relishing the *Hydriotaphia* is a biblioclast.

Too busy with philisters he can only spare several of his apocalyptic platitudes for American scribes. Wilson discloses that Allen Tate is "quite mature" and "older than Mr. Warren"; of Tate's eloquent volume, *The Forlorn Demon,* immensely above his own fustian, he has nothing to say. He has ignored William Carlos Williams' *In the American Grain* and Kenneth Burke's lapidary and gnomic declamations, *Towards a Better Life.* His allusion to Dos Passos is a misfortune to any novelist: "Dos Passos has perhaps gone to school to Ring Lardner and Anita Loos."

It is seasonable to consider Wilson's lucubrations; his style has no head, neck, arms, legs or feet. Mounted on his Pegasus his plight is worse than Voltaire's Cunegund's, who goes out into the world on a horse with one buttock. "The age of great men is going; the epoch of the ant-hill is beginning," lamented Amiel in the nineteenth century.

Once I had occasion to praise a little-read and remaindered book, D. H. Lawrence's *Studies in Classic American*

Literature to Wilson and Van Wyck Brooks, and both dismissed it with a flout. Lawrence's work had not moldered enough to be reckoned a posthumous commodity that could be marketed. Later Wilson included Lawrence's entire volume in his book, *The Shock of Recognition*. The inveterate opsimath, he has presently in his doughty seventies discovered the Elizabethans.

Edmund Wilson has always stood outside the Portal of Feeling, the mother of literature. A rationalist, he would turn the stones into bread, imagining this alone can bring about the apotheosis of the ravished lower classes. A positivist never understands the absurd needs of man. The touchless paranoiac abstract man must partake of the "inward food" because the economic question will never take care of the human one. To expect the mass-man to have an etiological soul is the refusal to see the individual person of flesh and bone. The abstract man is No-Body.

Alexander Herzen said, "Every foetus has a right to develop," but he added that it is false to suppose each foetus will ripen. Would that every human being were as cogitative as a pond, mere, glen, birch, moss, or a musk-ox; these are thinking animals, but man oftentimes is not.

Edmund Wilson has never had the intellectual power for a metamorphosis absolutely essential to the seer who must pass from one plane of thought and emotion to another. The terrible sin of the Laodicean, who is neither ice nor fire, is that he is No-Feeling.

33

---

*So then because thou art luke-
warm, and neither cold nor hot,
I will spew thee out of my
mouth.*

—Revelation

There is another who comes to mind at this time, although
actually we did not meet until some years later.

Around 1938, when I was living in East Gloucester, an
obscure youth came to my door and introduced himself as
Charles Olson. He was the son of a Swedish mailcarrier and
an Irish Catholic mother. He had noble brows, a nose finely
molded by Euclid, and he was a giant near seven foot high.
But his stature was his shame.

The young Olson knew pages of Shakespeare's *Measure
for Measure, Lear, Troilus and Cressida, Timon of Athens*
by rote. A perfervid disciple of Herman Melville, he had
devoured *Moby Dick, Mardi,* "The Encantadas," "Bartleby
the Scrivener," "Benito Cereno." He venerated that small
spermal candle in American literature, Melville's "Hawthorne and His Mosses," and was the first to excavate many
of Melville's epistles then in the possession of Mrs. Metcalf,
Melville's granddaughter. In the forties I introduced him to

ancient writers, and he chewed up Hesiod, Manetho, Statius, Apollodorus, Diodorus Siculus as if they were a broken shirt, unlaundered socks and a used-up catarrhal overcoat.

Soon I gave him complete devotion, immolating my own interests to his advantage. I published his essay, "Lear and Moby Dick," in *Twice a Year*, opposing a lioness with barking dogs for a belly to do it. Olson had two staunch friends who helped him: I and Charles Olson.

He was entangled in a love affair with a young woman who either impersonated Pasiphae or was her descendant; she was not enamored of a bull but of a horse. This was my earliest but nebulous glimpse into his nature. I thought of the centauri who were half-man, half-horse, and very insolent. His nature was thickly veiled from me.

Olson wrote an essay, his last piece of English, on Dostoevsky's Stavrogin in *The Possessed*. He was obsessed with Stavrogin, the ahuman, the intellectual neuter. What I had previously taken for light in him was a negative sun. I brooded over his Stavroginism. Had he fallen under a malignant black star that governed his mind? Was his intellection a nihilistic zero? What then? Maybe a man can water his sands, weeds and thorns, for his genius may lie in his wastes.

Olson's fervor for me ebbed, and I saw his scab of pride, the fleas of envy biting his entrails, and the putrid smoke of his jealousy. For the first time I noticed the hard demons that lay behind his pedantic spectacles; I had never observed his rapier eyes before. But then we alter a friend's features as our love for him rises and falls.

Bewildered I was slow to comprehend his fell purposes. He was lacerating himself, but I did not know he was a self-waster. Nor could I presume that he preferred to crush the few bare twigs within him and to stifle his faculties. Aside from annulling his intellect and abdicating the traditional language, his principal renunciation was myself. Let no one imagine you need him; it is more perilous than staring at the Gorgon Medusa.

There had been no fevered or scurfed quarrel between us. For seven years I had received two or three letters a week from him, with the salutation: "Edward, my Edward." Then one day he came to me, his head pained, the broad surfaces of his face gnarled and warped, and disclosed that he feared my influence was impeding him.

Taken aback, I mused: Few men can tolerate human kindness, and I said: "Don't fret. Let nature decide who is the better between us. Books are our chaff blown hither and thither by the wind, the aching rains, and the moist clouds."

I narrated his perplexities for three hours, and he desolately ruffled his hair, but was resolved to go away. I cited La Bruyère: "How difficult it is to be satisfied with any one," and I reminded him of André Gide's insight: "He who fears the influences of others makes a tacit avowal of the poverty of his own soul."

Olson venerated water, which is unstable, and according to Virgil "deceitful." What I had inferred was Jovian fire in his spirit was a plume of roaring blazing waves, and what I had not guessed was that his blood was frozen mildew. But "man is nimble, like a flea in a sheepskin," says Aristophanes.

After his commentary on Dostoevsky I had hinted to Olson that it was his confession, but I was unsure. More determined, he sacked his deserts and quenched his compassion. He had studied the Trimmers in Dante's *Inferno:* "Thou shouldst see the wretched people who have lost the good of the intellect," and regarded himself as one of those in the woeful circle.

Stavrogin's predicament is that he cannot and will not choose either to be good or bad, nor can he be pervious to people, their bleedings and their livid desolation. Pitilessness is the creed of the modern Stavrogin. Nature, man's foster mother, does not hear his heavy sighs, and what rock laments the scrannel surf at neap tide?

Stavrogin is not against God or for Him; Dante's Trimmer is paralyzed by inanition. Stavrogin declares: "Even negation does not come from me. Everything has always been petty and spiritless." Knowledge that is not action is bestial perversity. Stavrogin hurts others because he has neutral bowels; he wills nothing. His is a preterhuman detachment—what Charles Olson called the cannibalism of the self. In the *Gita* man is told to be rock and mountain, and not to be involved in the affections of men, for all attachment brings suffering. It is true, but such a doctrine is destructive to Occidental man. This is from *The Bhagavad-Gita:* "He who works without attachment, resigning his actions to Brahman, is untainted by sin, as a lotus leaf by water." It is a stony discipline, but adamant indifference to quivering flesh is modern Western narcissism. I have never sought the perverse way, the doleful ruinous road of Stavrogin, nor made the great refusal: "Behold, here is good and evil, choose." This is the moral injunction in Genesis. I may not understand good and evil, but I know what pains me and, I pray, others.

Olson harmed me because he said he did not know "how to exorcise his devils." When a woman is unfaithful to her lover he thinks himself a miserable ass, and shame covers his skin and stings him like a wasp. However, the cruelest form of infidelity and betrayal is intellectual cuckoldry, the perfidy of man, vowing the utmost fealty to a friend whilst breaking into his soul to get what he requires for his own ends, and then claims he has stolen nothing except empty gourds and cockles. Not even Lear's pelican daughters, Regan and Goneril, are such haggards.

Charles Olson abolished the memory of himself and of
me, hurling the latter, his monitor, into the gullet of Cocytus. Right up to his death he pretended I no longer was with
the green leaves and the grass that placate our short bitter
seasons. He is in the ground now. I have grieved over him,
and then again my soul has been dipped into the squalid
marshes of wrath. I have taken the oath never to allow a
stranger to cross the threshold of my fragile identity and
call me friend. Coleridge, after he had been puddled by another, made a similar vow.

It is not my purpose to resolve incomprehensible secrets
of the flesh but to record them. Anyway, soon as a man left
me or I him, and without any tincture of pride, I think I
always was ready to allow him to go away. Is this self-love?
I do not care for myself and I've never embraced that sorry
creature. Could I be self-sufficient? It is true, we are as
separated from others beneath the moon and the Pleiades as
we are when we are covered with earth: I can see no real
difference. This is involuntary; could I understand one human being I would know who commenced the universe.

Olson had to renounce me. He had an ungovernable im-
pulse to destroy himself. Is that bad? It was his inherent
conviction. Why then judge him? Let me admit, it is absurd, but unless man is bizarre, he is not worth noticing. I
shall always love Charles Olson and condemn him. Is that
senseless? Then "smite me on the other cheek" is the demand
of a great tragic Madman. Ordinary people will attribute
this to self-killing. It is far deeper than that. It is the human way.

34

> . . . *these foul snails leaving*
> *their spume and froth on the*
> *fairest flowers of literature.*
> —John Ruskin

Shame, according to Aristotle, is a corporal sensation. I would drink the cup of Lethe to forget the scorifying thirties.

Why did I become a Communist? All just men covet a utopia, although this is vain apocrypha. Though nothing is contrary to one's identity, man covers the Milky Way of his destiny with scoriae. The intelligentsia of America were powerfully stung by the sufferings of the humble people. The richest nation on the earth was afflicted with an artificial famine that bankrupted the shopkeepers and was at the same time a benison to industrialists who hoarded an immense store of gold, properties and land.

The poor were unlike dogs who could paw the ground and dig up bones that had been hid and saved against the day of hunger. The corporate farms were not choked with tares, but were overladen with wheat, barley, and the pastures were pestered with millions upon millions of kine, sheep and porkers.

The rulers went to the Pythian oracle to resolve the

riddle they had invented and received as an answer an economic sophism that must have baffled them as much as it did the twelve million unemployed and penniless workmen. Unable to sell the grain, milk, cheese and livestock the people desperately needed for a famished household table, the government burned the crops, the sheep, the pigs in order to increase the price and save the country. Who, pray, is the country? This was done at the behest of Henry A. Wallace, Roosevelt's Secretary of Agriculture. Later Wallace, desiring to become President, was supported by the Communists, who had earlier organized the hunger march to the Capitol (starvation having been created by the Washington, D.C., ephors). "Policy sits above conscience," says Shakespeare. Thus the Stalinists became the advocates of Henry A. Wallace, sacerdotal arsonist of the state, who put to the torch the food the hungry Americans needed.

What the rich had not learned by sitting on the monetary delphic tripod they garnered from Joseph's shrewd dream, paraphrased by the medieval poet, William Langland: the lean kine, Avarice, always in want, devour the fat kine. The workers who dress the earth, the vines, plow the tilth, labor at the lathes and the assembly lines, are themselves the manure of the politicians.

Pondering this I became one of the innocent altar boys of the lowest divinity, Matter. That such espousal of the New would turn me into a lotophagus I never conjectured. I endeavored to embrace the abstract mass-man, and renounced the "worship of Hermes and the hilly Muses." I adopted a gallimaufry of ferine neologisms and a drabbish language whilst abjuring the heroic English of former times. Worse, I held that the diction of the Elizabethans and the Restoration was obsolete.

Most of the writers were propertyless intellectuals—city anchorites stived up in an emboweled room no better than

Diogenes' tub, said to have been a Grecian burial vase. Sill, we did not cant and whine—Dr. Johnson's phrase— nor show any reluctance to abide by the ancient cynic tradition of frugality, and were satisfied with a cheese sandwich, a plate of beans and bread smeared with free mustard at Stewart's Cafeteria at Seventh Avenue near Fourteenth Street. We believed in Blake's "politics is brotherhood" and thought the Stalinists shared our vision.

Early in the thirties the publishers of Mae West's autobiography gave a trumpery party for her. America was already becoming, as Plato writes in the *Laws*, a theatocracy. Many poets and novelists thronged to see this dilapidated, synthetic doll of the theater. I looked at her with a few distempered reflections, and thought how the ideal American woman in the films was the glorious tart, the deified chit, the skeletal scrag.

At this gathering I met a lonely youth also fevered with poverty. At first I regarded Erskine Caldwell as a *tabula rasa* monument; he reminded me of Shakespeare's gaping mussel shell. A son of Georgia, he was more abstruse than the inscription on the Rosetta Stone.

With the exception of Theodore Dreiser, Sherwood Anderson, Allen Tate, Hart Crane, Kenneth Burke, Archibald MacLeish, William Carlos Williams and Erskine Caldwell, the writers of the thirties were militant illiterates. Caldwell's first and best book, *American Earth*, was almost unknown. In a chanting earthen prose he wrote about a full-bodiced tree or a sweet-teated jill, and aside from Sherwood Anderson was in that prose poem the most sensual singer in America. However, he pillaged his nature more cruelly than Achilles sacked Tenedos. He was wasted by an ungovernable nether lust, for his books gave off the fetid effluvium of the necropolis. His stories were filled with a dithyrambic love of corpses and the mutilation of human limbs. He lopped off the arm of a tenant farmer as one might decapitate the top of a corn stalk. He sang as a sow devoured the stomach of a Negro sharecropper.

Man changes his creed but never his character. "Men's minds vary like the daylight that Father Jupiter sends upon the fruitful lands," as it is said in the *Odyssey*. The emotions of the poet are quick and variable as a thunderclap, but he is never a dissembler. Caldwell, as a didactic leftist, amputated the hand or foot of a Georgia cracker to illustrate how brutally man was oppressed by the capitalists. But when he ceased to be a natural necrophile he also failed as an artist.

One assumes that Gustave Flaubert created *Madame Bovary* to depict the vapid everyday life of romantic Emma and her morbid fribbles. However, Flaubert was obsessed with a certain pigmentation: "In *Madame Bovary* what I was after was to render a special tone, that color of the mouldiness of a wood louse's existence."

Erskine Caldwell had no wish to be the mendicant novelist. In ancient Athens Crates, the philosopher, was content with apples, millet and acorns roasted on the ashes. In a frigid factory country an author has to maul his primy days for his barest needs.

My predicament was a painful one. After *American Earth* Caldwell published a humbug cash novel, *God's Little Acre*. He had written an encomium on *From Flushing to Calvary* for the *New Masses*. I impugned Caldwell's novel, John Don Passos', and the murrain fiction of eight others in *The Nation*, determined as Jonathan Swift was "to drag out lurking errors like Cacus from his den" in the mawky books of the thirties. I was not mistaken about Caldwell. He had made the most crafty pragmatic adjustment: he purposed to be a palmy denizen of Philistia, "swilling sack and sugar, and mowsing fat venison" and at the same time tithe his soul by giving a farthing of his fortune to "the Cause."

In George Grosz there was a similar strain of dualism. If one were a patron of the George Grosz proletcult museum he could gaze with a rising gorge at a pair of repulsive bourgeois women with fat blowsy posteriors. Should he afterwards step into a pornographer's book mart he could browse through a George Grosz portfolio of female nudes with immense blossoming buttocks created to inflame the erotic appetite of the viewer.

Obviously my hortatory invective had no effect upon Caldwell. It is impossible to give other people advice because you expect them to have your faults. I had to abide by my character; either I must cut off the head of the Hydra knowing beforehand that another will always sprout up in its place, or be a Tartuffe critic. Did Caldwell compromise, or had he quenched his gifts in a single book? Had he a choice: to be the literary underground pariah or a scribbling Caliban? He had to be what he is and I had to blame him for it. That's morality, a vain and heartbreak word; there's not a man on earth who lives by it. Why then abuse a man for his venal books? There are conundrums no one can answer, but he who declines to reply to metaphysical questions is a poltroon. I did what I am, am full of faults, but have not the disposition to be wily. "In wrong preisying is all his craft and arte," said Wyatt.

Fellow-travelers were common in our national brothel, Hollywood. A hack or a greedy doxy, a notorious film star, signed a Communist petition, appeared at a rally for the liberation of the Harlan miners, or cried out against pellagra in the South, but continued to provide scabrous and criminal entertainment for the hapless multitude. Whilst

266

they larded their gouty pockets they were reputed to be saviors of the American Republic.

Meantime I visited the canneries, and the miserable tenements in New York City to acquire proletarian experience. We were exhorted to look everywhere for the evidence save within ourselves. I covered the hunger march for *The Nation*. About three thousand delegates, conveyed in trucks and jalopies, rolled into the capital. They came from Seattle, Portland, San Francisco, Los Angeles, the midwest and the Atlantic seaboard. As they approached the outskirts of Washington they were met by the police, the military and the firemen. To spectators the unarmed delegation, surrounded by thousands of lawmen, must have looked like an Elks' parade or a fireman-and-policeman Mardi Gras.

The hunger marchers were herded into a sterile gully where they were kept from early dawn until night, without water, a toilet for women and children, or a cracknel to eat. On the top of a hill hanging over the ravine where the delegates quietly talked or squatted were machine guns. I was standing close by a rump-fed cossack with burly ruddled chops who was hovering over one of the guns. I felt so infuriated I wanted to throw it down the declivity. Had I done so I would have been shot to death by the gendarme.

The underpaid white-collar workers of a department store on Union Square went on strike, and authors banded together to picket. Among those I recall were Nathanael West, James T. Farrell and Sol Funaroff; of course there were others. It was an orderly procession, which did not prevent the police on horseback from galloping down the pavement and charging into us. Why I did not flee I shall never know; I am not particularly brave. Shortly thereafter I was in a cell and my sole mate was Nathanael West, author of *Miss Lonelyhearts* and *Day of the Locust*.

To earn his bread West was a clerk at a small hotel on Madison Square. My acquaintance with him was thin but friendly. About a year later I met him at the La Salle Station in Chicago, where I was waiting for a train. I was on my way to New York and he was going to Hollywood. He had a pavid soporific face, and we parted with a feeling of desolation neither one of us understood. He and his bride were to die on their honeymoon in an automobile accident. Nathanael West was another Maupassant, Jr., who renounced his iconoclastic hatred of a monied brute society to cog and lie for the Hollywood stews.

In 1933 or thereabouts I spent some time outside a company town at Paint Creek, nineteen miles from Charleston, West Virginia. The miners had been locked out by the coal operators. They and their families were dwelling in the tents of Kedar hard by a diphtheria stream. Neither the Red Cross nor the Salvation Army which had received donations from the coaldiggers for over a generation would furnish them with food; a strike, or a lockout, they said, was not an act of God. Indeed it wasn't; it was the malefic ropery of the coal barons. The miners apparently were expected to select their sublunary misfortunes. Why had they not the good sense to be blasted by a tornado, or driven from their company town hovels by a flood?

Each morning the evicted miners went to the slaughterhouse to collect mawky collops of meat for their wives and gaunt children. They had been forced to be tenants of shacks owned by the operators. The walls of the rooms were papered with newsprint, and the roofs were so leaky that when it rained a family had to move the table from one part of a room to another to be able to eat their scanty meal. After they had paid rent, medical and funeral expenses, and bought food at the company grocery store, where the staples cost as much as a hundred percent more than the same vegetables and products at a green-grocer's outside the confines of the operators' acreage, they had nothing. Their fortnightly wages were debts, pellagra, and graveclothes.

I had been writing occasional reviews for Malcolm Cowley, who had succeeded Edmund Wilson as book review editor of *The New Republic* and I received word from him that Hart Crane had committed suicide. This tragedy and the wretchedness of the miners so benumbed me that after three weeks with them I returned to New York, where I continued my parlous trade as a grub-street proser.

35

Thus me pileth the pore and
pyketh ful clene
The ryche raymeth withouten
any ryght.

—Anonymous

Those asleep suppose the thirties were dissimilar from the present cormorant decade, but the Past is the quartan ague of Now. There were the tatterdemalion hunger marches, the broken wage-earners in the foul canneries, funguses, starvation among miners (who still have black lungs), and the Stygian Dust Bowl. How was that period different from the plaguy agony of the untouchables dwelling in tenements scurvy as old London's Houndes Ditch where dead dogs and filth were deposited, or the cry of the scaly millions who share the vagabond's woe: "He hath made my gowne so bare that a louse can get no holde on it." Today millions of empty bellies wail like bagpipes.

An instance of baneful indigence in that era and ours is a cantle of Jack Conroy's *The Disinherited*. This is a passage of a miner's last rites in Moberly, Missouri: "There he lay like a trussed blue fowl, his feet protruding from beneath a cheap cotton shroud. His scarred hands were folded across his chest, coal dust still blackening his nails and show-ing between his toes."

Conroy furnishes us with a scene of his own childhood in Moberly, where he still lives: "We crept down the rotting steps at the side of the house and watched mosquito larvae wriggling about in the water, and there was a frog perched on a floating shingle. . . . Mosquitoes in a dense cloud swarmed about the shack; we burned rags to keep them away. . . . Screens were almost unheard of on miners' houses. . . . Sugar was precious. In lean times sorghum might be used for sweetening coffee."

The people in Washington, D.C., surfeited on quail, thrush, pheasants, fishes and musk-pears, are "surd as the adder" to thievish prices. Judge, O Minos, a civilization by its bread—the fruit of the meal, Homer calls it—and its cost. When the baking of bread is not a ritual the country is with-out justice and poets. The primitive Indians whom Colum-bus discovered in Hispaniola, now Haiti, would not look for gold until they had made their bread of yucca, called cazabi.

The following quotations come from the most famous an-cient cookbook, *The Deipnosophists*, authored by Athenaeus, who cites among others the Attic poet, Archestratus:

> *Here I come, bearing in my hands the offspring*
> *Of three months' wheat, not doughy, collabi,*
> *Mixed with the milk of the grass-feeding cow.*

Rolls were known as collabi. Then the same writer refers to Pherecrates and lists these two lines:

> *Olen, now roast a penny roll with ashes*
> *But take care, don't prefer it to a loaf.*

Again Athenaeus had occasion to allude to barley cake which Hesiod calls amolgae:

The amolgaean cake of barley made,
And milk of goats whose stream is nearly dry.

Robert Burton, reputed for his erudite *Anatomy of Melan-choly*, was deeply concerned with beverages and loaves. He thought "the thinnest whitest wine is best, not thick nor strong; and so of beer, the middling is the finest. Bread of good wheat, pure, well purged from the bran, is preferred"; and he goes on to say that Laurentius, an antique writer, showed a bias for bread kneaded with rain water.

Men will again overthrów Troy and spoil another Priam's seed for an honest loaf of bread. Does not the eye lag and the stomach rebel at the sight of our robber hemlock loaves, wrapped in winding sheets of cellophane and sold at twenty-five or thirty-eight cents? Who can drown his daily chaff in the chemical milk of Cacus at thirty-two cents a quart, or digest, without sodium bicarbonate, the cankered chickens and the tins of carrion soup and fruits.

The columns in the papers are gorged with flagitious tidbits about "the beautiful people," the deformed and hare-brained parasites "furyd with ermyn"; like the Prioress in Chaucer's Prologue they feed their hounds with the dain-tiest "wastel breed." The commoners are expected to sus-tain themselves on a plover's diet of "earthworms, slugs, testaceans and insects." In a just commonwealth an idler would be arraigned as a felon. According to the medievalist, William M. Ryan, in his volume, *William Langland*, one who did not earn his livelihood was considered a waster, a pillager of his own country.

The politicians feign that costs of simple fare cannot be regulated, but it was done in the reigns of Edward the Sec-ond and Henry the Eighth, and by other monarchs and mayors of former times in England. They severely corrected the baker who wrought bread with humbug ingredients, or a woman who made *myngd* (false) butter, by setting the malefactor upon the pillory. Swindlers were put in a cuck-ing-stool, the seat of shame, and exhibited to the ridicule and jeers of the public. I quote Stow's *Survey of London:* "And I have read, that in the 4th year of Edward II, Rich-ard Reffeham being Mayor, a baker named John of Strat-forde, for making bread less than the assize, was with a fool's hood on his head, and loaves of bread about his neck, drawn on a hurdle through the streets of this city. . . . In the twentieth year of Henry VIII six bakers of Stratforde were amerced in the Guild-hall of London for baking bread under the size appointed." In Langland's *Piers the Plough-man*, Avarice says: "I first learned to lie, then to give false measure of everything I sold."

The circumstances of the writers in the thirties were as bad as those of a ditcher or a street costermonger. Most were honest and poor as Piers attired in a workman's torn tabard, and their books brought them a tuppenny. How like Lang-land's mumpers they were, who "go with bordon and bagges" ("bordon," the staff; and "bagges," the wallets for holding pieces of victuals, in the manner of the Greek cynics). With-out sniveling they sacked their songless pockets to compose a a few humble truths, and fed on orts when they could. The Elizabethans were familiars of the same pinch, hunger, and a number of hallowed authors took up bastard underworld trades. Robert Greene, who wrote *The Art of Cony-Catch-ing*, was himself a confidence man. Thomas Nash called the hero of his novel Pierce Pennilesse; Nash was fortunate when he ate feeble meat and scummed a cup of small beer at a hedge-tavern. François Villon, prince of French poesy, was a cutpurse. Most scribes are "the children of Nemesis," as Isaac d'Israeli named them.

Many of the authors in the thirties were my companions; cankered by the dismal planet, Saturn, that brings ill-hap to men, "none of them was worth a couple of onions" to quote Villon once again. Among these were Josephine Herbst, Jack Conroy, Grace Lumpkin, Joseph Freeman, Joshua Kunitz, Lola Ridge, Mary Heaton Vorse, Joy Davidson. Alive or deceased they epitaphed our times and their lives: "Poverty and poetry this tomb doth inclose." They abhorred the grease of cupidity, which Langland regarded as the worst of the seven deadly sins. Langland hated the condescension of the upper classes and their euphemistic "vocabulary of poverty—want, hunger, privation, misery," in Dr. Ryan's words.

The books of the thirties are anguished statistics rather than marmoreal griefs; the language of raw prate piebald with the wrath of Agamemnon, lacking wit, learning and concinnity. Defiant opponents of the rotten sluttery of the times, their authors were not sages. Didactic zeal is ever blind, and wears the mourning weeds of the moralist, not the poet. Alexander Herzen affirmed that "the writings of the egoist Voltaire did more for liberation than those of the loving Rousseau did for brotherhood." As Herman Melville said, there may be Pierian volumes in the tomb of Shakespeare that were never made, but alas, these are a sunken Atlantis of unwritten lays.

36

---

*Homo homini lupus is one of
the most steadfast maxims of
eternal morality.*

—Shestov

In 1933 I wrote a piece on travel for a steamship line, urging
Americans to go to Europe while it was still extant. For this
writing I received a round-trip ticket to Germany and forthwith embarked for Hamburg and from thence by rail to
Berlin. Two days after the Reichstag fire I found myself in
Hitler's *Walpurgisnacht*. I talked to newspapermen, the
Kaiser's former pastor, Spartacists, Socialists, Communists.
Someone suggested that I see the foreign correspondent of
the Baltimore *Sun*, a man named Boulton. He disclosed that
he had been on friendly terms with Hitler, said the Führer
had read a good deal of ancient history, and that eighty-
three percent of the German students supported him. He
advised me to see Edgar Ansel Mowrer.

When I set foot in Mowrer's office he declined to present
himself. Baffled, I found the reason was most plausible. He
detested Boulton and so did I, and when I was able to explain that I had known nothing of Boulton until I met with
him, we became friendly. Mowrer was the dean of foreign

correspondents and his wife was Jewish. He invited me to tea at his home in the Tiergarten, and there I met another guest, Dorothy Thompson, the wife of Sinclair Lewis and herself an eminent columnist. Mowrer said one could hear the groans of tortured Nazi victims in Berlin every day.

During a hectic conversation about the worm-eaten Nazis, two storm troopers and a photographer entered the room. They asked Dorothy Thompson if she would go into the Tiergarten with them as they wished to take a picture of her. Shortly, in the papers throughout the world, there appeared a photograph of Miss Thompson standing between the two storm troopers.

One evening I sauntered out of a café on the Kurfurstendamm Strasse lost in reveries from which I was awakened by a youth in a brown shirt who was beating me about the face with a rubber truncheon. I was surrounded by Germans, some obviously sympathetic to me, but the storm trooper, a butcher's apprentice, continued to strike me even while I was showing my American passport to the police. The entire incident was anesthetic, but of a sudden I roused myself and punched my assailant. Apparently this was considered newsworthy, for when I returned to New York a reporter from the *World-Telegram* arrived on a cutter to interview me before I disembarked.

In Berlin I had spoken to a gentle author, a German Jew, whose father owned Wertheimer's, the largest department store in the city. Storm troopers were picketing the store, carrying placards that read: "*Juden Schweinerei.*" I pleaded with him to leave Germany, but he declined and was liquidated. I also had the opportunity to engage in a long conversation with a beautiful woman who had a salon in Berlin, to which Porto Riche, Romain Rolland and other celebrated people had come. She was a relative of mine through marriage and I importuned her to quit the country. She informed me that she had heard Hitler over the wireless a number of times and that he had a magnetic voice. Taken aback I replied: "My dear lady, Nero, Caligula and Commodus were good fellows compared with Hitler. He will wipe out you, your daughters and husband. Don't imagine he is insincere; murderers are very passionate about one thing, and that is to kill. You must believe every word of *Mein Kampf*." It was futile. She remained, and her husband, a scientist famous throughout Europe, and two of her daughters were murdered. Utterly broken, she came to New York with her two remaining daughters.

In articles I wrote for the *New York Times* and the *New Masses* on the savagery of Hitlerism I berated the German Communists for quarreling with the Socialists instead of uniting with them against the Nazis. The American Stalinists were no different; they condoned every stupid act of their political brethren abroad.

There was a tremendous anti-Nazi rally at Madison Square Garden; some twenty-five thousand people assembled to hear various speakers deride Hitler. When I rose to speak I received an ovation, but after I warned the audience that the Third Reich might last for twenty years a pall of silence hung over the arena. They had been informed by the functionaries that the terror would be over in three to six months. The word was passed about that I was a "defeatist."

During this period of darkling fright, Joseph Pass, a member of some small organization supported by the Stalinists, saw a trifling item about eight Negro boys who were to be executed for ravishing two Southern white women. The state of Alabama had been set for a Roman carnival by the lawmen. Thus began the famous Scottsboro case.

Eight black unschooled moujiks were to die because they were supposed to have assaulted two albic whores in a boxcar. The real question which nobody ever proposed was: "Is it possible to constuprate a couple of prostitutes?" Alexander Herzen might have described the situation as the "fifth act of a bloodstained drama set in a brothel." Nobody had ever proved that the harlots had been raped, a metaphysical quandary for the Duns Scotus or that they had been harmed in any way. The two women, who were for sale, had not been purchased.

Legislative grout-heads have a wily conception of morality. How many members of the Alabama State Legislature had lain with tarts? But they were ethical because they had paid for their squalid recreation.

A committee of writers, Communists and fellow-travelers met at Theodore Dreiser's manorial apartment on Fifty-seventh Street. How were these boys to be defended? Amidst sundry polemics and withered dialectical pronouncements, someone turned to Dreiser, the great pensive animal, and suggested that it was up to him to utter a recondite solution to the predicament. It was the first time I had seen the man, and I satiated my jejune eyes upon his massy physiognomy as Priam had when he came to Achilles, not able to fill his eyes or mind enough with his master. I listened with admiration to Dreiser's simple answer: "If it's brains and logic you're looking for, good God, don't expect them of me."

It had been suggested that the criminal lawyer, Samuel Leibowitz, be retained to go to Scottsboro to espouse the cause of the Negro prisoners. Several functionaries had grave moral doubts: should the party engage an attorney who had defended the most infamous criminal in America, Al Capone? Indeed, it was a very nice dilemma. The American law courts are often a stage, and the prosecuting attorney and the counsel for the defense wear mock buskins and will plead any way regardless of the crime. Isabella, Queen of Castile, had banished all lawyers from the New World. The legal casuist agreed to go to Scottsboro and without a fee. How astute he was.

Croton-on-the-Hudson, about an hour by train from Grand Central, was then a summer camp for radical artists, and I had rented a cottage there. Presently I was asked by party members to afford a night's lodging to one of the white women alleged to have been violated by the black Alabama peasants. When I laid eyes on her I was dumbfounded. She was the most rancid and used-up whore I had ever seen. Her face was laced with pimples and boils and she looked so diseased that after she used the toilet I would not go there until I had thoroughly disinfected it. When I related my disgust and clinical apprehensions to several Stalinists they tittered.

Alfred Stieglitz had mentioned the American smirk, but it is universal. Laughter is a form of convulsion; seldom have I heard people laugh without wincing. Nor have I witnessed Americans at a dance without imagining I was in a charnel house. Saint-Simon tells of a great lady at court who had been laid out with considerable pomp, and who was guarded by a group of royal personages. During the vigil the entrails of the corpse, deposited in an urn, fell on the floor and caused a vile stench. Instead of funeral tears there was hysterical laughter. How few understand Don Quixote who has windmills in his brain and appears to walk across the Iberian stage in comic socks. Once Dreiser said to me that when he read *Don Quixote* he wept. What a powerful and meditative insight! That, my unknown friends, is literary criticism.

Joshua Kunitz was living in Croton at the time and we spent many hours together. Kunitz had Slavic high cheekbones, and his cogitative face was as melancholy as the Russian steppes. Born in Russia, he spoke and read the language fluently and had translated the works of Lenin into English for International Publishers. Kunitz, the collectivist, was a solitary figure, and whenever I saw him in New York he was alone. What desert is so immense as a New York sidewalk; one is broken to pieces by crowds of people. What perplexed me was the apathy of the party to Kunitz's writings. One day I asked him to read aloud to me a part of his unpublished manuscript on Samarkand. It was an account of an Asian feudal society that had been transformed into an industrial country by the Soviets. The machine had taken the place of the camel, the horse, the burro, the farmlands, and the parables of the tares and the cumin seed.

There were many days of salt torpor and long summer worming ennui when Joshua and I would rummage our store of acquaintances at Croton. We knew beforehand the dolorous choice, and so with a heavy, resigned groan we picked up our morose bodies and said, "What's the use? Life's over anyway. Let's go and see Bill Gropper." We wear out our friends as we do heavy unwanted hours, mute and thick-headed doors and thresholds that resent our uninvited feet, and finally everybody, and then who is exhausting whom?

William Gropper was of a rather short stolid stature, with wide lumpish shoulders. He was a plain homespun man without a single affectation; his dullness was positively honest. That no one knows anything about people can be endlessly repeated.

Gropper's cabin resembled a tin of Log Cabin syrup. The great Dreiser also had a house that looked like this silly geewgaw. How well I recall getting on a train at Grand Central and passing through a dozen cemetery hamlets until I reached the ultimate graveyard, Mount Kisco, where Theodore Dreiser lived.

The interior of Gropper's dwelling place contained the

EDWARD DAHLBERG

usual gimcrack factory furniture. Why a remarkable artisan should purchase stupid machine-made tables and chairs is another enigma. In the entire setting one could not discover the genius of the human hand. The large room was Gropper's private art gallery and the walls were covered with his oils, actually penciled squibs upon which he had dropped listless inert paint. Gropper showed us many of his drawings of consumptive tailors, hard-working laundresses with rough, corrugated arms, scrubwomen with pendulous breasts, and shirt-makers with peaked hopeless noses. Nobody had ever defined radical art but here it was. With a few pencil strokes he had depicted a disgusting swag-bellied landlord eructating, or a congressional lubber yawning. In pathos he was superior to George Grosz, and aside from Kathe Kollwitz' lyrical lithographs of German coaldiggers there were no caricatures so eloquent as Gropper's.

When I returned to New York I urged Harry Block, the editor at Covici-Friede, to consider Kunitz's manuscript. He obligingly requested that I bring it to him at once. That proved no easy matter, for though Kunitz promised many times to deliver the Samarkand papers to Block, he didn't. Delay is an impostume in the soul. He who does not whet his will every hour perishes of velleity. I have no clear or good purpose save in exercising my will, for nothing I do appears right to me, but I must do it. Unless I go to my table and work each day the stars disappear, the heavens go out, and the world vanishes. He who does nothing kills the sprouting bubbling plants; his foot is dead and his neck is froward. As is said in the *Gita:*

If I did not always work unwearying,
Men would follow my ways,
The world would perish if I did not work—
I should bring back chaos, and all beings would suffer.

Eventually the manuscript was produced and Covici-Friede published the book under the title, *Dawn Over Samarkand*. One day at the *New Masses* office the editors and several Party members gathered around Kunitz and informed him they wished to give a party to honor the publication of his book. Kunitz's sunken Slavic wrinkles glowed. Then they added: "Our party objective, comrade, is to encourage our Negro brother, Angelo Herndon, the heroic strike leader who is being persecuted by the Southern white medievalists. We think it would be a fine black and white gesture if you would dedicate your book to Angelo Herndon."

Kunitz had never met the man, and had only vaguely heard of him, but he acquiesced and there the party's interest in the book ended. Only when an author received considerable attention in the capitalist press did the Communists deem him important. Success was their touchstone. Apostles of expediency, they courted a writer until he became a Marxist thinker, that is, one who had gulped down thirty slogans which he picked up by hearsay or from the exsanguious tracts of Lenin, Stalin, Bukharin, or Radek. A piacular detective story hack was more significant to the Stalinists than a poet. They decoyed and corrupted the people they proposed to redeem.

Archibald MacLeish was one of the editors of *Fortune*. He had a sharp artillery visage, well-arranged features, short-cropped hair, and went about in a quick smart suit. I asked him if he would speak at a gathering to celebrate the publication of Kenneth Fearing's poems. He unhesitatingly accepted, although he had been vehemently impugned by Mike Gold as an anti-Semite. It should be added that Fearing was half-Scotch and half-Jew.

Sol Funaroff, a young Communist, and I published Fearing's first book of poems. Funaroff designed the volume and took care of the type and I raised the money from editors of publishing houses and magazines. Penniless Funaroff was ready to print any Marxist's verse but his own. He had a pimply face, a long gummy nose, a rounded chin and a chemical breath, not offensive but symptomatic of arcane diseases which were to bring his life to an end before his thirtieth year.

Funaroff and I had the same malaise, and I quote what was in ancient times ascribed to Epicharmus: "It is not kindness in you but disease, this itch of giving." I am a becrazed valetudinary who'll never recover since I'm always trying to be the good Samaritan for some unknown writer. Funaroff would have been as much an invalid as I had he continued to live.

Comrade aesthete V. J. Jerome reproved me for having asked MacLeish to speak before a left-wing group. I replied I considered MacLeish a distinguished American poet. Comrade Jerome, who had a bulbous head set on a short square body, frowned. "MacLeish runs with the Christian Wall Street money brokers," he said. "He belongs to the wolvish social Fascist pack."

I disagreed: "There is far more political energy in friendship than in ideology. Besides, would it not be more profitable to pour Marxian thoughts into his bourgeois opinions in much the same way as the poor Jersey farmers of England, according to Peter Kropotkin, fertilized their scanty soil with refuse, bones, and the mummies of cats they imported from Egypt."

"Kropotkin, that petit-bourgeois anarchist," fumed the Hegelian seer. "I detect a certain taint of reaction and Trotskyite infantilism in your irresponsible approach. Friendship, comrade, is subjective, and smacks of *lumpenproletariat* solitude."

37

*We write books, paint pictures,
compose symphonies—but is that
labor?*

—Shestov

The Communists had recherché dicta concerning poverty. There were various categories of indigence; penury was not highly esteemed by the functionaries of the party unless it was enjoyed by a drayman, hodcarrier, steamfitter or riveter, a longshoreman, millhand, or steelworker. The party was especially anxious to attract Irish laborers and there was a report that a genuine Irish-American had become a member. His name was A. B. Magil, the son of a rabbi.

No matter what hardships the *lumpenproletariat* suffered such people did not count. The Stalinists were also reluctant to admit that a man who employed his brains did any work at all.

There were seizures of despondency. I could see no real distinction between Dostoevsky's unfilial nihilist Stavrogin in *The Possessed* and the Stalinists who viewed the Old as the nemesis of the New. Lenin had rebuked his comrades because they could not go back on their memories. Nostalgia

284

is the stumblig block to perception, but he who has no memory is without affection.

Centuries earlier the same dispute had been carried on by Aristophanes, who defended the ancient customs redolent of thyme, nard, yews, poplars, modesty and the chaste cestus of the virgin. The comic Greek poet had parodied the dialectical "thinking shop" of Socrates and ridiculed the low-born pleb, Euripides, whose mother peddled herbs and watercresses in the Athenian agora, and who was up to date and questioned the gods. Plato's Socrates says to his accusers, the two poetasters and the dikasts, the Greek senators: "Do you really believe I do not venerate Helios, the Sun, and the goddess, Selene, the moon?"

The old traditional style of feeling, embodied in such words as morals, good, evil, honesty, kindness, pity, and principles, was now deemed sick symptoms and the cant shibboleths of the middle class. Gratitude was tabu or regarded as sycophancy. Sallust affirmed that "mercy" and "mildness" had long ago lost the true etymologies of those words. And La Bruyère: "There is no excess in the world so commendable as the excess of gratitude."

True, I could not truckle to the shopkeeper's code of deportment; moreover, an overplus of moralizing is frequently a sign of spleen, as is displayed by D. H. Lawrence. There's the busybody and the gossip in the Doric moralist. Where is there a virtue without a vice in it?

The writers of the Left had fallen into a utopian oscitancy —a sort of political nympholepsy had taken hold of the intelligentsia. We were in such a drowsy state of madness that we looked upon the proletariat as a sublime superhuman race. We were grieved and felt degraded because we were not the regal progeny of peasants, colliers, or sharecroppers. How unlucky it was not to have been a cotton picker, or never to have been inside a shoe factory or a laborer in a sweatshop.

Despite this zeal, and although the Stalinists were eager to attract authors, intellectuals were viewed as a suspicious Bohemian band. Sometimes the sin of class origin was venial; an Anglo-Saxon writer was a minion, almost a pillicock, of the Stalinist ephors. A son of a multimillionaire was likewise an hors d'oeuvre of the party.

Authors were often attacked for producing petit-bourgeois and "defeatist" literature. Nobody knew how to describe a proletarian novel. Most of the strictures by Mike Gold, the barking Cerberus of pleb fiction, were a knot of cavils and quibbles. All the tenets he prescribed for novelists he was incapable of following in his own narrative, *Jews Without Money*. Moreover, those who perused such fiction felt no less persecuted than the workers who were forced to exist under such conditions.

In working-class fiction, one never saw a laborer smile, laugh, or seated at table with his jovial family. The political pamphleteers had neither the wit nor the nobility of language to create Shakespeare's Feeble or an Elizabethan Mistress Overdone or a Doll Tearsheet or the commoner Silence who, as Hazlitt mentions, sits "in the orchard and eats his caraways and pippins."

The quandary was never resolved. Some advised writers to cheer up the oppressed toilers; others asserted that aside from a few muddle-headed rank-and-file members, nobody read these works except those who wrote them. The coal-diggers and steelworkers in West Virginia and Pennsylvania, the toilers in the New Jersey canneries and the farmers had never heard of the class struggle.

The perplexities deepened. Robert Cantwell, author of *Laugh and Lie Down*, confessed he was not sufficiently familiar with certain laws of nature; he divulged he was overcome with a passionate urgency to write about death, and didn't know how to describe it since he had never died. One or two comrades wryly suggested that he ought to try the experiment.

The general feeling among the Stalinist clerks was that the intellectuals were politically ill, and should purge themselves with *lapis lazuli* and a deep study of Stalin's treatises, also the tracts of Bukharin, Radek and Plekhanov. The arguments were continued at the John Reed Club, an artistic and Bohemian organization founded by Communists. At one meeting, heavily attended by authors, painters, and cartoonists, the society was harangued by a working-class guest. He was a small thewy man with a lagging mouth. Consumed with hatred for the decaying capitalist system and inflamed by the Third International he commenced his oration in a high Ciceronian tone:

"Comrades, I'm just a simple garment worker, and I don't know anything about literature. Still I confess I owe it to our glorious party and to Stalinist ideology to ask comrade John Dos Passos, who unfortunately is not present, why he wrote the decadent *Manhattan Transfer*. With all due respect to this master of our revolutionary novel, I must say I find much infantile adventurism in the manner he expresses himself. Although I don't understand what our comrade is aiming at, it is my objective and doctrinaire opinion that he uses big Hamlet-like words of the reactionary and feudalistic tradition. For example, I quote from our leading party fiction-writer."

Before making this illustrious citation, the garment worker wiped his sweaty spectacles. Then drawing a piece of paper out of his coat pocket he asked the assembly of radicals: "What does comrade Dos Passos mean by . . . I haven't found a single one of these hard words in the dictionary . . . 'compan yunion, prosecutin gattorney, screwd river, firt rees, firn eedles.' "

A John Reed member took the sheet of paper from him and obligingly acted as his dragoman: "Comrades, the words are company union, prosecuting attorney, screw driver, fir trees and fir needles. Dos Passos is a fast machine-gun prose stylist who is hastening the revolution by joining separate sluggish words together. He has adopted the aesthetic of speed of the syndicalists to energize the weary factory laborer. As you well know, comrades, the toiling masses are too tired to read each single word in a novel. I maintain this is class struggle art. Dos Passos' prose is a Bonapartist forced march, the origin of the syndicalist military tactics in Sorel's *Reflections on Violence*, which Dos Passos has used to fashion the novel to ambush the middle-class reader."

The garment worker gave him a fierce Stalinist visage. His glasses were steaming again and he had to remove them, but he quickly responded: "From my point of view, as a humble workman, Dos Passos displays the degenerate tendency of a collapsing society." He snatched the scrap of paper from the John Reed member and demanded: "Explain, comrade intellectuals, what does novelist Dos Passos mean by the following: 'Their shoulders smile thinly our eyes look.' " He paused, his own pin-buttocks triumphant, then vociferated: "Either the author must write a plain clear prose a cutter, a furrier or a needle-worker can understand, or else he is an *agent-provocateur*, a Trotskyite, no better than the shopkeeping philosopher, Sidney Hook, the enemy of the revolutionary movement, or he must take up a trade. As matters now stand I cannot prove that Dos Passos is honest, but who's got time in our Marxist-Leninist crisis to prove it? As comrade Lenin pointed out in his manifesto to the Mensheviks, June 27, 1918, a Bolshevist cannot test each person with a sincereometer."

He continued: "A leading theoretician of our great party,

also a strict student of Plekhanov, the Russian aesthete, told me that a bad figure of speech is as much the foe of the workers as the imperialist warmongers. Having read one of Dos Passos' masterpieces from cover to cover this scholarly member of the Central Committee gave me the following words which I shall now quote aloud to you: '. . . on the broken floor of a lurchedover cabin a man halfsits halflies, propped up by an old woman two wrinkled girls that might be young.' Any dialectician knows this is a classic instance of the brutal advertising style employed by the ruling cliques to deceive and exploit the toiling masses. I hold that Dos Passos lacks revolutionary orientation and shows taints of revisionism. He also lacks a working class environment.

"I would like to suggest that comrade intellectual Dos Passos go into the field for a year to organize the millworkers in Fall River, or be a common laborer on a railroad section gang. After he has acquired a firsthand experience of the sweating proletariat, he should then be able to write a clear sentence a tailor, a steam-presser, or a suffering longshoreman can understand. I would also advise comrade intellectual Dos Passos to model himself upon Gladkov's immortal Soviet book, *Cement*. However, I'm just a pure and simple garment worker and don't know anything about what the diseased upper classes refer to as literary technique or genres of writing. I am just a rank and file member of our great party. I thank all of you for your kind proletarian patience."

He sat down amidst tremendous noise. A fiery adherent of *Manhattan Transfer* was ready to beat him, but he was restrained by the Herculean Hegelian of the party, V. J. Jerome, who said that to lay a finger on a garment worker would be an act of Fascist sensationalism.

In such a movement there were bound to be a number of zanies and nuisances. One of these hawked Chinese cherry-blossom doggerel. The Stalinists were proud to have an Oriental in the party and no one dared to criticize his verse lest he be denounced as a white chauvinist. The Chinese poet used to sell his rueful nonsense at left-wing rallies in Union Square, and offer his chapbooks to fellow-travelers and Communist sitters at the Waldorf Cafeteria on Sixth Avenue near Eighth Street. He asked a dollar for each pamphlet, but who had a dollar? Shortly, he vanished. James T. Farrell, whose novel, *Young Lonigan*, was then regarded as hoodlum scribblings, referred to him as the yellow peril.

Now let me chronicle the small beer of Farrell's puddly fooleries and japish writings. Farrell had thick shaggy hair, ragged teeth, and at first bluish I supposed he was good-natured. It took me a while to discover how shrewd is an amiable man. Vacquerie, the French litterateur, says that he who loves everybody hates everybody. Farrell, and his wife Dorothy, lived in a bare scathed room, subsisting on tins of tomato juice and crackers. His beggary was deplorable. No one would review his work. With what ardor I could muster I endeavored to convince William Soskin that he should give some notice to the novel in the *Post*, but he said he wanted no part of Farrell's cloacal words.

When a second fiction, *Gas House McGinty*, was published, Henry Hazlitt said I could review it for *The Nation*. But after I had read it I was so appalled by the pleurisy of profanity and unlettered pages that I went to see Farrell and asserted it would be unkind of me to fatten his obscurity by attacking the book, and rank falsehood of me to say one good word for it.

Still, I wanted to assist him, and I wrote a lengthy article on his works for the *New Masses*. Farrell was presently embraced as a convivial and waggish Irish fellow-traveler. As his reputation increased his attachment to me dwindled, until I could no longer countenance him. He seemed to me surreptitiously overbearing, and I find it impossible to patronize even a maggot.

Farrell and his wife had separated, and at that time he was pursuing a Texas beauty. She would have kindled my own blood had she not such fragile legs. It pained me to observe her standing or walking, for I was certain she would crumble to pieces. She was an unadulterated dizzard, but unusual. One month she was enraptured with Karl Marx and felt it her bounden duty to lie with a Stalinist in order to understand more minutely *Das Kapital.* Again, she fell in love with Dostoevsky and insisted upon having sexual commerce with a commentator on *Notes from Underground.*

The last time I saw her she was under the spell of William Blake's poems. Always puzzled by her I never knew whether she was a nymphomaniac or an erotical laboratory worker. She had resolved that she could never interpret Marxist culture unless she had connection with one who possessed the tool to produce it.

About 1966 or so, two years before her agonizing death, Josephine Herbst was at a party I gave. We had been friends since the thirties, sometimes very close, and both of us had sought a truthful fame; we were determined, as Sallust says, "Not to die in Silence or Oblivion, like Beasts of the field."

Now she was tormented with cancer and her sturdy carnal frame was ravished, the face seamed by the cankerworm and the mouth of Venus Genetrix almost clean gone. I looked at her with terror knowing she would soon be wrapped in a winding sheet. However, her sky-gray eyes were firm, and she had retained her robustious manner that concealed iron negations. "Don't worry about me," she chuckled. "I'm a real tough bird." A festered lily, she remained undaunted.

That night I asked Josephine: "What the devil did you ever see in Farrell? Didn't you suspect a writer who calls his central figure a stud?" With a cigarette hanging from her famished lips, she poked a bony sibylline finger into my chest, as she would do whenever she was at a mirthful gathering, and exclaimed: "I was charitable."

Josephine Herbst was a tragic victim of "the Cause"; it had been her funeral toll and hurried the last rites apace. When she could flesh her pages she composed very sensual passages, and writing that is not physical is gibberish. I never weigh a real author's wares in Themis' scales, that is, by the pound, but I must mournfully state that her good work was scanty. Aside from her Communist activities her other phlebotomist was poverty. She really fell, I assume, on the battlefield in Spain during the Civil War; she was the only woman permitted to stand at the front line. Although she returned to the States to resume her vocation, authorship, and to publish her tender book on the American naturalist, Bartram, *New Green World*, she lacked the strength to sustain another work. A brave literary soldier, she expired in a New York hospital, holding close to her bosom a manuscript, the unfinished Memoirs. She was a political Demeter of whom Schiller says: "In all Ceres' wanderings she found misery everywhere, and her great spirit wept for man's fate."

38

What potions have I drunk of siren tears.

—Shakespeare

I had delivered an address at the first Writers Congress stating that Hemingway, Caldwell and Dos Passos considered ignorance a kind of genius, and that they were anti-heroical novelists who worshipped the villainy of the Little: their dimensions were pygmean. Shortly afterward I was subjected to a catechism by a member of the Central Committee: "Did I not realize that the party was doing its utmost to attract Hemingway and Caldwell?" I said: "No, I did not," and I asked: "Comrade, what is your occupation?" "I am a needle worker," he replied, to which I retorted, "My trade is chagrin." He gave me a fuddled glance and I continued: "Comrade, you ply your needle and I'll take care of literature."

The Communist tactic was simple; anyone who disagreed with the policy of the Stalinists was a reactionary, a counter-revolutionary, and a Fascist. I abhorred the flag of Bread and the creed of the New proclaimed by the left-wing intellectual rout. Like any other class they were a mob. Nor would I have any part in their incurable boyism. Porphyry refers to cantles of the *Enneads* of Plotinus, composed when he was between fifty and sixty years of age, as the work of the philosopher's "early youth." Neither could I hold with the upstarts whose shibboleth was Originality. All wise books are writ by one man, sometimes called Homer, then Aeschylus, Horace or Shakespeare. I am not contemporary for I am unhistorical. The Muses existed before Creation which is said to have taken place when the sun was in Aries.

Guilty of cacodoxy I had sinned against the cult of the Same. As a result I was already a banished man; I bore the mark of the beast on my forehead.

Aristotle states that at Syracuse the names of those who were ostracized were inscribed on the leaves of an olive tree and this was called Petalism. Men who formerly were glad to shake my hand now pretended they did not know me as they passed me on the street. A base man steps upon a bug and his nerves quiver as he quashes it; this toad-spotted creature must rule something, a fly, an insect, a chair, for power over anything at all is his cornucopia of musk. No brute on the earth enjoys hurting others as does man. One of his honeyed pleasures is to harm a helpless fellow.

When I left the party I was first denounced as a Trotskyite, although I had never attended a single meeting of that clique, and a Fascist, and even charged with being an *agent-provocateur*. Could I ever spy upon my own chameleon emotions or capture one obscure feeling I might be a Chaldaic diviner. That the accusations were canards was patent to all except dizzards and maniacs.

I was the woodcock of the Stalinist epigones, for I have always suffered for what I have never done. I am too impressionable to suppose I couldn't do something bad. One's moral position is always precarious. An evil person is sure to tell you how good he is. I can only hope no one will be so unkind as to claim I have committed a gross deed that was never in my head, for then I am certain to think of it. No moralizer, I cannot stand on my feet under any strict surveillance; I am no better than the worst man in the world. Besides, I am too weak to trust myself. Who can believe in his scruples, or say to another, Trust me? What a knavish demand.

Terrible as the situation is it is also bizarre. Were I to ransack a single virtuous motive I suspect I've had I would go mad. Should I vapor about my scruples Cain would fetch his ladle, dip it into my blood, stir and taste it, and then give me the most leering grin. I cannot maintain such a pose without being shattered.

I had fled from the universal theology of lucre but could not avoid the snare of politics. I had reached the end, which is another path to perception. My skies were sackcloth, my distempered lakes were dried up, my body a dead gully. The abyss is no-feeling, that is the ultimate despondency. When I'm cauterized, flea'd or bled, I want to feel it.

The first intimation of my condition came not from my intellect but from my foot. Ill luck had been settling in my joints and unsinging knees; worst of all, my feet were force-less sinking shadows. When the feet despair the mind is a Tartarus of black humors. The neck, the arms, the elbows, and especially the feet know what is going on long before the head has intelligence of it. One thing I want to make plain is that the mind is the most ignorant part of the body. Could I only forget my old footsteps I might cure a jot of my nature.

Realizing I could cony-catch myself better than any enemy, I came to another indecision. I resolved to make the journey alone, with nothing to guide me except the oar of the prophet Tiresias, also blind, which Odysseus had gotten.

I saw it was either the Many or the Socratic hemlock of ostracism—a ticklish choice, but life took care of that.

I dimly understood I would never be out of the forest, so deep and wild was the dusky foliage of Nodh in my breast. As a writer I had not even begun my apprenticeship. It took more than the strength of the phoenix for me to raise my maimed pinions from the ashes of my brute scrawl.

Wherever I went I was the victim of a doltish Communist Ajax ready to slay me with his dullness. Everything got worse though nothing was ever any good. Unable to escape my persecutors I brooded over the disappearing American earth; as Péguy said, the world had become a peopleless land. The machine had displaced human beings.

Would to heaven I could spy upon my own feelings. I could not eschew their fangs of malice. "Thy reason, dear venom, give thy reason," laments Shakespeare and Ben Jonson asserts: "I am beholden to calumny."

The Stalinist book-slayers were stationed on almost every paper and magazine that claimed importance. What wolves were the Communist lambs who spoiled the vines of any writer who abhorred the banner of homogeneity. They pretended my volumes did not exist, and cast them into Sheol without a reviewer's obituary notice. "As good almost kill a man as kill a good book," it is written in Milton's *Areopagitica*. Whether I was in New York, Los Angeles or San Francisco, I was pursued by the beagles, the Stalinists and F.B.I. agents.

Man covers the planet with gore for justice, but where is it? Tamburlaine spilled far less blood than Stalin. Can anybody imagine that Brezhnev, the czarist clerk garbed in the drab vestments and chasuble, the double-breasted suit of the assassin businessman, who impudently intones "Holy Russia" and "Our Mother Land," is a Lycurgus or an Agesilaus? Little wonder that Leopardi saw the world as a vast league

EDWARD DAHLBERG

of criminals ruthlessly warring against a few virtuous madmen. The soul pants for the tender frolicking hills, the small
meditative brooks, the miracle of human warmth, and an
apocryphal Eden. In the Jewish legends it is said that dying
Adam asked Seth his son to fetch oil from the tree of knowledge, but Paradise had vanished.

39

The whole of this material universe of ours, with all its suns and its milky ways—is nothing.
—Tolstoy

I fell into hourless Orcus, and the leaden fog on the rigging of my soul was frozen hard. I saw that the Barren Grounds is not the coldest region on the earth; it is the human heart. I stuffed my naked ribs and moaned: "My name, my name, thou hast been besmirched, every rogue has bayed thee. Be quiet, poor flensed waif, and sit in the dusty dry corner of thy self." I shrouded myself in seven syllables of silence, in seven leaves of years, within seven Ephesian graves.

Would I ever find a northwest passage to the Moluccas? That could not be. I've always been a helpless ninny, an inexplicable ludicrous one. Imagine I sought affection from people I never needed; they were senseless and droll enough to suppose I required them. That was the only hoax I was ever able to impose upon these average unfeeling noddles. Naturally I gather together a few persons now and then to decoy me. A man has to provide himself with a covey of Judases; that's what is called life.

Then I wrote books, a useless occupation, and I would have done something else had I thought of it. Seneca advises his readers that a man must do something though it be to no purpose. Besides, I got into a squabble with myself about truth and justice. Am I really serious about this? How should I know? All I can say is though I am no astute worldly Pontius Pilate, I ask what is truth since no one lives by it. " 'And there is some good in the world,' replied Candide. 'Maybe so,' said Martin, 'but it has escaped my knowledge.' "

No matter how often I studied Homer I could not be sane about the vain and imbecile pursuit of wisdom. The Sirens endeavor to tempt Odysseus to approach the perfidious rocks by offering him what no mortal can attain, knowledge.

Then I fell into another predicament: What mite of consciousness could ever be mine? The more I am on guard against my emptiness and fatuity the more obtuse I am. How can one be vigilant twenty-four hours of the day? Not even the disciples could remain awake long enough for the vigil. I am sure they were automatic. Did they walk to Capernaum? I doubt it; they thought they did. They never lived; nobody has. No, I am not quibbling: I do not believe I exist. The thinker who thinks he exists is no thinker. Suppose I'm wrong, it won't be momentous anyway. The universe is a slumbering animal that has visions. "I think the world's asleep," says Lear.

Descartes was sure of his paltry dictum: "I think, therefore I am." But I think and am not. I grant either way there is no evidence. Our short pilgrimage is obviously one of renunciations. At first we trust what we are sure we see, but this is a seminal delusion. Then little by little, as our rude and coarse physical forces dwindle, we become extremely suspicious, and begin to assume the earth's a ruse and that we have been taken in all the while. What are these things since everyone perceives them differently? I came to feel that space is a void and time the flux and ebb of a dying dream.

When people die we very soon forget how they looked.

Did they ever live is our unrelieved groan. It never occurred to me that I would regard trees, the ground, a shingle, the sea as God's baubles. Heraclitus states: "All things we see when awake are death." One can go on and on.

Meanwhile I have accumulated a pile of wrinkles which are basely attributed to time by sick-winged heads. Once in a while I regard a new crease around my mouth as a frightful defeat and my downfall. I have another fear which contradicts whatever I have said. Although I have confessed I don't care a tittle for my intelligence, what will happen if my faculties begin to flag? Lucretius revealed that "when Democritus was warned by his ripe old age that the memory-bringing motions of his mind were languishing, he spontaneously offered his head to death."

What has the Worm taught me? I believe that Shakespeare's hundred and fifty-four sonnets were a hundred and fifty-four Gethsemane nights. Is that all? Is there nothing else? I pity the squalid drabs of the bribed Muses who pick-thank feelings and have never been ripened by shame, mire, the ditch of humiliation. Not one author has sung the song of the dying swan, what Socrates referred to as the thinker's last senilia. They linger on, their wings shriveled, dissipated echoes of their youthful dotages. "Many a one, alas, waxeth too old for his truths," said Nietzsche. Would that I weren't a writer; since I am, I'd like to produce one page that is a replica of the handkerchief of St. Veronica upon which was impressed the divine and tragic features of Jesus.

I have another pelting vexation. Suppose there is a Creator, or a Demiurge who framed day and night, will it make any difference? Won't I arise in the morning petulant because there is rime on the window sill, a cramp in the small part of my back, acid mildew in my lungs, or my head is clogged with fenny yesterdays? And if there is no God, will it not be the same? I'll die anyway.

Would I had a dram of calm. Will the grave provide it?

Is death total cessation, or may it not be a wailing and gnashing of the grieving bones? There might be a grain of truth in this, for the body is no liar. Let me taste the constellations when I go my way unhindered to the great Worm, enjoy one infinite second of quiet.

Since there's no solution I stalk the stage in buskins though I speak in my comic socks, and I dismiss the immense self-delusion, life, and bid farewell to the world with: "Sir, money is a whore."

This is not all. Another small matter frets me: why am I obscure to myself? Could I understand my experiences I would annihilate myself. However, as nature will do it for me, I shan't bother. It just occurred to me: Is God acquainted with Himself? All He can utter is: I am that I am. Is that a great revelation? Shakespeare, a better poet than God, is as vague; he merely mimicks the Lord and says: I am that I am.

That picklock I venerate, François Villon, palmed off this mournful stave: "I know the doublet by its collar; I know the monk by his habit; I know the master by his servant; I know the nun by her veil; I know the sharper by his jargon; I know fools fed on creams; I know wine by its barrel; I know all, except myself."

What else? I'm as lost as I was. Nobody has ever found himself. What I am searching for is a man with an unbearable void within him. I am seeking myself.

I confess I do not know my own bounds. Be gone, ye caitiff cowards who announce your limits. I need stellar etiologies.

No secular person, I am the small gleanings of many devout sages. This book has been hanging over my head like the rock of Tantalus. I have battered mountains, torn up seas as elephants in rage break grass by the roots, for a metaphor.

This is a song of no-knowledge, a chant of shame. What

else can a memoir be but an enchiridion of chagrins. If I have not divulged all, it is that life is illicit. St. Paul saw in a vision things "unlawful to utter." I walk upon my hurts which readers entitle my books. Sunset writes for me, and rain scribbles my woes. Forgive me, dear unknown readers, for I cannot pardon myself nor life.

Before it's all over with me I am going out into the world to swear at the most depraved and cunning of all harlots, Reason. Ye who demand evidence are the culprits, for I am the proof. When I am clean out of reason I am out of guile. Have you not learned that a logician will cut your heart into a thousand gammons and languorously champ it. Does this make me a weeping trunk of dust? Only a rationalist would so affront me.

In one respect I am resigned to be the staunch companion of Alone. A writer is a banished man. Euripides died in Macedonia; Thucydides wrote his history of the war between the Athenians and the Peloponnesians near the forest Scapte; Herodotus migrated to Thurii. While the "fishes are quivering on the horizon, and all the Wain lies over Taurus," I sacrifice reverently "to the shade of holy outcast Spinoza."

In bringing this trembling exile book to a close, I pray it is the clay that smells of the flesh from which Prometheus molded man. My own darkness, my wilderness, and the black Cain leaves crying in my breast, are Odysseus' apostrophe to his own nature: "Endure, my soul, endure."

New York, Dublin, Barcelona,
Tel Aviv, Geneva
1966–1970

INDEX

Hollywood, California, 28, 105, 114, 199, 251, 266, 268
Holofernes, 138
Holy Ghost, 17, 44, 103, 231
"Holy Russia," 296
Homer, 43, 62, 126, 143, 194, 223, 245, 254, 271, 294, 299
Hook, Sidney, 288
Horace, 8, 28, 94, 101, 171, 207, 216, 222, 294
Horus, 219
Houdini, 254
Huntington, Constant, 215, 216, 217, 221
Hurried Man, The, 197, 221
Hurst, Fannie, 254
Huxley, Aldous, 216
Huysmans, Joris Karl, 251, 252
Hydiotaphia, 255
Hydra, 266

I Kan, 17
Iliad, the, 8, 38, 171
Ilium, *see* Troy
Incas, 13
Ince, Thomas, 108
Inferno, the, 259
Insanity of Genius, The, 111
International Ladies Garment Workers Union, 88
In the American Grain, 255
Intimate Journals, 240
Iron Heel, The, 147
Isaac, 16, 95
Isabella, 278
Ishmael, 95
Isis, 144, 162
Ithaca, 146

"Jacataqua," 137
Jacob, 16, 95
Jacob's ladder, 14, 149
James, Henry, 215, 220
James, William, 58, 163
Janus, 208
Japeth, 31
Jehovah, 90, 102, 157
Jerome, V. J., 283, 289
Jerusalem, 25, 232
Jeshurum, 56
Jesus Christ, 17, 28, 39, 86, 114, 150, 172, 202, 230, 231, 232, 300
Jew of Malta, The, 222
Jews, 192, 195, 204, 217, 222, 232, 276, 282, 297
Jews Without Money, 286
Job, 5, 82, 115
John Reed Club, 287, 289
Johns, Richard, 250
Johnson, Samuel, 227, 235, 253, 264
Jonah, 196
Jonson, Ben, 6–7, 69, 113, 123, 144, 145, 146, 147, 185, 207, 296

Joseph, 114, 263
Josephus, David, 58
Journal (of Amiel), 111, 152
Journal to Stella, 223
Jove, 101, 259
Joyce, James, 189, 192, 193, 194, 197, 198, 201, 225, 226, 245
Judas Iscariot, 24, 29, 99, 298
Jude the Obscure, 115
Judea, 173
Judith, 26
Julian calendar, 189
Jungle, The, 147
Juvenal, 207

Kansas City, 11, 59, 235
Kaufman, George S., 255
Keats, John, 121
Kedar, 63, 268
Kidron River, 150
Kierkegaard, Soren, 252
King Lear, 149, 257
Kollowitz, Kathe, 281
Kroeber, 149
Kropotkin, Peter, 283
Kunitz, Joshua, 274, 279, 281, 282

Laban, 252
La Bruyère, Jean de, 208, 222, 240, 244, 245, 259, 285
Lady Chatterly's Lover, 217, 218–19, 227
Laforgue, Jules, 207
Lais of Corinth, 36, 141
Lamech, 15
Lancelot of the Lake, 114
Langland, William, 121, 143, 200, 263, 273, 274
Laodicea, 252, 256
Lao-tsu, 56, 61
Lardner, Ring, 254, 255
La Salle, R. R. C., 39
Laugh and Lie Down, 286
Laurentius, 272
Lawrence, D. H., 39, 195, 201, 203, 211, 212, 213, 215, 216, 217, 218, 219, 222, 225, 226, 227, 237, 255, 256, 285
Lawrence, Frieda, 195, 211, 226
Laws, the, 264
Leah, 252
"Lear and Moby Dick," 258
Le Disciple, 36, 111
L'Éducation Sentimentale, 29, 150
Left Bank, 193, 195, 200
Leibowitz, Samuel, 278
Lenin, Nikolai, 133, 280, 282, 284, 288
Leopardi, Count Giacomo, 296
Le Sage, Alain René, 115, 117, 220
Lethe River, 228, 262
Letters (of Rosa Luxemburg), 128
Lewis, Meriwether, 39

EDWARD DAHLBERG